CULTIVATING
DEMOCRACY

CULTIVATING DEMOCRACY

Civic Environments and Political Socialization in America

James G. Gimpel

J. Celeste Lay

Jason E. Schuknecht

BROOKINGS INSTITUTION PRESS
Washington, D.C.

Copyright © 2003
THE BROOKINGS INSTITUTION
1775 Massachusetts Avenue, N.W., Washington, D.C. 20036
www.brookings.edu

Library of Congress Cataloging-in-Publication data

Gimpel, James G.
  Cultivating democracy : civic environments and political socialization in America / James G. Gimpel, J. Celeste Lay, Jason E. Schuknecht.
    p. cm.
  Includes bibliographical references (p.) and index.
  ISBN 0-8157-3154-X (cloth : alk. paper)
    1. Youth—United States—Political activity.   2. Students—United States—Political activity.   3. Political socialization—United States.
  4. Youth—United States—Attitudes.   5. United States—Politics and government—Public opinion.   6. Public opinion—United States.   I. Lay, J. Celeste.   II. Schuknecht, Jason E., 1973–   III. Title.

  HQ799.2.P6G55 2003
  305.235—dc22   2003016810
                        9 8 7 6 5 4 3 2 1

The paper used in this publication meets minimum requirements of the American National Standard for Information Sciences—Permanence of Paper for Printed Library Materials: ANSI Z39.48-1992.

Typeset in Adobe Garamond

Composition by R. Lynn Rivenbark
Macon, Georgia

Printed by R. R. Donnelley
Harrisonburg, Virginia

For our social studies teachers

Contents

Appendixes

Acknowledgments

A small army of people has been involved in this project since its inception in January 1999. We want to take a little space to thank these individuals for the ideas they brought to the project and for their enthusiastic participation. Diana Lin and Kristie Curameng were members of the original research team who traveled to sites to collect data, make presentations about our work, and record careful field notes. Dania Shami and Marsha Talento joined the team to help code and enter data, always with a good attitude. Elizabeth McQuinn and Matthew Crouch toiled over the occupation coding for more than a month to derive a reliable socioeconomic status measure. Mike Berry and Andrea Miller assisted in the data collection for the 2001 follow-up survey in four Maryland high schools. We thank Barbara Segnetelli for allowing us to pilot the survey at classrooms in Severna Park High School in February 1999 and for giving us helpful feedback on the survey design. Substantive discussions with all of the above greatly advanced the maturity of the ideas we present here, as did classroom discussions with graduate students and undergraduates.

We have derived enormous personal benefit from doing the field investigations and meeting the teachers and students who made this work possible. We are grateful to the teachers and administrators in the fourteen cooperating school districts and twenty-nine schools for making their classrooms available, and of course, we thank the over 3,050 students who always willingly participated and gave us insightful feedback in the focused discussion sessions. Conducting this research has been a perspective-changing, even life-changing experience.

A number of our academic colleagues have read and commented on pieces of this manuscript or otherwise discussed major ideas with us. This does not mean that they agree with our conclusions or even liked what they read of our work. They include Kent Jennings, Richard Niemi, W. Phillips Shively, Judith Torney-Purta, Jane Junn, Eric Plutzer, David Campbell, Diana Mutz, David Armstrong, Karen Kaufmann, Eric Uslaner, Irwin Morris, and Marco Steenbergen.

Support for our research effort was generously provided by the William T. Grant Foundation. We thank Lonnie Sherrod, Bob Granger, and Tom Weisner at W. T. Grant for believing that we would eventually produce something. Professor William A. Galston of the Pew Charitable Trusts' CIRCLE project at the University of Maryland provided funding for course release time to complete the manuscript. Roberta Green Ahmanson and the Ahmanson Community Trust have supported an extension of this research that is ongoing.

Christopher Kelaher, the editor at Brookings, located three brilliant, highly critical reviewers and provided helpful guidance as we marched through the steps of the editorial process. Starr Belsky provided highly competent editorial advice, and Janet Walker deserves thanks for efficiently marshalling the manuscript through the publication process. We also thank our families and those closest to us for their patience as we jumped through all of the hoops necessary to arrive at this point.

Finally, this book is dedicated to our social studies teachers, especially those in junior high and high school, who sparked our interest in politics and government.

1 Becoming Political: Local Environments and Political Socialization

Approaching the town of Dundalk, Maryland, on the I-695 bridge over the Patapsco River inlet to the Chesapeake Bay is truly a breathtaking experience. Eastbound I-695 winds its way through southern Baltimore County, passing through relatively open, rural land before descending toward the river. But as one drives up to the mid-point of the bridge, the horizon suddenly drops away to reveal the vast superstructure of the Bethlehem Steel works at Sparrow's Point on the right, along with associated chemical and manufacturing plants on both sides of the highway. Belching smokestacks, gigantic warehouses, and vast marine shipping terminals dominate the view. A large number of hulking, dingy brick buildings with shattered windows, spray-painted with graffiti, have long since been abandoned. A sign in the middle of the bridge warns, "This Area Is Subject to Dense Smoke."

Behind this imposing view of what can only be described as industrial sprawl sits the town of Dundalk, compressed on jagged pieces of land east of Baltimore, where inlets slice into the bay like miniature fjords. Its streets are lined with 1940s and 1950s era cottages and row houses—two and three bedrooms—some with water access and boats docked in the rear. Some of these homes are clearly showing their age, but the residents are proud and try to keep the lawns neatly trimmed. If it were not for some late-model cars on the streets, one would almost guess that the bridge traversed a time warp, taking travelers back to 1955. Except that in 1955, the town was doing far better than it is today. Dundalk has suffered along with the rest of the Rust Belt economies of the Northeast. At its peak, the Bethlehem Steel plant employed 38,000 workers; now that number has dropped to 4,000.

Growing up in Dundalk, young men soon learn that for the most part their destiny lies in a few working-class options: the DAP caulk and chemical factory, Sparrow's Point (the Bethlehem Steel mill), the docks in Baltimore, or low-paying jobs in the service sector. Military service is an alternative for the more adventurous, and military recruiters have what is virtually a permanent station in Patapsco High School, where recruitment posters plaster the school walls. Predictably, Patapsco High also has one of the strongest industrial arts programs in the area. Girls have more educational ambitions than boys, realizing that because male-dominated factory work generally is not an option, they will have to go to a community college to get the training to do office work, perhaps as a bookkeeper, bank clerk, or administrative assistant. Others seek advanced training in cosmetology. Rather few go on to a four-year college, although the numbers are growing as the realities of the post-industrial economy set in.

A place as distinctive as Dundalk also breeds a distinctive politics. The population is working-class white, hostile to diversity, baffled by sustained immigration in the wake of September 11, pro-union, pro-death penalty, not highly confident that it has a voice in government, generally unsure of the value of its opinions, and Democrat by identification but not strongly loyal to either party. A Republican represented the area in Congress through the 1980s and 1990s, usually winning the vote of the "Dundalk Democrats" by a comfortable margin. Voting is an irregular act, a habit acquired slowly, although most residents will be regular voters by middle age. The people here are entirely educable and can be mobilized, but whether they get to the polls is contingent on the closeness of the contest and whether anyone reminds them.

Contrast this setting with that of Churchill High School in the Washington suburb of Potomac, Maryland. Churchill sits among homes that sell for hundreds of thousands of dollars on a winding stretch of a thickly wooded residential lane. Students from some of the metro area's wealthiest families go to school here, and the parking lot, with its Land Rovers, Mercedes-Benz convertibles, and BMW sedans, proves it. Here, an American-made sport utility vehicle would be considered low end. Churchill students are so serious about academic performance that it is hard to field a competitive sports team, and the football team typically maintains a losing record, sometimes going for seasons without a victory. The school shows some diversity in that it has a substantial Asian American population, but very few African American or Hispanic students attend.

In Potomac, students are politically socialized both inside and outside of school. They hear about politics from their white-collar professional parents, and they bring newspaper articles to school that are relevant to the subjects being studied. These teens ask such challenging questions that some teachers are forced to transfer because they cannot keep up with them. There are few discipline problems, and the students are polite. But these teens also are under a lot of pressure. This was the only school where we saw students carrying expensive "white-out" pens to correct any mistakes that they made while doing class work. More kids are hospitalized for depression and more attempt suicide in Potomac than elsewhere in the area. While parents are highly supportive of the teachers, they are incredibly meddlesome; calling, for example, to harass teachers about any unacceptable grades their children receive.

These kids grow up to see government as highly responsive to what few demands their parents make. Candidates ply their neighborhoods during fund-raisers, knowing that the residents have deep pockets. Churchill High students consider the police merely a minor irritant, out to bust their parties and arrest their friends for drinking and drug use. One female student mentioned speed bumps as the most salient local issue in her neighborhood. Students pick up their political orientation and attitudes, a mix of liberal and conservative, from their parents. Many students see their tax money as being wasted on programs that do not work, but their attitudes about diversity and immigration are ambivalent. Immigration is not a prominent issue for the super rich. Churchill students express their opinions on virtually any topic, but their views usually are not deeply seated in a hurtful personal experience of threat or injustice. The political socialization experience in Potomac produces both Republicans and Democrats of a fiscally conservative and socially liberal stripe. Most Potomac teens will become regular voters when they settle down after college and postgraduate school.

A world away from Churchill High is Southern High School, which is within walking distance of Baltimore's touristy Inner Harbor. From the school's front steps, students can look down on marinas crowded with sailboats, but inside the school, built in the early 1970s to serve a predominantly black and impoverished population, the halls are dark. The brick walls are gray; the floors are of brown brick tile. There are few windows, and those in the classrooms that do have them do not open. From three to six full-time Baltimore police officers patrol the halls; others are called in from street patrol if needed.

When our two-person research team entered the classrooms at Southern High, the students greeted us with stares and gaping mouths, astonished that anyone had come to visit them. After looking us over (one of the team that visited the school that day is white, the other Asian American), one boy observed that we certainly had "come a long way from outside District 1"—a reference to the police precinct in which the school and his home are located. When we informed him that we were from College Park, just forty miles away, he returned a blank stare. When we told him that it was near Washington, it became clear that he did not know where the nation's capital was either. He asked then whether College Park was "where the Terps play," referring to the University of Maryland's basketball team, usually one of the best in the nation. We found out later that in his fourteen years of life he had never left the Baltimore city limits. This is truly an insular and isolated population.

The students who showed up were amazed to see us because that year Southern High had the worst reputation for gang violence of any school in the city. There were certain stairwells that the teachers warned us not to go to, certainly not alone. African American youth from the Cherry Hill and East Baltimore neighborhoods had used Southern High as a staging ground for turf wars through much of the preceding fall, and the fighting and disruption in the school had been so bad that seventy-five students were kicked out, most of them permanently. One teacher was seriously injured when some students slammed his hand in a door; several of his fingers had to be amputated. Some teachers quit, and others were forced out by school administrators. Most of the remaining teachers were close to retirement age, and several in the social studies department were counting the days. The Baltimore City school system has a difficult time keeping young teachers. The older teachers, most of whom are white, remain only because they are so vested in the system that another jurisdiction cannot offer them comparable compensation. They are nice people, but few are highly motivated.

But who can blame them? Truancy is a serious problem. In any given day, 30 percent of the students fail to attend class, and 70 percent of the students are chronic truants. Of 700 students who begin in ninth grade, only 120 to 150 earn a diploma. Teachers have adjusted their expectations accordingly, and they readily admitted that students did not have to come to class every day to keep up. There are a few working-class white students in the school, but most of the white youth from south Baltimore now attend magnet schools or private schools.

The black students we talked to in class were surprised by our presence because the white people they encounter typically shun them or fear them. They were not at all accustomed to having white people ask their opinions. And they did have opinions. Their views were most intense on issues relating to diversity and to local law enforcement and the court system. They shared many personal stories about ways in which they had been badly treated in stores owned by Asian immigrants. Asian immigrants, regardless of nationality, were broadly characterized by the youth as "Chinese" or "whatever . . . " and deeply resented for their inability or unwillingness to communicate in English when the kids shop in their stores.

These teens pay almost no attention to what is going on in the world apart from issues that directly touch their lives or the lives of their family members. Civic engagement and political participation are completely alien notions to them, yet they were lively when asked to express their views and eager to share their experiences with us. We left surprised not by how bad the kids were but rather by how well they were doing given the obstacles they face. If their participation in class is any indication, very little is standing in the way of their good citizenship other than the fact that no one has come along to tell them that their voice matters, that someone is listening. We concluded that in order to become engaged, these youth simply had to be asked. No one around them, however, was doing any asking.

These are three different high schools in different communities where the experience of growing up could hardly be more different. Each of the twenty-nine places we visited was distinctive in at least a few ways from the ones before it. To be sure, not every feature of the local environments we have studied has an influence on an adolescent's political life, but we wanted to know which ones did.

Places and Political Socialization

This book is about the local sources of variation in the political socialization of young Americans early in the twenty-first century. Our work takes up many of the classic questions about socialization in an effort to determine what contributes to an adolescent's development of a wide variety of viewpoints and dispositions germane to his or her civic engagement and political behavior later in life. Numerous social scientists have indicated that the behavior described by the term "civic engagement" is undergirded by a set of attitudes that demonstrate knowledge about and positive evaluations of government and politics.[1] This book builds on the previous research by examining the sources of those attitudes, not just in the individual characteristics of survey respondents but also in the characteristics of the local environments that shape their experiences during late adolescence.

Surprisingly little research has been done on the role of the local context in the political socialization process.[2] Where the local context has been examined, the focus has been on adults rather than adolescents.[3] Theoretically, our effort will merge two large bodies of research that have been independent of each other: the growing literature on contextual effects and the traditional literature on political socialization, which has its roots in political science and developmental psychology.

Fresh research on the topic of adolescent socialization is needed because previous research cannot necessarily be trusted to explain the attitudes and behavior of later generations, including the one that came of age in the late 1990s and early 2000s. While we believe that the previous body of research provides ample material for hypothesis testing—and we reviewed much of that literature in the course of writing this book—we also have good reasons to believe that the causal relationships are not the same today as they were in 1975 or 1955.

To sum up, our motivation for revisiting the topic of political socialization came in part from the belief that the effects of local context on political socialization had been overlooked and also from the conviction that what was true of previous generations would be less true today, because the nature of the stimuli has changed. For example, news media exposure today cannot mean what it meant thirty years ago, given the way in which news content has changed and media choices have multiplied. The most recent birth cohorts may begin their political lives much later than their parents and grandparents did. If feeling rooted in one's community is necessary to recognize one's stake in political life and this feeling does not appear in contemporary adolescents until they reach thirty years of age,

---

1. Abramson and Aldrich (1982); Delli Carpini and Keeter (1996); Jennings and Niemi (1974, 1981); Nie, Junn, and Stehlik-Barry (1996); Niemi and Junn (1998); Putnam (2000).

2. But see Garcia (1973); Litt (1963); Sanchez-Jankowski (1986).

3. Huckfeldt and Sprague (1995); Huckfeldt (1986).

their participation is going to lag behind that of previous generations, whose life was well established by age twenty-one.[4]

The demographic composition of the nation also has changed considerably in the last fifteen years. Literature from the 1960s and 1970s suggested that white children exhibit more trust than black children and that ethnic background was a good predictor of adolescent political values.[5] With some of the highest levels of immigration in over a century, we stand at an excellent point in history to retest old hypotheses on new immigrant and second-generation populations. Family structure has undergone a complete revolution in the thirty years since Clarke found that the absence of a father among black children led to increased cynicism about politics.[6] The relationships between the new generation of youth and the primary agents of socialization—parents, schools, media, and peers—have been altered in many important ways.

People are politically socialized by the information they receive. This information certainly varies over time, but it varies more regularly across space, as communities and their constituent parts structure the content and flow of politically relevant messages in distinctive ways. Within a particular age cohort, socializing messages will be received differently, with greater impact on some than on others depending on the attributes of the individuals themselves and characteristics of the places where they live.[7]

The extensive literature on political socialization has about as many explanatory models as there are articles on the subject, testimony to the complexity of the phenomenon itself. No simple modeling exercise can possibly capture this complexity, but our explanatory framework has several major themes, which are developed in the chapters to come. First, children are raised within a specific structural context, a local social environment, that influences the political attitudes and values that they develop. This environment comprises the forces working at the top of the "funnel of causality" described by Campbell and colleagues in their landmark work, *The American Voter*, including community resources (income, education), diversity (racial and ethnic groups), political engagement (voter turnout), and political leaning (Republican, Democrat, or competitive).[8] While these

4. Schneider and Stevenson (1999); Deufel (2002).
5. Greenberg (1970); Lyons (1970); Greeley (1975).
6. Clarke (1973).
7. Schuman and Corning (2000, p. 921).
8. Campbell and others (1960, pp. 24–32).

environmental forces might have only a small *direct* impact on an adolescent's political development, their indirect impact could be quite profound.

Social context is an important element of our approach to socialization because it structures the quantity and flow of information. An individual is "embedded within a particular context," which "structures social interaction patterns."[9] These interactions communicate political information on which the individual bases an attitudinal response. While many locations in which the interactions take place are self-selected—a neighborhood, for instance—there are constraints on the selection itself (income, housing market), and the choice leads to non-self-selected exposure to information. If one's neighbors are mostly Republicans, one is likely to pass by Republican yard signs and to talk with Republican neighbors whether one wants to or not. Work settings often are sources of cross-cutting, non-self-selected information exposure as most people rarely have complete power to determine the views of those around whom they work.[10]

We know from volumes of previous work that certain attributes of a person's identity and personal history shape the likelihood that he or she will participate in politics, feel efficacious, and be tolerant of others. The classic survey research in socialization has focused on individual characteristics as causes of the attitudes and behaviors of interest.[11] For example, a staple finding of public opinion research from the discipline of political science is that individuals who are more knowledgeable and interested in politics are more likely to participate. Our point is to remind readers that people do not become interested in politics within a vacuum. In technical terms we would say that political knowledge and interest are not exogenous variables—they do not appear in the universe without prior cause. Instead, certain social contexts stimulate interest and mobilize people for political action better than others. A major theme that we pursue is that contextual variables that capture aspects of the individual's political environment have an impact on how much adolescents learn, what opinions they form, and how they express themselves politically.

For example, some previous research suggests that a child who is inclined toward one party but grows up in a social environment dominated by adherents of another party may be more reserved about express-

9. Huckfeldt and Sprague (1995, p. 8).

10. Mutz and Mondak (2001).

11. Campbell and others (1960); Miller and Shanks (1996); Nie, Verba, and Petrocik (1979).

ing his viewpoints than if he were surrounded by like-minded partisans.[12] One might hypothesize then that homogeneous political environments encourage more political discussion than heterogeneous ones because people feel safer talking about politics when they are among those who agree with them.[13] Heterogeneous social environments, while potentially more stimulating, may ironically retard the political socialization process by squelching discussion and limiting what a person learns through it, leading eventually to depressed political participation.[14]

But there also are compelling reasons for believing the opposite—that heterogeneous environments stimulate discussion because controversy fills the air. A consistent series of findings in the political participation literature suggests that competitive, politically diverse environments produce higher turnout in elections than lopsided, one-party settings.[15] Even though individuals may prefer to discuss politics with people who are most like them, they also are more inclined to participate when they think that their vote counts or when an important outcome hangs in the balance.[16] Competitive elections not only stimulate higher interest among voters, they also bring mobilization efforts to life, in the form of voter outreach activities by parties, interest groups, and candidates.[17] What can be surmised from this fascinating mix of research findings is that citizen interest is piqued by political conflict and that competitive political environments generally have a positive effect on political socialization. At the same time, young people are probably no more desirous than adults of having high levels of political conflict among their closest associates or regular discussion partners. A competitive and conflictual environment is positive so long as there remains a safe place for political discussion within one's immediate constellation of associates.

Another theme in our explanatory framework is that the direct impact of structural environmental factors is mediated through family and school relationships, which are more immediate sources of causal influence on an individual's sense of efficacy, political knowledge, nationalistic sentiment, tolerance of diversity, and other dispositions germane to the political socialization process. We do not argue that political behavior and attitudes are

---

12. Berelson, Lazarsfeld, and McPhee (1954, chap. 6).
13. Mutz (2002a).
14. Mutz (2002b).
15. Key (1949).
16. Rosenstone and Hansen (1993).
17. Huckfeldt and Sprague (1992).

completely structurally determined but rather that the range of individual freedom is restricted by the political and social aspects of the nurturing environment in the family and the community.

Setting and Design of This Study

Against this background we set out to collect data on the attitudes of adolescents, bearing in mind the need to gather information about the communities in which they grow up. While previous research provides excellent material for testing hypotheses, we had good reasons for believing that the causal relationships today are not the same as in previous decades. But implicit contrasts and explicit hypothesis tests are two different things. This book focuses mainly on hypothesis testing of cross-sectional data on ninth through twelfth graders surveyed in 1999 and 2000.

The design for our research is based on our general theory that political socialization is not uniform within a society but is shaped by the local political and social circumstances in which individuals find themselves. Our research strategy did not guarantee that we would succeed in finding evidence to support that notion. It was clearly possible that once we controlled for relevant individual traits, social and political environments would have no impact whatsoever. To test for causal influences across communities, we studied twenty-nine distinct schools in twenty-nine different communities within or just outside the Baltimore and Washington, D.C., metropolitan area. The academic community has needed further research on the neighborhood and community influences on political socialization for a long time. Many previous studies were limited by the fact that they did not capture enough variation across neighborhoods and communities; research carried out in one, two, or a few schools of necessity treats community characteristics as a constant, missing whatever causal impact they may have. Other studies simply failed to record neighborhood and community information that could be used to investigate the effects of these variables on attitudes and behavior. Still other studies gathered some limited contextual information, but it has not been sufficiently detailed to be of much explanatory value.

In the spring of 1999 and of 2000, we surveyed 3,060 students in high schools scattered throughout the greater Baltimore-Washington metro area (see figure 1-1). The schools were selected by random sampling of fourteen separate school districts—rural, suburban, and urban—in order to represent the area's public high school population by social, economic, and political characteristics. While the focus of this study was on examining relationships rather than representing a specific population, the classes chosen within schools ensured representation by race of student and academic standing. In spite of the fact that it was not feasible to choose a strict random probability sample of the student population from enrollment lists, the resulting sample was remarkably representative of the underlying population (see appendix A for details on sample selection and representation).

The area's high schools generally track students into two or three groups; "honors" and "standard" tracks were most common, with the standard track less oriented toward preparing students for college. Often more than half of a school's students were in honors courses, with more than one-third of all students aiming at advanced placement (AP) college credit. We typically chose no more than two honors courses at each school, and at least half of each school's subjects came from the standard academic track. In almost all cases, we obtained a representative sample of students of varying grade and achievement levels, although at one school we surveyed only tenth graders—nearly the entire tenth-grade class. We generally sought to survey between 70 and 150 students at each school, depending largely on the school's size. High schools in the metropolitan Washington-Baltimore area range in size from a low of about 500 students to a high of about 3,000.

A small research team of between two and four people traveled to each school, briefed teachers on the purposes and goals of the study, and administered the questionnaire to classes of ninth, tenth, eleventh, and twelfth graders in classes of mixed achievement. The survey research team included two Caucasian males and two Asian American females. Usually the research was carried out in each classroom in teams of two, and the teams were mixed by gender and race.

Schools included four all-black high schools in Prince George's County, Maryland, and inner-city Baltimore, Maryland, and three predominantly black high schools in Prince George's County. The Asian respondents were heavily represented in the five Montgomery County, Maryland, high schools. Maryland has a small Hispanic population, but it was best represented in the Prince George's County schools. Arlington County, Virginia, also contributed many Hispanic respondents. The sites also included two rural schools in areas where immigrant farm labor is widely used but where few immigrants are enrolled in the schools. Two schools situated in extremely affluent areas of Montgomery County, Maryland, also were included in the sample. The resulting sample represents a broad cross-section

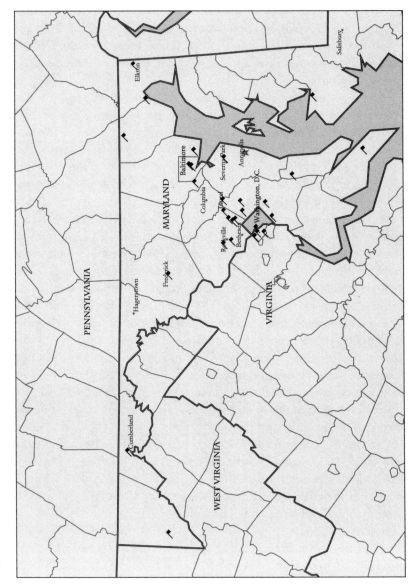

Figure 1-1. *Location of Participating Schools in the Metro Civic Values Study, 1999–2000*

of economic, political, and demographic contexts that should provide sufficient variation to test hypotheses about the effects of social and economic context on the attitudes of both immigrant and native-born youth.[18]

Outcomes of the Socialization Process

Political socialization is the process by which new generations are inducted into political culture, learning the knowledge, values, and attitudes that contribute to support of the political system.[19] Through exposure to various socialization agents, citizens develop a relationship with their government and political leaders, although nothing inherent in the process ensures that the relationship will be "healthy" or "good." Even so, political socialization research as it has been carried out in the United States has always built on an implicit normative foundation. The content of what is transmitted is of critical importance since the goal of socialization is the perpetuation of values consistent with the governance of the nation.[20] Hence, in a constitutionally democratic republic, we have judged that it is better to develop attitudes that favor political participation than to develop cynical, nonparticipatory ones. Similarly, being knowledgeable about the system and how it works is viewed as superior to being ignorant of its workings. More generally, successful socialization ought to involve the formation of crystallized, stable opinions on issues.[21] Respect for the outcomes of the political process also is integral to support of the political system, especially when those outcomes may not be in one's personal interest. Practices that further the goals of participation, knowledge, opinion holding, and support for the democratic process are judged to be superior to practices that undermine those goals. It is possible then to speak of defective or "bad" socialization just as we speak of effective or "good" socialization.

We stand to gain considerable insight about the potential for civic engagement among individuals and social groups by taking a careful inventory of the forces that contribute to bad socialization. It is clear that political learning and socialization do not end when a person graduates from high school.[22] However, there is ample evidence to support the conclusion

---

18. Comparisons of our sample populations to the school populations by the key characteristic of race or ethnicity with and without sample weights are available from the authors.

19. Almond and Coleman (1960); Almond and Verba (1963); Jennings and Niemi (1974, p. 5).

20. Dennis (1968).

21. Sears and Valentino (1997).

22. Searing, Schwartz, and Lind (1973); Searing, Wright, and Rabinowitz (1976); Markus (1979).

that what is learned during adolescence predicts adult political behavior and opinions.[23] The accumulation of risk factors in a particular population of adolescents may well doom that group to a lifetime of civic inactivity and irrelevance while the absence of those factors frees another group to realize its political potential. Identifying the risk factors that predict non-participation has some policy relevance because it would help to identify individuals and populations that may need compensatory guidance and mentoring. The effects of one or a few of these handicaps can be overcome by more positive environmental forces and interventions, but to achieve that end, the risk factors first must be identified. We address this after first detailing the outcomes we measured.

Political Knowledge

Nothing is more central to democratic theory than the idea of an informed, knowledgeable citizenry. By knowledge, we mean the capacity of citizens to recall facts about what government is and does.[24] Our main concern is with *fundamental* knowledge relating to political structures, historically significant developments, and the identities and roles of officeholders in the political system.[25] To measure knowledge, we used a seven-item political knowledge test and scored results from 0 to 100 percent (see appendix B). Knowledge of fundamental facts about government and politics is essential for interpreting information in news broadcasts, understanding details about important events and actions taken by public figures, and making inferences from news stories that translate into judgments about whom or what to support or oppose.[26]

When asked, high school students even as young as ninth graders recognize that political knowledge counts, yet an amazing number of them will fail to acquire much of it by the time they reach adulthood. Consequently, knowledge probably is one of the most variable constructs that we examine and one that is likely to have many causal covariates among individual traits and community characteristics. While there is pretty solid evidence that the level of political knowledge has dropped over time, our focus is on differences in political knowledge across our study population.[27]

23. Beck and Jennings (1982); Jennings and Markus (1984); Green and Palmquist (1994); Alwin and Krosnick (1991); Plutzer (2002).

24. Delli Carpini and Keeter (1993; 1996).

25. Garramone and Atkin (1986).

26. Miller and Krosnick (2000, p. 312).

27. Delli Carpini and Keeter (1996).

Citizens who possess the least political knowledge are those who are least likely to participate in a wide variety of political activities; their needs, therefore, are not expressed to officeholders.[28] Adolescence is one of the few periods during the life cycle when there are nearly universal opportunities to collect and absorb political facts and information through coursework in social studies and history. Understanding the sources of variation in the retention and recall of political information is critical because it predicts levels of political interest and participation later in life.

Frequency of Political Discussion

People who know more about politics are much more willing to engage in political discussions. Knowledge and discussion of a subject are reciprocally related: discussion of politics has long been considered both a function of one's level of political knowledge and a means of obtaining additional information.[29] But even though political knowledge and frequency of discussion are related, it is worth considering them separately because they may have different causes. Discussion is a social activity, knowledge a measure of what people remember. Our measure of political discussion frequency was a survey question about the number of times students engaged in political discussion with family members or friends in the previous week (see appendix B).

We found that many youth refused to engage in discussions of politics because they failed to see its relevance to their lives. We witnessed the following exchange among ninth graders on the subject of why young people do not take more of an interest:

> *Sam*: Government doesn't directly affect us all the time. Usually you don't realize how government affects your life until later, after high school.
>
> *Julie*: After a certain age, you learn that you need to vote.
>
> *John*: Older people have seen more how government affects their lives.
>
> *Ryan*: Older people need to have something to complain about. Every old person I know is always talking about politics.

The consensus among these ninth graders was that politics is relevant only for older people, that eventually it might become important to them

---

28. Verba and others (1993b).
29. Delli Carpini and Keeter (1996).

to take more of an interest, but that it was not important to them at their age. Just when one reaches this age-relevance threshold was unclear; the students could not agree on when that happened. Age eighteen, however, clearly was not where the bright line was drawn:

> *Question*: Do you consider age eighteen to give you a special status because you can then vote?
>
> *John*: No, I wouldn't think of this as all that special—not like driving!

On one hand, it seems unreasonable to expect fourteen-year-old freshmen in high school to have developed an adult interest in politics and to have reached a high level of civic engagement. To some extent, these kids are right in saying that politics and government is not as relevant to them as it is to older people. Nor should we expect politicians to be especially concerned about what kids are thinking. What concerns us is that many of these youth never cross that elusive age-relevance threshold when they believe it is time to discuss politics. They will spend their lifetimes as non-participants.

The good news is that some of the youth we surveyed had developed an interest in politics well before they turned eighteen. What forces predict the extent of political talk going on outside the classroom? We will answer this question in the chapters to come, but we anticipate that higher levels of political discussion are likely to be reported among those living in well-educated communities that have more resources to expend on providing access to information. Likewise, it is a good bet that settings that have highly competitive elections stimulate more discussion about politics than those with predictable, one-sided contests. Similarly, communities with higher levels of voter turnout have adult populations with greater levels of knowledge about politics than do those with low turnout. Participation and discussion are linked as closely as discussion and knowledge.

Political Efficacy

A sense of political efficacy is one of the more thoroughly examined concepts in the study of political socialization. Efficacy justifiably attracts attention because it is thought to be central to political participation, a necessary prerequisite to taking an action as simple as voting or as complex as contacting government officials or volunteering for a campaign.[30] "Internal" efficacy refers to the perception that one has the necessary resources

---

30. Campbell, Gurin, and Miller (1954); Abramson and Aldrich (1982).

and knowledge to have an impact on the political process—the sense that one can perform civic duties adequately or even with a high degree of competence. It could be characterized as one's self-confidence regarding involvement in politics.[31] A person who is inefficacious feels powerless and in response becomes apathetic and inattentive to political matters.[32] Internal efficacy is highly associated with political participation in the form of voting and campaigning, especially among those with lower levels of education.[33] Our measures of internal and external efficacy are detailed in appendix B.

"External" efficacy is the perception that government is responsive to whatever efforts one makes to exercise influence. It is not simply a reflection of what one thinks of incumbent officeholders at a given moment; it reflects a more enduring attitude toward the system.[34] Among the youth we surveyed, cynicism rooted in low external efficacy was an abundant commodity:

> *Tambra*: Actions speak louder than words. Most of these politicians are in it for the money, that's all. They say one thing but never do anything.
>
> *Eric*: I can't believe them when they say things. I'll believe it when I see it. They have to do something.
>
> *Chris*: Sometimes a candidate comes up with an idea but it comes so late that you think he's just saying it to get reelected. There are all these last-minute antics to draw voters.

These young people, like adults, widely believed that politicians seek office for personal gain, not to serve the public interest—that politicians pander, making empty promises that they never intend to fulfill. Some simply dismissed government as corrupt, period, offering neither evidence nor explanation. Do such young people ever shelve their cynicism and become participants? Perhaps, but someone probably has to activate them. If they are activated even once, it may alter their attitudes about government performance.[35] Political involvement gives citizens the opportunity to test the system's responsiveness directly, and they generally conclude from their trials that it works.

31. Almond and Verba (1963).
32. Seeman (1966).
33. Finkel (1985).
34. Iyengar (1980).
35. Finkel (1985).

With political participation on the decline, it is no surprise that aggregate levels of external efficacy have shriveled as well.[36] With more people withdrawing from political participation, fewer seize the opportunity to test the system's responsiveness for themselves. Still, there are wide variations in participation levels across neighborhoods and communities, suggesting that underlying efficacy levels vary widely and that the variation may be at least as important as the temporal drop in efficacy that we have observed over several decades.

Tolerance for Immigration-Induced Diversity

In many areas, the social conditions in which adolescents are being raised are very different from the conditions that prevailed in previous generations. That conditions have changed so drastically provides us with an excellent reason for posing questions about tolerance and openness to immigration. The continuing controversy surrounding civil rights for African Americans has generated a wealth of fascinating studies about black-white relations over the last thirty years. Much of that research has construed tolerance for diversity to mean acceptance of African Americans and the civil rights agenda: school desegregation, affirmative action, ending discrimination in housing and employment, and spending on programs favoring blacks.[37]

Here we ask how tolerance for ethnic diversity and immigration varies among the current generation of native and foreign-born adolescents in a variety of social contexts, some with high levels of immigration, others with little or no immigrant presence. The extent of exposure to diversity varied highly across the locations we visited. One of our primary dependent variables, then, is tolerance for the ethnic diversity resulting from the nation's high immigration levels. We dub this construct "immigration-induced diversity," as opposed to ethnic diversity that may not have immigration at its core. We use a number of survey items to gauge reactions to diversity (see appendix B).

Visits to the high schools in our study area revealed a wide variety of viewpoints, at least some of which seemed to be determined by local context. Some striking examples of anxiety and ambivalence about immigration came from African American students in our inner-city black schools:

36. Lipset and Schneider (1983); Uslaner (2002).

37. Glaser (1994); Kinder and Sanders (1996); Kinder and Sears (1981); Sears, Sidanius, and Bobo (2000); Schuman and Bobo (1988); Schuman, Steeh, and Bobo (1985); Smith (1981a, 1981b); Steeh and Schumann (1992).

Question: Would more immigrants make Baltimore a better place to live?

James: What makes you think another culture would make it better here?

Darryl: It would make it worse, because people would want stuff.

Cedric: Yeah, we fight ourselves right now. If they moved in, we would be fighting them and us.

Aleshea: We have enough problems as it is. They wouldn't want us to move into their country.

Tamelyn: But you can't stop people from moving where they want to move.

Aleshea: You sure can, you can meet them at the border with guns.

Tamelyn: Foreigners aren't wanted around here because they take up jobs and work hard. But people need the competition they bring. People here are just lazy. Bring the immigrants in and give them a run for their money. Everything in life ain't free.

Lanelle: We are already overpopulated. There isn't enough space, they'll take all the jobs, there isn't enough room. They gotta go. Look at [Washington] D.C., it's crowded there.

Cedric: They open up stores in the neighborhood that we would otherwise open up.

Lanelle: How can an immigrant be here for just a few months and they open up a business, but it's hard for a black person to open up a store who's been here for their whole lives?

Tamelyn: Well, maybe we're lazy.

Teya: Black people don't want to do nothing. They're just lazy. They don't want to earn anything themselves, they want it given to them.

Ashata: There's a lot of immigration in my family. My dad and my relatives are from Trinidad and Barbados, and that's not right that we say they shouldn't come here because maybe some Caucasian people say we ought to go back to Africa. You know that's not right.

The African American students who opposed immigration framed their objections primarily in terms of the economic threat that immigration posed, but some also referred to overcrowding and cultural conflict. Those who were more open to immigration mentioned the immigrant ancestry of African Americans and underlined the importance of a free and open society, where people could move about as they pleased. Notably few of the black youth we encountered argued for diversity in terms of civil rights or on the grounds that there is a right to immigrate.

Among white youth, our field notes indicated the most hostility in areas that were close to but did not necessarily include diverse populations, usually inner-ring suburbs where students associated diversity with the inner-city problems of joblessness, crime, and even sanitation and health. The following exchange from a Baltimore suburban high school is illustrative:

Jacob: I know that immigrants are supposed to bring in new culture and yadda yadda yadda, but I've had enough new culture. They're taking up all the jobs, flippin' burgers and doing construction.

Andrew: They may bring in foreign diseases that we don't have here. We don't need that.

Michael: Immigrants are people so how can you say they will improve things? It'll be neutral, some will improve things, others won't.

Justin: California is nice because it's diverse, but immigration brings other problems. On main streets, it's fine, but you go down a side street and everyone is speaking Spanish. There's a language barrier, and I can't communicate with them. There is also crime associated with immigration. I wouldn't want Catonsville to be like California.

Michael: There are good people and bad people all over.

Jacob: Okay, I would like to amend what I said earlier. Legal immigrants are okay, but there are those illegals who are jumping over fences and using up my welfare money. That I just can't take.

We were struck by the confidence and forcefulness with which these white suburban students expressed their reservations about diversity. There were no tentative pauses in response to the questions we asked. The students pounced immediately, providing evidence that they had considered the issues at some length and had well-formulated opinions. Here the sentiment ranged from keeping immigrants out because they might pose a threat to the prosperity and health of native-born Americans to letting them come in to be evaluated on the basis of individual merit. There certainly was no sentiment, among any of the students who spoke up, favoring a broad right to immigrate.

The views of suburban youth who felt threatened by diversity differed considerably from those of rural youth who had rarely given it much thought or were simply ignorant of the subject. One student from a small-town high school on the distant metropolitan fringe even approached a member of our research team to ask what the term "immigrants" meant.

Billy: Who cares if immigrants move in? It's okay.

Joseph: It would give us more ideas on how different people live and different religions and different cultures, but it would cause conflict too.

Billy: It wouldn't matter, it would be the same.

Some rural youth approached the question of an immigration influx with a mixture of mockery and disbelief at the very suggestion:

Jennifer: Where are they going to move here?! There are more gas stations than stores. There's nothing for them here.

Sarah: The main reason people come in is because of jobs, and we ain't got no jobs. Americans are losin' their jobs.

Ronald: If you look at transportation, the roads here are terrible.

Daniel: There's not much up here. There's nutin' for 'em to do.

Ronald: All we got here is farms and hicks. This is the middle of nowhere. It wouldn't make much difference.

Rural students were slower to respond to our questions about diversity. It was obvious from the coaxing we had to do that they had never really considered the issue before. They also were more reluctant than the suburban youth to say anything that could be construed as critical of or prejudiced toward racial minorities. Even though they may have harbored prejudiced views, they were far more reluctant to express them, perhaps reflecting a social constraint akin to politeness that was not present in the suburban schools. From these informal discussions we received the distinct impression, to be tested more rigorously later, that proximity to diverse populations influenced adolescent attitudes about immigration-induced diversity.

Nationalism and Chauvinism

Not since the mid-1970s, at the close of the Vietnam War, has there been so much interest in young Americans' attitudes toward the U.S. political system. The terrorist attacks of September 11, 2001, have renewed interest in patriotism and nationalism and how these sentiments vary across the population. The impetus for research on this subject during the Vietnam War era was to understand the foundations of the antigovernment sentiment being expressed on university campuses throughout the nation at that time. During this turbulent period, liberal scholars adopted the term "chauvinism" to describe devout loyalty to U.S. government institutions and policies, such as that expressed in the motto "My country, right or wrong."

As characterized by the previous generation of research, chauvinism is the belief that one's nation and government are superior to others, a belief closely related to ethnocentrism and nationalism. According to this interpretation, one who is willing to criticize the American political system is not a chauvinist. Chauvinists not only are unlikely to engage in criticism of their own government, they probably are disdainful of those who do. In earlier research, chauvinism was associated with intolerance of political nonconformists (for example, communists, socialists, and campus radicals) who might attack the justice and fairness of American political and economic institutions. Education that inculcated nationalistic sentiment was widely thought to be akin to teaching bigotry—that America is superior to other nations and so are Americans. This sort of favoritism for one's own political community often is considered to be contrary to the liberal virtues of impartiality and tolerance.[38]

On the other hand, some modicum of nationalistic sentiment may be necessary to stimulate respect for and trust in the institutions and political processes established by the U.S. Constitution. Arguably, the only way people can understand their responsibilities to their community is through patriotic education: a positive emotional attachment to one's country is often considered to be a necessary condition for civic engagement.[39] Love for one's country need not lead to bigotry or intolerance. Social psychologists have found that a strong in-group identification (for example, love for one's nation) does not necessarily accompany hostility to those outside one's group.[40] Nor do patriotic individuals become uncritical followers. On the contrary, without patriotic education, many schools fail to provide students with the knowledge and skills necessary to be critical citizens, and also ignore opportunities to teach the liberal standards of tolerance and objectivity.

With these opposing views firmly in mind, we examine the sources and effects of nationalistic sentiment because we believe that expressions of support for the American political system are associated with other important

38. MacIntyre (1995, p. 225).
39. Damon (2001, p. 135).
40. Brewer (1999).

attitudes toward policy and could be related to a person's level of political awareness and civic engagement.

Among the youth we met, few were willing to think very globally about the American political system, much less offer any criticism of it through comparison with some other institutional design. Students sometimes complained about government performance and about taxes being wasted, and some occasionally asked why our system of government is shaped the way that it is, but none held up an alternative model. Students have a hard time grasping the difference between proportional representation and single-member, winner-take-all election districts, and many teachers themselves are fuzzy on the details. When students ask why there are not more political parties in the United States, few teachers can provide a straightforward explanation. Unlike their parents' generation, these kids do not have protestors in their midst calling for a revolution, and no one is stretching (or attempting to contract) the limits of political speech. With few challenges to the existing political order in the postcommunist era, there just isn't much to be chauvinistic about.

We were interested in whether nationalism is an attitude that fosters or retards the political socialization process. Does nationalism influence efficacy or participation? Does a feeling of national pride generate interest in politics and government? To the extent that nationalism fosters knowledge and participation, it might be something to encourage.

Attitudes toward the Police and the Courts

Maintaining a healthy suspicion of official power is a venerable American tradition that did not begin with the antiwar protests of the 1960s or with the public's reaction to the Watergate scandal. Nor was the public's suspicious reaction to the federal law enforcement actions at Waco and Ruby Ridge in the early 1990s especially out of line with the nation's heritage.[41] The widespread inclination to view police action with distrust predates the nation's founding. The commitment of the founders to protecting the citizenry from overbearing police power was underscored by the passage of the Bill of Rights.

Highly publicized accounts of police misconduct and of negligence of the courts have sparked public furor in the last two decades. The fallout from the 1992 Rodney King beating in Los Angeles was extraordinary,

---

41. Brewer and Willnat (2001).

demonstrating the damage that police brutality can inflict on police-community relations.[42] The not-guilty verdicts initially handed down to the policemen who brutalized King further strained relations between Los Angelenos and the police; they also caused people to question the fundamental fairness of the court system. The King beating and subsequent police trials provide an infamous instance in which the public eye was quickly and coldly trained on police and courts.[43] More recent incidents of police brutality in New York City and reports of police corruption in Los Angeles further eroded the public's trust. African Americans and other minority groups are quick to highlight evidence of police brutality as proof of how the police cannot be trusted to protect everyone and how some communities may even be threatened by police action.

Our measure of attitudes toward police and law enforcement was derived from two survey questions detailed in appendix B. What is curious to us is the extent to which the variation in attitudes toward the police and courts could be predicted by an adolescent's race, neighborhood of residence, and other traits. Adolescents, in general, often are described as "oppositional" vis-à-vis authority, of both parents and others. But while many high school youth may express a general contempt for local law enforcement, that disdain is likely to run much deeper and wider in some communities than in others. African American students in the majority black schools we visited guffawed with laughter at the idea that they might trust the police to protect them. Even their teachers laughed. The following comments were typical and show the extent of opinion formation on this issue, even among the female students, who presumably had less contact with the police than the males:

> *Latisha*: It takes them an hour to go somewhere where someone's been shot in a black neighborhood, but it takes like three minutes for them to respond to a call from a white neighborhood.
> *Lashonda*: My uncle got beat up. The Caucasian police will try to make a black man look bad.
> *Kedron*: The cops will think I'm the criminal when they arrive, and yet I'm the one who called in the first place.
> *Tiffany*: Cops have way too much attitude in the performance of their duties. And the black police are just as bad as the white police.

---

42. See Tuch and Weitzer (1997).
43. Baldassare (1994).

Robert: The cops target minorities. They pull you over for nothin' and question you just because of the way you look. They harass you for petty things.

Latisha: I've seen them watching a fight from a distance rather than go in and break it up.

Robert: The only ones the cops respect are old people and people with money. Unless you're black with money, then it doesn't count.

These students were almost equally skeptical of securing a fair trial from the local court system:

Robert: The public defenders don't work for you. They're workin' for them. They're paid by them. And they don't care because they get paid even if you're not free.

Juan: [Getting a fair trial] depends on what you did. If you stole a bike, maybe.

Kedron: Yeah, if you kill a cop, forget it. You're finished. A big deal is made of a couple of white kids who dress up in trench coats, but no one talks about an innocent brother who is shot.

Latisha: It takes money—money, and you have to know how to talk to people.

The students in this predominantly black and Hispanic school viewed the police and local court system as stacked against them in about every conceivable way. Their beliefs about the police and the courts were rife with the perception of racial and socioeconomic inequality.

The white suburban youth expressed a much smaller set of complaints—mostly that the police harassed them and had nothing else to do but chase after minor drug and alcohol offenses. Absent from their comments was any sense that the police enforce the law unequally or target certain groups over others on the basis of race or socioeconomic status. They complained about police competence and the fact that police do so little in these relatively crime-free neighborhoods:

Emily: The cops mostly hang out at Dunkin Donuts. They don't want to face any real crime.

Kathleen: There's not much to protect, not much crime to protect us from. They enforce the basic laws around here.

John: At our age, you don't think of the police for protection, you
   think of them for busting our parties and arresting our friends for
   drinking and drugs.
Emily: The cops protect you from things that aren't dangerous.
Ann-Marie: I feel bad for cops. There are no easy solutions. They
   aren't going to get it right every time, but it would be worse without them.

Suburban and small-town youth also were more optimistic about their
ability to obtain a fair trial.

Nerissa: I would never get into trouble with the law; that's not my
   thing. But if I did I'm sure I could get a fair trial.
Question: How sure?
Nerissa: Pretty sure, I guess. But that's different than when you asked
   if we can trust the police. You know that they are always looking
   to get after teenagers. Like there's nothing better to do, you know?

There can be little question that there were enormous racial differences
in these adolescents' attitudes toward the police. But our interview notes
also suggest that their attitudes toward local police and courts were subject
to strong contextual influences that can be traced to the ethnic and economic character of their neighborhoods. Because information about police
and court misconduct usually is local, we fully expected our survey data to
show that attitudes vary across communities.

The Clinton Impeachment

Events are a catalyst for the development of political values, offering
"occasions for socialization."[44] Prominent socializing events can be of two
types: some have the effect of stimulating national unity, while others
divide the nation, sharpening and even redefining partisanship. Among
those that count as unifying are the two world wars, the Persian Gulf war
of 1991, and the Oklahoma City bombing; one also could count the terrorist attacks on the World Trade Center and the Pentagon in this category.
These events are important because they galvanize the nation to fight
against a common enemy for an unquestioned cause. Among examples of
events that produce division and sharpen partisanship are the Vietnam
War, the Watergate scandal, the civil rights protests of the 1960s, the O. J.

44. Beck and Jennings (1991); Sears and Valentino (1997).

Simpson trial, the Los Angeles riots, and the shootings at Columbine High School. In these cases, universal alarm about a major problem soon gave way to policy judgments that were sharply divided. These events are important for political socialization because they deepen cleavages during a time when young people are beginning to understand and remember political events and their outcomes.

Another divisive socializing event was the impeachment of President William Jefferson Clinton. With the major exception of the terrorist attacks, few political events of the millennial generation were as visible as the House impeachment and Senate trial of President Clinton at the close of his second term in 1998. The Clinton impeachment will be remembered because it had all the features of good political theater: sex, intense partisan conflict, good guys versus bad guys—and debate about who the good and bad guys were. Because of its sensational, titillating content, media coverage was round-the-clock, and it was virtually impossible for even the most irregular of television viewers to avoid it.[45] Yet how adolescents responded to that barrage is likely to vary highly across individual and community characteristics, depending primarily on partisan orientations. Our measure of response to the impeachment process is derived from two survey questions (see appendix B), one tapping reaction to the principal offense itself (lying to the grand jury) and the other asking whether the impeachment process discouraged interest in politics because of the purportedly "trivial" nature of the sexual indiscretions that precipitated it.

At each school site, the most vocal students were highly aware of the impeachment process and generally opposed it. Informal polls of our classrooms indicated 2-to-1 opposition to the impeachment proceedings. The following exchange among ethnic minority students in a predominantly Democratic area was typical:

Darnell: The president's personal life is no one's business but his own.
Tamika: He's doing a good job as president, so who cares if he made a human mistake?
Steven: The whole process is a joke. This is a total distraction away from important matters.
Jorge: It's nobody's business. You're human. It's your nature to lie.
Darnell: He's not God.

45. Morris (2002); Rozell and Wilcox (2000); Quirk (2000).

Steven: But he shouldn't have lied about it. He should have been up front from the beginning.

Kedron: It was a waste of money. But he lied under oath and got special treatment. The president shouldn't have gotten special treatment; that wasn't right.

Darnell: The Republicans were just out to get the man.

But we also sensed that the adolescents' views of the impeachment were probably less context dependent than many other attitudes we tapped. Even in schools situated in more heavily Republican neighborhoods, there was substantial sympathy for the president's acquittal, mixed with sarcasm, sexual innuendo, and traditional morality:

Daniel: It probably wasn't worth impeachment, but he's made us the laughing stock of the world.

Mary: He's not fit to be the head of state. He has everyone laughing at us.

Brenda: You have to separate someone's private life from what they do in public. He's still a good president.

Barry: People lie under oath all the time, but when it's the president they make a big deal out of it.

Angel: And what's this thing he has for such large women? (titters of laughter across the room)

Kristin: I think it was disgusting that Monica Lewinsky was so young.

Mary: I think it is a moral issue. The president has to set a good example.

We found that the impeachment was something that the white students very much enjoyed joking about. Many felt that Clinton's affair with Monica Lewinsky was a comical event and that the impeachment process was excessive hoopla over a trivial matter. A few would occasionally speak of the events leading to the impeachment as a justification for their cynicism: "It just goes to show you that you can't trust our leaders," insisted one suburban white female. Our qualitative notes showed that a clear cultural divide, independent of partisanship, was present between white students from small towns with more blue-collar and service sector employment and white students from affluent suburban areas whose parents were high-achieving professionals. The former took more conservative positions on the impeachment while the latter were willing to join the majority of black inner-city students in dismissing the president's conduct.

Reaction to the Events of September 11, 2001

The destruction of the World Trade Center towers in New York, in which more than 3,000 people died, was the most shocking event to occur on American soil since Pearl Harbor. Its potential as an agent of socialization should not be overlooked. For one thing, the sheer quantity of media coverage following the attack and the subsequent attack on the Pentagon gave adolescents an unprecedented opportunity to learn more about American governing institutions and officeholders.

To examine the reaction to terrorism, we followed up our 1999–2000 research with a second round of surveys in four of our Maryland schools in the fall of 2001 and the spring of 2002, drawing on very similar samples. We compared the before-and-after results from those schools in an effort to draw inferences about the impact of the terrorist incidents on adolescents' attitudes toward government. To begin, we compared before-and-after observations on the amount of political discussion, political knowledge, and news media consumption in these adolescent populations. We then examined variations in the responses to questions about efficacy according to the amount of news broadcasts students watched and the amount of political discussions in which they engaged in the aftermath of the attacks.

Measurement of the Dependent Variables

Six of the dependent variables described above are formulated as principal components scores from sets of survey items, rescaled to range between 0 and 100 in order to ease interpretation in statistical analysis. Briefly, principal components is a statistical method used to take multiple survey items and identify overlap among them as a means of determining whether they are measuring a common theoretical concept (such as attitudes toward equality, or diversity).[46] In survey research, some variant of principal components or factor analysis is commonly used when researchers are not confident that a single survey question is sufficient to capture a complex theoretical concept. In order to measure internal efficacy, for example, one survey item probably is not satisfactory. Nor would a single question be adequate to capture such complex ideas as "opposition to diversity," "nationalism," or many of the other attitudes customarily examined in political socialization research.

---

46. Kline (1994); Maruyama (1998).

By using principal components, we can identify whether there is a single, more basic or unique variable or "factor," say, internal efficacy, lying at the intersection of the responses to a number of survey questions. The resulting factor is defined by what the separate measures of internal efficacy have in common, and it can be used to calculate a factor score for each respondent that provides some indication of the respondent's level of internal efficacy.[47]

The details for the factor analyses are reported in appendix C. In our research the dependent variables formulated within the factor analytic framework are internal political efficacy, external political efficacy, opposition to diversity, nationalistic feeling or chauvinism, negativity toward local police and courts, and support for the Clinton impeachment. The factor analyses and factor loadings for each question from which these latent variables were constructed are reported in appendix C. In addition, two other variables from specific survey items are treated as dependent variables in our analysis: the amount of political discussion in the last week (in number of days) and the students' scores on the seven-item factual knowledge test, expressed as the percentage of correct answers. The questions on the knowledge test are listed in appendix B.

Elements of the Explanatory Framework

So far we have detailed the outcome variables we were interested in explaining and how we measured them. But what of the explanations themselves? Just how are the participation-enabling and side-taking dimensions of the socialization process conditioned by neighborhood characteristics? Individual choice is not strictly determined by environmental influences, but clearly one's environment limits the choices one can make.

Social Environment

Parents, teachers, clergy, the media, and children's peers are themselves a product of local social and political environments, and they reinforce the political values of the community.[48] The social composition of the community, then, plays a role in predicting what is taught, preached, and otherwise communicated to children.[49]

---

47. Maruyama (1998, p. 133).
48. Sanchez-Jankowski (1992, p. 88).
49. Jencks and Mayer (1990).

Political efficacy, for example, is conditioned by ecological or neighborhood influences because many elements of an individual's personal (and family) history are tied to the histories of the people (and families) living nearby.[50] The development of many individual traits and habits is expressly attributable to characteristics of the social environment: for example, for attendance at religious services to register on children's attitudes and behavior, churches and church members must be available to do the socializing.

Again, taking the sense of political efficacy as an example, we should not be surprised to find that efficacy is higher among children when parents and other adults in the community model efficacious behavior through their own involvement in politics. When a clear majority of adults in the community identify with one of the two major parties and when parents and neighbors take an active part in politics, offspring come to the conclusion that involvement is worthwhile. Political involvement by friends and neighbors also increases the amount of political discussion in the home—a valuable instrument for learning political values. A reasonable starting hypothesis is that students should score highly on efficacy indicators in communities where information and participation levels are high and lower in communities that exhibit considerable political apathy. We may find that efficacy levels are higher in smaller rather than larger community settings because individuals are more likely to feel a sense of belonging in small towns than in large cities and congested, transient, and sprawling suburbs. In part, this effect can be traced to the greater stability of the populations in small towns compared with those in suburbs and cities.[51]

Our measure of the social environment is based on U.S. Census Bureau information for the zip codes in which the schools are located. Zip codes seem to be an appropriate measure of community context because many of the alternative geographies seem much less optimal. Counties usually are too expansive, particularly in the study area, where living conditions can vary widely within a few miles and getting from one place to another can be complicated. While some adults may have a social network that spreads across a large geographic area because they work at a location far from home, few adolescents interact with peers or other citizens on a truly countywide basis.

50. Huckfeldt and Sprague (1995); Putnam (1966).
51. Steinberger (1981); Finifter and Abramson (1975).

Other units of analysis that might capture context seem either too compact (census blocks and block groups), or again, too diffuse (census-defined places) to capture the effects of local community influence. Census tracts have been widely used as measures of neighborhood context in many sociological studies and perhaps come closest to zip code areas in terms of typical size and population. We decided on zip codes because we found that they came consistently close to capturing the size of the catchment areas of high schools—the zone that encompasses the residences of students served by a school. To be sure, zip codes were not always perfect substitutes for the school's catchment areas. In some cases a catchment area included addresses from several adjacent zip codes, but we were informed by school authorities that the vast majority of students came from within the same zip code in which the school was located. In the four schools with magnet programs that attracted students from outside the immediate vicinity, those students constituted no more than 20 percent of the student body. And in all cases, the magnet programs drew students who were from areas close to the zip code in which the school was located, suggesting that living conditions would be highly similar to those in the zip code of the school.

Political Environment

The political diversity that comes with two locally competitive parties proves to be the optimal setting for political learning. Young people acquire partisan identities by making the connection between the social groups with which they identify and the social groups that undergird the major parties.[52] In single-party environments, socialization is commonly defective because the opposition party's social groups are rarely observed or well understood. One may comprehend the local social profile of one's own party but have no inkling of whom or what the other one stands for. The presence of members of the opposition party forces young people to reflect on and defend, if only to themselves, their reasons for choosing their party. A mountain of political science evidence points to the competitiveness of the party system as a powerful influence on the level of political activism, heightening the sense that one's vote counts.[53] The obvious psychological link between partisan heterogeneity and engagement is through efficacy: if voters believe their vote counts, they feel capable of influencing the election

52. Green, Palmquist, and Schickler (2002).
53. Rosenstone and Hansen (1993); Hill and Leighley (1993); Patterson and Caldeira (1983); Key (1949).

outcome. Competition also produces campaign activities, turning candidates and parties into agents of political socialization. Competitiveness fuels media coverage of especially close contests, creating greater opportunities to learn about politics and government. Citizens also are more likely to discuss closely contested elections than ones in which the winner is a foregone conclusion.

Related to party competition is voters' sense that they are represented at some level of government by officeholders who are like minded—or that with reasonable effort they *could be* represented by such a person. Simply the prospect that Jesse Jackson could be the Democratic Party's presidential nominee led to record levels of black mobilization.[54] In related research, there is evidence that blacks living in cities that have elected African Americans to prominent political office feel more efficacious and are more attentive to politics than those living in areas where blacks are not among the visible officeholders.[55] Having minority political representatives, then, is instrumental to minorities' feeling that they can trust the system and count on it to be responsive to them. Empowerment leads to higher efficacy.[56]

The generalization that the political efficacy of minority group members is contingent on their ability to elect at least some representatives of their group to public office may apply to other politicized, but not necessarily racial, identities. There is a similar effect for gender, for example. Women are more likely to talk to others about politics and feel more politically efficacious during election campaigns in which women are on the ballot.[57] The competitive status of any number of salient identities may act as a stimulus to higher turnout.

Given that the federal system permits substantial autonomy among local units of government in the conduct of elections, it is not difficult to imagine that one could belong to a local political minority while being a member of a national political majority. For example, Republicans may be the dominant partisan group in a community while being in the minority at the statewide or national level. Which partisan context matters most to one's political behavior and attitudes—the local or the national? We would agree with a long line of others that it is one's local political status that counts most and that locality is even more important for adolescents who

---

54. Tate (1991).
55. Bobo and Gilliam (1990); Browning, Marshall, and Tabb (1984).
56. Bobo and Gilliam (1990, p. 387).
57. Hansen (1997); Sapiro and Conover (1997).

are unlikely to be aware of their position in broader opinion distributions. If one's local minority status in political affairs is acute, it erodes the prospect of finding safe, compatible discussion partners and heightens the prospect that one's minority status will lead to silence, ignorance, and non-participation in regard to politics. Finding no social support for one's views easily translates into the sense that one's voice does not count, diminishing one's sense of efficacy. Citizens living under conditions in which their policy interests are consistently shouted down or defeated feel less efficacious than citizens whose interests dominate.[58] One might predict that Democrats living in areas of long-standing Republican dominance would exhibit lower efficacy and express fewer opinions than their Republican counterparts, and vice versa. Majority partisans in one-sided political environments are likely to have many congenial discussion partners, whereas minority partisans may assiduously avoid discussions of politics and miss opportunities to learn.

At the same time, we recognize that there is more to the decision to participate in politics than competitive calculations of advantage. Some participate not because they believe that their vote might decide a close election but simply out of a sense of civic obligation and pride, or due to strongly held political convictions.[59] How else can we explain the turnout of voters in one-party political settings where the election outcome is always known well in advance? General elections in large cities usually are not known for being competitive, and one may question why anyone bothers to show up at all. Because turnout is motivated by forces other than the competitiveness of the contest, we examine the effects of not just local party diversity but also voter turnout. Areas of high voter turnout rooted in a strong sense of civic engagement among adults are likely to have a strong socializing impact on young people, giving them first-hand examples of what participatory behavior looks like and how one gets involved.

Our measures for local political environment could not be drawn from zip code or census data because the Census Bureau does not collect and record political information. Instead, we collected precinct maps for each of our twenty-nine school locations and aggregated precinct data to the catchment area of each high school. For the most part, we did this by hand, although in the late stages we used a GIS (geographic information system)

---

58. Weissberg (1975); Iyengar (1980).
59. Campbell (2002).

program, a computer program designed for mapping. The procedure we followed was simply to trace in the catchment boundaries over the more granular precinct geographies. We then aggregated the precinct data to calculate measures of political party diversity, turnout, and Democratic and Republican Party bias for the 1996 presidential race, the 1998 gubernatorial race (1997 in Virginia), and the 1998 state legislative contests (see appendix B for measures).

Media Exposure

A series of studies has been made of the impact of news media on adolescent socialization.[60] News consumption rises steadily as children grow up. Inasmuch as the news media are a primary source of political information for adults, it is not surprising that children who see informational programs on television typically wind up being more knowledgeable about politics and current events than those who do not.[61] Even so, as the number of mass media outlets has multiplied, knowledge about politics and current events has diminished.[62]

Viewing television news sometimes is thought to increase political knowledge and interest in politics, but it is also usually considered to reinforce existing attitudes.[63] We believe that consumption of television news may well lower an adolescent's sense of efficacy given that the broadcast media have a stake in maintaining public doubts about government.[64] Because people pay more attention to negative information or "bad news" and are less likely to absorb "good news," network television news organizations have a strategic interest in covering negative news: it helps them maintain market share. Exposure to television news also has been previously associated with political malaise.[65] Some have suggested that it is the media's scandal-obsessed coverage of politics and politicians that contributes most directly to citizens' cynical and passive attitudes about public life.[66]

---

60. Conway, Stevens, and Smith (1975); Conway and others (1981); Garramone and Atkin (1986).

61. See Zaller (1992) regarding media, politics, and adults. For a discussion of media and the political socialization of children, see Chafee, Ward, and Tipton (1970) and Garramone and Atkin (1986).

62. Zukin (2000).

63. Chafee, Ward, and Tipton (1970); Atkin and Gantz (1978).

64. Fallows (1996); Lipset and Schneider (1983).

65. Berman and Stookey (1980); Robinson (1975, 1976).

66. Bennett (1997); Ansolabehere and Iyengar (1995).

No doubt the suggestion that information conveyed through television might diminish political efficacy and discourage participation will strike some as controversial. Such coverage probably contributes to political knowledge, and one might guess that greater political knowledge inexorably yields more efficacious feelings. But what is it that adolescents learn from the mass media? While exposure to some types of information may build their basic knowledge of government—that the president has veto authority, what the role of the chief justice on the Supreme Court is, the date of the next primary election—exposure to television news is likely to increase their knowledge of scandals and the most intractable of government problems, generating a different type of knowledge. Bill Clinton's affair with Monica Lewinsky may have been newsworthy by most measures, but it was certainly negative and did nothing to reinforce public confidence in the presidency. A steady bombardment of scandal coverage can leave the impression that government problems are insoluble. A regular diet of such information could easily lead one to take a despairing view of the value of citizens' input in government. Our measure of news exposure is a question about the number of days in the previous week in which students watched a news broadcast on television at home.

Family Characteristics and Parental Resources

Early studies of socialization focused on the role of parents as key agents in the transmission of political values to children.[67] In the 1960s, parents appeared to consistently transfer their party identification to their children, but little else.[68] Subsequent research has indicated that the transmission of political values from parent to child is strong among highly politicized parents but not among those who are apolitical or inconsistently political.[69]

We believe that parents' most important role in political socialization is that of material and moral provider. This emphasis places the explanatory weight squarely on parental socioeconomic status and religious values. A family's economic resources have been widely understood as influential in shaping a child's educational aspirations and academic achievement after high school. The socioeconomic status of individuals influences their sense of control over the larger environment because others infer from their sta-

---

67. Hyman (1959).
68. Sears (1975); Jennings and Niemi (1981).
69. Jennings, Stoker, and Bowers (1999); Beck and Jennings (1991).

tus the worth of their contributions to the political system. Uneven evaluations of political efficacy across a population, then, are rooted in social and economic inequality.[70]

Family structure is thought to be related to key socialization variables such as self-efficacy and self-esteem. Children raised in single-parent homes, usually with the father absent, are likely to have lower feelings of efficacy than those raised in two-parent homes, and they are disadvantaged in a myriad of ways that reduce their educational achievement and probability of economic success.[71] Given that children's attitudes toward authority are determined at least partly by their experiences at home, family structure has political implications.[72] An earlier generation of research suggested that fathers were more responsible for politically socializing their children than mothers, possibly because fathers may have more leisure time to devote to political and community affairs.[73] Along with lower self-esteem and educational aspirations, children in single-parent homes develop less confidence in their capacity to influence the political system than those in two-parent homes. Political efficacy is simply an attitudinal subset of a larger sense of self-efficacy formed by parental and other environmental influences.[74] Since self-efficacy is developed through the experience of accomplishing one's goals or attaining personal mastery of a subject or skill, parents' support and encouragement, along with demands for achievement, are significant.[75] Inasmuch as political discussion in the home is an instrument for building efficacy, the two-parent home has a distinct advantage over the single-parent home. In two-parent homes, a child is likely to hear more adult discussion on a large number of topics, politics included.

School Experiences

Many early studies found that schools—specifically civics courses—contributed little to students' political awareness or participation.[76] A more

---

70. Della Fave (1980; 1986).

71. Clarke (1973); Coleman (1988); McLanahan (1985); McLanahan and Bumpass (1988); McLanahan and Sandefur (1994); Yakibu, Axinn, and Thornton (1999).

72. Easton and Hess (1962); Hess and Torney (1967); Jennings and Niemi (1971); Langton (1969).

73. Jennings and Niemi (1971); Burns, Schlozman, and Verba (1997).

74. Gecas (1989).

75. Bandura (1977).

76. Langton and Jennings (1968); Litt (1963); Jennings and Niemi (1968); but see Hess and Torney (1967).

recent consideration of the effect of schooling suggests that students do gain political knowledge from civics courses but that the gains vary across student subgroups.[77]

In addition to the amount of civics coursework, students' affinity for civics courses is a critical ingredient in the socialization process. Teaching the subject or simply exposing the student to information about government is not enough to generate positive political socialization. Students must acquire a liking for the material in order for the school experience of taking government classes to pay off in greater levels of civic engagement and participation.

Schools transmit information about politics in more ways than through formal coursework in civics. We examine one aspect of the school climate—students' assessments of the way in which they are evaluated by school authorities. School authorities usually are the first nonparent authorities a child confronts, often as early as three or four years of age. Children eventually will evaluate their teachers and administrators as fair or unfair, and they may generalize those evaluations to other authorities, including the government and its officials. The tendency to generalize from one's experience of local authority to higher level officeholders often is described as "diffusion." Diffuse support is the tendency to be supportive of the entire political system based on one's judgments of the fairness of local officials, including teachers and school administrators.[78]

Race, Ethnicity, Immigrant Status, and Gender

A string of prominent studies of racial differences in political socialization have found that black children have a consistently lower sense of efficacy and know less about politics than white children.[79] There is nothing inherent in being identified as black that causes a lower sense of efficacy; rather it is the myriad of attributes closely associated with growing up as a black person in the United States that contributes to defective socialization. Levels of internal efficacy among African Americans have been shown to be quite high once socioeconomic variables have been held constant, suggesting that it is mainly economic inequality that deprives blacks of the opportunities to build efficacy.[80] At the same time, feelings of external efficacy

77. Niemi and Junn (1998).
78. Easton and Dennis (1969).
79. Abramson (1972); Clarke (1973); Greenberg (1970); Langton and Jennings (1968); Lyons (1970); Pierce and Carey (1971); Rodgers (1974).
80. Hughes and Demo (1989).

remain low. African Americans often doubt that the system works for them, but many more remain confident that concerted action can make a difference.[81]

Perhaps the most notable difference between members of Generation Y and previous generations is the rapid change that they have experienced in the social environment. The unprecedented flows of immigrants from Latin America and Asia have raised questions of multiculturalism, diversity, and tolerance to a degree that was unknown to the protest generation. The nation's ethnic and racial complexion changed dramatically between the 1970s and the end of the century.[82] Cultural pluralism is at its historical peak, and we have little knowledge about how the experiences of immigrant, second-generation, and native-born children contribute to their political socialization in this new setting.

The interaction of natives and immigrants in impoverished areas raises questions about "downward assimilation," usually conceived of in an economic sense. But downward assimilation also may involve the learning of moral and political values; economic progress, after all, is only one aspect of immigrant adaptation. Because a large proportion of the immigrants arriving since the late 1960s have not been Caucasian, important questions arise about the extent to which they have faced discrimination and how it has shaped their stance toward the U.S. political system. Previous research indicates that some immigrants may learn to identify with native-born minority groups, picking up the social and political values prevalent in existing Hispanic, black, and Asian communities.[83] Consequently, they may feel politically inefficacious, alienated from the political system, and cynical about the benefits of participating.[84] Others who may have acquired a sense of efficacy may express their political demands in racial terms, taking their cue from the black civil rights movement.[85] Many unanswered questions remain about the way in which heightened levels of ethnic diversity have influenced political socialization.

Sex or gender differences in political learning have been noted by a number of scholars since the 1960s.[86] A gender gap in political knowledge and interest has persisted for decades, and the female deficit can be traced

---

81. Shingles (1981); Reese and Brown (1995).
82. Gimpel (1999).
83. Fernandez-Kelly and Schauffler (1996).
84. Cohen and Dawson (1993); Waters (1996).
85. Skerry (1993).
86. Hess and Torney (1967, chap. 8); Hahn (1998).

to their different information-seeking behavior, founded on the different socialization of the sexes.[87] The gender gap in political knowledge has closed over the years, but women still are widely viewed as properly occupying nonpolitical roles in society, a legacy from earlier times when women were prohibited from voting or holding office altogether. Gender role socialization steers girls away from conflict and toward consensual issues where rules to regulate competitive interaction are less important.[88] As a result, women wind up less interested in politics than men, affecting their propensity, for example, to engage in discussions of politics, enroll in social studies courses, and watch news broadcasts. Women remain more likely to be in social settings where there is less political information and work in jobs that are less affected by political issues.[89]

Direction and Plan of the Book

Political socialization, as we understand it, is a learning process largely linked to the experiences of adolescence and young adulthood. Socialization has two fundamental components that are not totally independent of each other: a participation-enabling component and a side-taking component that involves the formation of attitudes. Participation is enabled most directly through discussion, knowledge, and efficacy. It also can be facilitated by the crystallization of opinions on divisive issues that adolescents learn to care about.

Our research is founded on the notion that socialization experiences vary among subgroups of the adolescent population: blacks, females, children with immigrant parents, the affluent, those living in large cities, those living in single-parent homes, Democrats, the nonreligious, and so forth. We have highlighted these subgroup differences with survey data and then done our best to explain them through the understanding we have developed from our field investigations and observations as well as from what others have written. By the end of the book, our understanding of the political socialization process still may be incomplete, but we have made some progress and charted some new directions.[90]

---

87. Hansen (1997); Jennings and Niemi (1968); Burns, Schlozman, and Verba (1997).

88. Delli Carpini and Keeter (1996, p. 206).

89. Atkin (1978); Delli Carpini and Keeter (1991; 1996); Garramone and Atkin (1986); Burns, Schlozman, and Verba (1997).

90. In deliberating among ourselves about the outline for the book, we pondered several organizing schemata for the presentation of our results. One obvious choice was to move from dependent vari-

To examine our theory that context counts, we begin in chapter 2 with a study of how attitudes are shaped by the social and political context in which individuals live, measured at the community level. These causal factors are the most remote from the individual attitudes being explained, but ultimately they structure the interpersonal interactions that drive the communication of information in the socialization process. We try to understand the meaning and significance of urban, suburban, and rural differences as well as differences within these three subgroups. We also examine the effects of living in an ethnically and politically diverse rather than homogeneous community.

In chapter 3 we consider the effects of race and immigration status on adolescent political socialization. Race and ethnicity structure the interactions of individuals within their environments, which in turn determine exposure to alternative cultural values, influence the nature of peer relationships, and play a major role in the development of a wide range of political attitudes. While we believed that the influence of race and ethnicity would be strongest on attitudes toward tolerance of diversity, we also had reasons to expect that racial heterogeneity would explain efficacy, knowledge, and even nationalism. To avoid confounding racial and socioeconomic effects, we controlled for the socioeconomic status of families. In this chapter we also pause to consider the effects of family structure on political socialization.

Chapter 4 considers the explicitly political foundations of attitudes toward diversity, political efficacy, political knowledge, and the other outcomes we have mentioned. Political partisans and ideologues are made, not born, and it is worth spending some time simply to giving a thorough description of the way various population subgroups label themselves, including those that do not identify with a party or political ideology. The remainder of the chapter examines the effects of partisan identification, controlling for socioeconomic status. We consider the interaction of individual partisanship and the partisan composition of neighborhoods on attitudes.

---

able to dependent variable, chapter by chapter. But the disadvantage of that approach is that it makes the explanatory framework very repetitive and formulaic. Most of the same causal factors for efficacy, nationalism, tolerance for diversity, and so on would be recited in each chapter and only the statistical results would vary. Instead, we opted to place more weight on the independent variables, organizing the manuscript according to the explanations and processes behind the acquisition of dispositions toward politics and governing institutions. This way of writing the book places more emphasis on theory-driven explanations for the outcomes of interest.

In chapter 5 we examine the family's contribution to the socialization process, focusing on one key carrier of intergenerational influence: religious teaching. Parents are the most important factor in shaping the religious commitments of children. Religion, in turn, is an important teacher of moral virtues such as self-sacrifice and altruism, and religious participation is a widely recognized means of building social capital. As in chapters 3 and 4, we control for socioeconomic status because high income can compensate for a multitude of deficits in a child's background, counteracting forces that otherwise guarantee deficient socialization.

Chapter 6 examines the impact of several school-related variables. First among them is simple exposure to the civics curriculum. Students who have had more civics instruction often are thought to be better informed and more opinionated than those who have had less. We also consider whether students had developed an appreciation for the subject matter of government since exposure to required coursework still may leave them disdainful of government and politics. Students must develop a liking for the subject matter in order for formal instruction to have its desired impact.

A third school-related variable is students' educational aspirations, an indicator of whether they intend to go on to a four-year college after graduating from high school. Finally, we evaluate the extent to which students trust their teachers and school administrators to evaluate them fairly. Students who do not develop trust in school authorities are slow to develop trust in and respect for other governing authorities.

In chapter 7 we address the effects of the terrorist attacks of September 11, 2001, on the attitudes of adolescents from a small subset of the schools visited in 1999 that we revisited in the fall of 2001. Contextual effects are not only geographic but temporal. Socialization can be linked to events that trigger greater-than-ordinary information flows. Knowing that the terrorist attacks stimulated greater public attention to mass media, we were particularly interested in knowing whether the youth surveyed in 2001 scored higher on measures of political knowledge, efficacy, and nationalism than those surveyed in 1999.

In chapter 8 we consider relationships among our dependent variables and evaluate the experiences and attitudes that shape intentions to vote. We also consider the implications of our findings for public policy discussions. We argue that the focus on ways to enhance formal education is of critical importance from a policy standpoint but that other means for inculcating positive socializing messages have been ignored. The effects of additional years of schooling on participation levels are undeniable, but a prescription for more formal schooling will never be filled by the legions of students who do not go beyond high school. Realizing that improving the educational experience is only a single tool with limited reach, we search elsewhere for compensatory strategies to promote civic engagement among those who otherwise appear destined for nonparticipation.

2 Communities and Political Socialization

One's community consists of the people with whom one lives and interacts most frequently, including family members, neighbors, classmates, coworkers, members of one's church or social club, and people who work in the stores at which one shops. Social bonds can be either strong or weak; people typically have some of each tying them to particular places. Taken together, this collection of associates possesses a set of characteristics that define the community, setting it apart from other places, near and far. Each community has a certain average income and education level, a particular ethnic complexion, and a prevailing set of political beliefs and opinions. In the opening chapter, we suggested that local social, economic, and political characteristics structure the flow of information and the character of interpersonal interaction in a place.

A substantial body of literature has found that what we have labeled "community" does have an impact on political attitudes and behavior that is independent of the effects of individual characteristics such as race, occupation, income, and party identification.[1] People within a community are likely to develop similar attitudes and political dispositions germane to political socialization, regardless of other dissimilarities. Geography and proximity can sometimes trump economic distinctions, as when bankers,

1. Gimpel and Schuknecht (2003); Huckfeldt and Sprague (1995); Beck and others (2002).

lawyers, merchants, and laborers band together to vote alike in spite of their seemingly contrary visions for public policy.[2]

To take another example, it is common to find two groups of voters with similar backgrounds but from distinct geographic settings. One group may participate at a rate of 51 percent, the other at a rate of only 33 percent. Holding the relevant individual traits constant—for example, socioeconomic status, occupation, race and ethnicity—the big difference between the two groups may be accounted for by "neighborhood effects," the tendency for people to be socialized by those around whom they live. According to a growing body of research, people's political thinking is influenced by their local social interactions.[3] Even after researchers control for the usual individual attributes considered relevant to political judgments, contextual effects remain significant predictors of a wide range of behavior and attitudes.[4] Contextual explanations work especially well in accounting for the attitudes and behavior of individuals who are socially connected and receptive to political communication.[5]

Some might argue that social and political contexts do not matter in an era in which people can receive information directly from television or through the Internet. Our suggestion is that messages conveyed through broadcast media are refracted through and transformed by local agents of political socialization, including peers, parents and other family members, school authorities, religious authorities, and local news media. The effect of some events may be greatly magnified when local agents find them to be important or squelched entirely when judged to be unimportant. Local agents also may judge some messages to be positive, some to be negative, and others to be neutral. Places absorb and react differently to news events according to the color of local opinion, which undoubtedly steers the socialization process toward place-distinct outcomes.

Although individual characteristics such as socioeconomic status, race, and partisan identification certainly have strong and direct influences on political socialization, in this chapter we examine the influence of communities' ethnic and racial composition, economic resources, and political tradition in the absence of individual characteristics. We take particular

---

2. Key (1956); Gimpel and Schuknecht (2002).

3. Beck and others (2002); Huckfeldt (1986); Huckfeldt and others (1995); Huckfeldt and Sprague (1995); MacKuen and Brown (1987); Putnam (1966).

4. Huckfeldt (1986); Kuklinski, Cobb, and Gilens (1997, pp. 336–38).

5. Huckfeldt and others (1995); Johnson, Shively, and Stein (2002).

note of the political environment and how partisan politics and turnout stimulate interest and build a sense of efficacy.

To clarify our undertaking, suppose that we had no personal information by which to classify the responses to our queries except the name of the place where each respondent lived. We would then have to take the responses and look for possible explanations by using "ecological" variables describing the neighborhood or town in which the school was located. That would hardly satisfy the demand for a complete, psychologically based account of the sources of political efficacy, level of knowledge, attitudes toward diversity, and so forth, but it would at least give us some picture of what typically is observed in particular settings, without committing the fallacy of concluding that community characteristics become direct causes of individual behavior. In this chapter, then, we initiate our analysis of the survey data as if we had nothing to go on except the most general characteristics of the communities in which our individual respondents were observed. In later chapters, we build on this basic understanding, controlling for the causes that are more immediate and proximate to the outcomes we investigated.

Community Characteristics

To capture the ethnic and immigrant composition of communities, we include four variables: the percent of the community that is of Asian ancestry, the percent African American, the percent Hispanic, and the percent foreign born. Explanatory variables that signal community resources include median family income and the percentage of those over age twenty-five that have a four-year college degree or higher. Political characteristics of communities include the percent of the community that is registered with the Democratic Party, the extent of evenness in the vote between Republicans and Democrats for major offices, and the level of voter turnout in the previous presidential election.

The dependent variables that we consider include the eight constructs from our political socialization survey identified in the first chapter and described further in appendixes B and C: frequency of political discussion, level of factual political knowledge, internal and external senses of political efficacy, opposition to diversity, nationalism or "chauvinism," attitudes toward the police and the courts, and support for the Clinton impeachment. Except for the knowledge and frequency of discussion variables, the dependent variables were constructed on the basis of principal components scores derived from questions on the survey (see appendix C for a complete description).

Ethnic Diversity and Political Discussion, Knowledge, and Efficacy

If communities structure the flow of event-specific information in distinctive ways, our variables capturing community characteristics should go some distance toward explaining the political socialization outcomes we studied. And indeed we found support for the idea that the racial composition, community resources, and political orientation of places leave an imprint on adolescent political socialization.

The results in table 2-1 show that discussion, knowledge, and efficacy are the product of some staple local characteristics. For example, communities with large proportions of Asian residents show remarkably high levels of political discussion, knowledge, and internal and external efficacy. Of course, that is not necessarily a sign that Asian adolescents themselves are knowledgeable and efficacious. In the study area, the locations with the largest Asian populations were, for the most part, suburbs lying directly north of Washington, D.C., in Montgomery County, Maryland, one of the most affluent counties in the nation. So it is clearly possible that the Asian population variable is standing in for some other politically relevant characteristic. We discover in the next chapter that the high levels of knowledge and discussion in areas with large Asian populations are not due to the Asian residents per se but instead to the fact that Asians seek to live in areas with better schools near middle- and upper-income whites.

Foreign-born adults and their children often exhibit ignorance and suspicion more than negativity and cynicism. Because foreign-born parents usually have less knowledge about and less interest in American politics than native-born parents, their children grow up in homes where the subject is rarely raised and the parents are rarely observed exercising their franchise, much less donating their time and money to a campaign or a political cause. Some foreign-born parents also are highly suspicious of government, generalizing from memories of corruption in their home country to the conclusion that the U.S. government also must be corrupt.

The presence of an immigrant population is associated with lower levels of political discussion, knowledge, and efficacy, but especially of discussion (table 2-1). With each 10 percentage point increase in the proportion of the local population that is foreign born, we see a considerable 5 percentage point drop in the frequency of political discussion. Communication flows are likely to be disrupted in immigrant-heavy communities

Table 2-1. *Influence of Community Economic, Social, and Political Characteristics on Political Socialization*[a]
Units as indicated

Explanatory variable	Frequency of political discussion	β	Level of political knowledge	β	Internal political efficacy	β	External political efficacy	β
Population density (thousands)	1.701** (0.300)	.16	1.876** (0.297)	.21	0.810** (0.229)	.13	0.214 (0.224)	.03
Percent Asian	0.709** (0.366)	.15	0.668** (0.279)	.19	0.199 (0.214)	.07	0.467** (0.211)	.18
Percent black	−0.046 (0.066)	−.04	0.054 (0.050)	.06	−0.062* (0.039)	−.09	−0.035 (0.039)	−.06
Percent Hispanic	0.224 (0.323)	.06	−0.406* (0.246)	−.14	−0.171 (0.190)	−.08	−0.095 (0.186)	−.05
Percent foreign born	−0.509** (0.248)	−.23	−0.106 (0.189)	−.06	−0.083 (0.146)	−.06	−0.055 (0.143)	−.04
Median income (thousands)	−0.031 (0.041)	−.03	−0.010 (0.032)	−.02	−0.027 (0.024)	−.04	0.011 (0.024)	.02
Percent with four years or more of college	−0.189 (0.178)	−.06	−0.372** (.136)	−.14	−0.038 (0.104)	−.03	−0.079 (0.103)	−.04
Percent Democratic	0.001 (0.133)	.01	−0.276** (0.102)	−.19	0.126 (0.078)	.11	0.140* (0.078)	.13
Party diversity	0.103 (0.123)	.04	0.202** (0.094)	.11	0.161** (0.072)	.12	0.132* (0.076)	.10
Percent turnout	1.085** (0.146)	.24	0.933** (0.111)	.27	0.379** (0.086)	.14	0.041 (0.084)	.02
Magnet program[b]	5.009** (1.715)	.08	9.944** (1.304)	.19	4.519** (1.003)	.12	2.883** (0.982)	.08
Constant	−1.477		7.031		5.877		10.719	
Summary statistic								
R^2	.056		.106		.064		.039	
F test (*p* value)	14.79 (≤.0001)		29.57 (≤.0001)		17.22 (≤.0001)		10.00 (≤.0001)	
N	3,006		2,992		3,011		3,011	

Explanatory variable	Negativity about courts/police	β	Opposition to diversity	β	Nationalism/ chauvinism	β	Support Clinton impeachment	β
Population density (thousands)	-0.635** (0.311)	-.07	-1.021** (0.242)	-.09	-0.131* (0.081)	-.06	-0.550* (0.312)	-.01
Percent Asian	-1.072** (0.293)	-.29	-0.423* (0.207)	-.16	0.837** (0.260)	.26	-0.354 (0.294)	-.10
Percent black	-0.094* (0.053)	-.11	-0.025 (0.037)	-.04	-0.006 (0.047)	-.01	-0.140** (0.053)	-.16
Percent Hispanic	-0.318 (0.259)	-.11	-0.133 (0.183)	-.06	0.338 (0.230)	.13	-0.704** (0.229)	-.24
Percent foreign born	0.442** (0.199)	.25	0.116 (0.141)	.09	-0.309** (0.177)	-.20	0.385** (0.199)	.22
Median income (thousands)	-0.061* (0.033)	-.07	0.027 (0.023)	.04	0.009 (0.029)	.01	-0.043 (0.033)	-.05
Percent with four years or more of college	0.247* (0.143)	.09	-0.124 (0.101)	-.06	-0.215* (0.126)	-.09	-0.138 (0.143)	-.05
Percent Democratic	0.278** (0.107)	.18	-0.095 (0.075)	-.09	-0.121 (0.095)	-.10	0.104 (0.107)	.07
Party diversity	-0.162* (0.098)	-.09	-0.231** (0.069)	-.18	0.006 (0.087)	.00	0.182* (0.098)	.10
Percent turnout	-0.480** (0.117)	-.13	-0.117 (0.082)	-.05	0.197* (0.103)	.06	0.089 (0.117)	.03
Magnet program[b]	-4.434** (1.369)	-.08	-2.324** (0.967)	-.06	2.409** (1.215)	.05	-1.046 (1.372)	-.02
Constant	79.615		84.420		69.277		38.884	
Summary statistic								
R^2	.071		.050		.049		.038	
F test (p value)	19.06 (≤.0001)		13.04 (≤.0001)		12.79 (≤.0001)		10.02 (≤.0001)	
N	3,026		3,001		3,021		3,022	

Source: Metro Civic Values Survey, 1999–2000.

$*p \leq .10$; $**p \leq .05$.

a. Multiple linear regression, weighted least squares estimation. Cases are weighted for the inverse probability of selection. Values are regression coefficients with standard errors shown in parentheses. β, standardized regression coefficients. Control variable not reported is for survey question order.

b. Magnet programs draw a significant but minority percentage (<20 percent) of their students from outside the immediate school vicinity.

due to language barriers; to the irrelevance of elections to noncitizens, who cannot vote; and perhaps to ignorance and lack of familiarity with American political processes and institutions. Sampson and colleagues point out that immigrant neighborhoods are lacking in social capital because of the prevalence of communication barriers in multilingual settings.[6] The inability to communicate may prevent many politically related messages from reaching children of both immigrant and nonimmigrant parents.

We find that the presence of significant black and Hispanic populations reduces internal and external efficacy scores, although not always to a statistically significant extent in multivariate models. Adolescents from communities with large Hispanic populations show significantly lower political knowledge scores, even after controlling for the foreign-born population. Our results suggest that the combination of large Hispanic and foreign-born populations in a location appears to be especially unlikely to contribute to a positive political socialization experience.

Community Resources and Political Discussion, Knowledge, and Efficacy

As measures of community resources, we consider the community's income level and the proportion of local residents with four years or more of college (table 2-1). These are indicators of information and financial capital, variables usually associated with high social capital. We predicted that education and income would be associated with greater knowledge, efficacy, and discussion levels. Better-educated people are more likely than the less educated to engage in information exchange of all types. Higher-income communities have superior means for spreading information, including a greater variety of mediums of exchange: libraries, newspaper subscriptions, television news channels, and bookstores.

One of the more surprising findings reported in table 2-1 is that community resource levels do not have a clear and direct impact on efficacy, knowledge, or the frequency of discussion. If anything, communities with greater wealth seem to produce offspring who exhibit marginally less interest in political discussion and lower levels of knowledge. This is due to the fact that the rural areas in our study are home to youth with high levels of knowledge and efficacy but much lower standards of living than those enjoyed by residents in our suburban and urban locations. We find that there is nothing about lower-income communities that predetermines low

6. Sampson and Bartusch (1998); Sampson, Raudenbush, and Earls (1997).

levels of knowledge and efficacy among younger generations, and the studies that conclude otherwise usually have ignored rural populations that are highly participatory but economically strapped. Parents in small towns also may have high goals and ambitions for their children, and the slower pace of rural and small-town life permits more communication about all subjects, politics included.[7] We will probe this finding in more detail, but at this point it seems fair to say that creating greater wealth in a community is not the obvious pathway to the successful political socialization of youth that some have suggested. Our results suggest that the socioeconomic status of neighborhoods has been overblown as a source of political socialization. Most of the studies that have shown poor neighborhoods to be the heart of bad socialization have drawn their samples of poor people (usually adults) from inner-city neighborhoods. Including low-income rural populations in these studies might change the results entirely. Just as affluent suburban areas can show substantial political apathy, low-income rural areas often show high levels of civic engagement.[8]

Interestingly, the educational resource argument does not hold much water either, as those locations with the largest shares of college-educated residents show no decisive tendency to produce politically knowledgeable and efficacious adolescents. Indeed, our findings suggest that adolescents in areas with the most highly educated residents are marginally less knowledgeable than those in places with fewer college-educated adults. A one standard deviation increase in the percentage of residents with a four-year degree drops the political knowledge test score by about three points. Many of our best-educated communities were located in the affluent suburbs where the level of political engagement was middling—neither exceptionally high nor in the basement. Busy professionals and business managers may not engage in much political discussion or knowledge exchange about politics; if they do not, they are not likely to transmit a high level of political efficacy to the adolescents in their midst. High residential mobility in suburbs often has conspired to erode the social capital of suburban families, undercutting their sense of having a stake in the community and their political participation.

If there is one aspect of the resource argument that does hold up, it is the density or accessibility aspect, perhaps qualifying our observations about the apparent superiority of rural to suburban and urban areas. These results

7. Putnam (2000).
8. Putnam (2000); Campbell (2002).

suggest that if the environment provides more potential discussion partners, positive socialization outcomes are more likely to emerge. A twenty-point increase in population density increased the extent of political discussion by about 3 percent (table 2-1). Generally we found that students in areas with greater population density also demonstrated considerably greater political knowledge and internal efficacy levels. What this suggests is that there is nothing about the size or concentration of the population in urban and suburban areas that militates against their being acceptable environments for positive political socialization; indeed, they even may have some advantages over sparsely populated rural communities.

Political Orientation of Neighborhoods and Political Discussion, Knowledge, and Efficacy

When it comes to *political* socialization, attributes of the *political* environment are most likely to have an influence on shaping the attitudes we studied. In table 2-1, we put three characteristics of the community's political makeup to the test: the percentage of the local population that voted Democratic in the prior gubernatorial, state legislative, and presidential elections; the partisan diversity of the local vote for those offices; and the level of local voter turnout in the previous presidential race. The effect of turnout on political discussion and political knowledge is substantial, easily exceeding the influence of community resources and ethnic diversity. Figure 2-1 presents the bivariate relationship between average school test score and voter turnout in each school's catchment area. The relationship is strongly positive, with Montgomery Blair High School in Silver Spring, Maryland, exhibiting the highest average test score in a community where local participation exceeded 70 percent of registered voters. Still, part of the reason for the impressive test performance of Montgomery Blair students is that the school has a magnet social studies/journalism program, which attracts a small proportion of its more gifted students from outside the immediate vicinity of the school. At the other end of the distribution are a predominantly black inner-city school in Baltimore and a heavily Hispanic school in Northern Virginia, both exhibiting rock-bottom turnout and poor average test scores.

Turnout, along with partisan diversity, also has a positive impact on internal political efficacy—the propensity for youth to conclude that their voice matters. Some might object at this point, insisting that turnout is itself caused by discussion, knowledge, and efficacy and should not be used

Figure 2-1. *Relationship between Voter Turnout and Average Level of Political Knowledge, by School*[a]

Test score

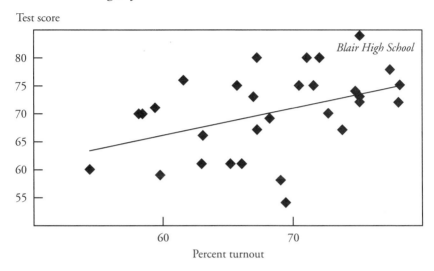

Percent turnout

Source: Metro Civic Values Survey, 1999–2000.
a. $y = 0.4833x + 37.091$; $R^2 = 0.1712$.

to predict such outcomes. Our results in table 2-1, therefore, present a thorny causal direction problem. But the idea that efficacy, knowledge, and discussion predict political diversity and turnout (and not the reverse) is likely to be true only of adult populations, who are engaged in the act of participating on election day. Among the youth we surveyed, rather few were eligible to vote, suggesting that there is little chance that the community's level of turnout was the result of our subjects' feelings of efficacy, political discussion, and knowledge.

Young people are able to acquire stronger partisan identities when they are in a setting in which there is a real choice between the two major parties. The presence of adherents of the opposition party forces more students to consider carefully the reasons for identifying themselves as Democrat or Republican. We should not be surprised to find a positive relationship between the partisan diversity of neighborhoods and the average political knowledge test score at each school we visited. The relationship shown in figure 2-2 is unmistakably positive, although not as strong as the relationship in figure 2-1 between local voter turnout and test scores.

Figure 2-2. *Relationship between Level of Local Partisan Diversity and Average Level of Political Knowledge, by School*[a]

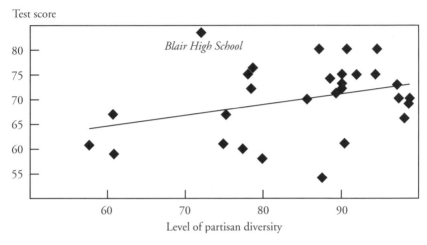

Test score

Level of partisan diversity

Source: Metro Civic Values Survey, 1999–2000.
a. Local party diversity formulated as 100 – [absolute(50 – percent Democratic)].
y = 0.2078x + 52.325; R^2 = 0.1036.

Clearly there are some locations where election results predictably advantage one party but test scores remain high, including Blair High School. Usually, though, these locations are generating high turnout either through strong political competition or other sources of high engagement, such as impressive levels of education among the adult population.

Why did partisan diversity have a significant positive impact on the level of political knowledge, increasing it by two points for each standard deviation increase in the level of local party diversity (table 2-1)? We can only fall back on an information-stimulus explanation for this intriguing finding. Localities in which the parties are evenly matched are full of citizens who perceive that their voice matters, making them more attentive to elections than they would be otherwise. Local political diversity, then, serves as an accelerant to the diffusion of political information. This diffusion may not occur through an individual's discussion networks, as recent evidence suggests that politically diverse networks have a demobilizing impact. Rather, information diffusion occurs because of the greater intensity of party and candidate activity in general elections, which lowers the cost of information acquisition and may render extensive interpersonal communications superfluous.

Equally important is the perception by local citizens of whichever party that the system works and that they have a voice. In politically competitive settings, both sides occasionally win elections, at least locally, leading all but the most cynical to the conclusion that the government is responsive. By contrast, in areas lacking partisan diversity, adherents of the minority party may conclude that they are not represented, generating low efficacy among a sizable bloc of such voters.

Partisan bias, as measured by the Democratic vote in state and national elections, diminishes the level of political knowledge, suggesting that the heavily GOP locations in our study area produce the most informed adolescents (see table 2-1). This finding is certainly consistent with the results from surveys of adults showing that Democrats are less knowledgeable about politics than Republicans. Nevertheless, a Republican partisan orientation is associated with lower internal and external efficacy, probably due to the fact that Republicans are a minority party in the study area generally, particularly in their state legislative delegations, and had won few of the most visible offices (U.S. senator, governor) in the dozen years up to the time that our survey was conducted.

We gather from this summary of our findings so far that the level of a community's political activity structures the adolescent socialization experience more than anything else. Presumably even places that are not especially competitive can produce knowledgeable and efficacious citizens if the level of civic activity is sufficiently high. Partisan diversity is not the only instrument of high turnout. Still, the extent of political heterogeneity matters, not only in the indirect sense that it drives up turnout but also in that it enhances internal efficacy by giving young citizens the impression that participation matters to electoral outcomes, and it increases knowledge by stimulating the flow of information. We did not find that the lopsided Democratic Party bias of an area diminished efficacy or discussion frequency, although it was associated with depressed levels of political knowledge.

Ethnic Diversity and Attitudes toward Law Enforcement

Attitudes toward the police and local trial courts have long been linked to race, and allegations of discrimination by mostly white police forces against minority suspects are commonplace. It is somewhat of a surprise, then, that the places with more diverse populations exhibited more trusting attitudes toward police and courts than our most homogeneously white areas. Specifically, Asian communities produced the most trusting attitudes, followed by Hispanic and then black communities. For every 10 percent rise in the proportion of Asians living in a community, for example, there was a 10 percentage point drop in negative assessments of the police and local courts. Perhaps the tendency for Asian locales to evaluate the police more favorably than Hispanic areas and for Hispanic communities to be more satisfied than black areas reflects the fact that Asians in our study area are wealthier—and have better educated neighbors—than either Hispanics or blacks. We found these results to be consistent with the other parts of our analysis showing that an Asian presence in these communities was associated with higher efficacy and knowledge levels. Perhaps this high efficaciousness is derived partly through positive contact with local police and courts, or at least less negative contact. Notably, however, we did find that suspicions of police and courts were considerably greater among youth living in communities with larger foreign-born populations. Diverse communities per se did not appear to structure negative attitudes toward the police, but immigrant communities did.

Community Resources and Attitudes toward Law Enforcement

We might expect that wealthy and well-educated people would be much more satisfied with their level of police protection than those living in poor, underserved places. Because they have the resources to pay higher taxes and the education to articulate greater demands, the rich and well educated can trust their local police and courts. In communities where the public demands a high level of public service and can afford to pay for it, institutions generally respond accordingly.

What we found, however, was that community financial and education resources had only a modest role in structuring youthful attitudes toward the police and courts (table 2-1). In general, adolescents living in wealthier communities did provide marginally more favorable assessments of the police and the courts than those living in poorer ones. Respondents in areas with highly educated populations, on the other hand, reported considerable negativity toward law enforcement.

Greater population density produces a less hostile stance toward police and courts, on average, apparently because high school students in low-density rural and suburban locales often complained loudly about police incompetence and laziness. These concerns rarely reflected a concern for uncontrolled criminal activity but instead showed a widespread teenage contempt for police harassment. We often found that youth from our more rural and low-density suburban communities complained about the police having nothing to do and being overly concerned with petty offenses. Rural youth, in particular, had a "Barney Fife" image of their local police, referring to the bumbling deputy sheriff from the old Andy Griffith TV show.

Urban youth also frequently expressed complaints, but they were of a very different character.[9] In our big-city neighborhoods, the police were perceived as corrupt, highly prejudiced, and intimidating. In predominantly black areas, police were faulted for being afraid to grapple with serious crime, for corruption, and for a general lack of responsiveness to minority populations. In rural and affluent suburban schools, low confidence in the police stemmed from the perception that they were overly zealous and preoccupied with traffic violations, and marijuana and alcohol possession. In the most urban schools, low trust was expressed because police were thought to engage in criminal and corrupt practices and in racial profiling. Contempt for police among adolescents should be seen at least partly as a developmental phase, reflecting the pervasive culture of opposition to adult authority among adolescents, but the rationale students provided for their resentment of law enforcement authority clearly varied depending upon their environment.

Political Orientation of Neighborhoods and Attitudes toward Law Enforcement

Not only was voter turnout closely linked to greater political knowledge and higher internal efficacy, it was also associated with greater satisfaction with local courts and the police. We were not surprised by this result, as it indicates that more highly engaged locales are more demanding of their local police and court systems and usually get what they want. The most politically active areas, in turn, produced youth who were learned and critical in their assessments of government functioning and who also were confident that government can be service oriented if political pressure is brought to bear. Apparently, local government institutions mostly live up to these expectations, so positive evaluations go hand in hand with a high sense of political efficacy and knowledge.

---

9. See chapter 1 for specific examples of these types of comments from youth in urban areas.

Democratic party bias was unmistakably associated with more negative assessments of local institutions, suggesting that one-party areas may be poorly served by their local governments, a finding as old as V. O. Key's *Southern Politics*.[10] What this indicates, conversely, is that GOP-dominant areas produced youth who were less suspicious and critical of their local governments. Youth in Republican-identifying locales apparently concluded that while most levels of state and local government in the study area are one-party enterprises in which they have little voice, they could expect some measure of responsiveness from their local institutions, where friendly majorities prevail. Another explanation is that the most Democratic communities in the area we investigated are more threatened by crime and related policy problems. Youth in these locations voiced more complaints about the unresponsiveness of police to persistent and serious criminal activity.

Ethnic Diversity and Tolerance of Diversity

One would think that no aspect of a community would be more highly relevant to its attitudes toward diversity than its ethnic composition. But what we found is that this relevance lay not in unqualified support but in the highly ambivalent views of youth raised in diverse communities. We found support for immigration-induced diversity to run consistently higher only in areas with large Asian populations. Black and Hispanic population concentrations had no effect on attitudes toward diversity. What this suggests, interestingly, is that some of the most ethnically mixed communities are among the most divided about the value of immigration. Whether students from ethnic minority backgrounds or students from the white majority harbor the most reservations about diversity is explored in the next chapter, but what this set of findings suggests is that ethnic diversity in a community does not immediately resolve questions, divisions, and doubts about its value.

Community Resources and Tolerance of Diversity

The material and educational resources in a community do not necessarily lead to positive attitudes toward diversity, either. Children being raised among highly educated adults wound up rather divided about the value of immigration, as evidenced by the statistical insignificance of local

10. Key (1949).

education levels in table 2-1. Higher-income areas were expected to be more supportive of diversity than lower-income areas because they are more insulated from any threats posed by it, but we found that opposition *rose* slightly with median household income. This result may be simply a function of having a larger number of ethnic minority respondents in our lower- and middle-income communities than in the wealthier ones, a possibility we investigate later. We did find that higher-density areas were associated with more positive views of immigration than lower-density ones, but this too may be simply a function of the higher number of immigrant youth represented in the suburban and urban subsamples.

Political Orientation of Neighborhoods and Tolerance of Diversity

The political environment turned out to be the most potent predictor of attitudes toward diversity, and the degree of local political party diversity appeared to be especially critical. In two-party competitive settings, we found greater tolerance for immigration than in lopsided one-party settings. Of the one-party settings, however, we found marginally greater tolerance in Democratic than in Republican locales. The association of high voter turnout (independent of partisan diversity) with more tolerant attitudes was not statistically significant.

That partisan political diversity would promote greater tolerance makes some sense if we consider that in fiercely contested political battlegrounds, there is a need to enlist the support of minority nonvoters in order to craft a winning majority coalition. Moreover, Asians, Hispanics, blacks, and immigrants are more likely to be a part of the active electorate in areas of local party diversity than in locations where a single party dominates in the midst of low turnout. A less charitable interpretation of this finding is that the most highly competitive environments contain fewer partisans and ideologues who harbor reservations about racial and ethnic change.

Ethnic Diversity and Nationalism

Our nationalism questions gauged support for the belief that American institutions and values are superior to those elsewhere in the world. Our general expectation was that ethnically diverse locations would show less inclination to label the United States as superior to other nations, partly because ethnic minority populations may have less trust and confidence in the American system generally, particularly those that have experienced persistent discrimination. In this case, the results for nationalism should be similar to those for external efficacy. The results in table 2-1 do suggest that external efficacy and expressions of nationalistic support for the American system have an important common root. Communities with large Asian populations were significantly more chauvinistic than other locations, and these same communities showed far higher levels of external efficacy than locations with concentrations of African Americans and Hispanics. In fact, the communities in the study area with established black and Hispanic populations appeared quite ambivalent or mixed in the extent of their nationalism.

Respondents from locations with large foreign-born populations clearly rejected the notion that American institutions and values are superior. These results lead us to probe more deeply for an association between fresh immigrant roots and nationalistic sentiment. Foreign-born residents may not be more positive and nationalistic than the native born and may be less inclined to take the virtues of the American system for granted. What our results presently show is that not all types of diversity in a community conspired against the production of nationalistic sentiment among younger generations but that fresh immigrant communities were likely to produce less chauvinistic views among adolescents than more established ones.

Community Resources and Nationalism

It is easy to be nationalistic when things have gone well in one's life, and it was along this line of reasoning that we hypothesized that the wealthy would express greater nationalistic fervor than the poor. We found no statistically significant differences, however, between wealthy and impoverished communities in the propensity of their youth to express chauvinistic views. The relative wealth of the neighborhood did little to structure attitudes about the superiority of the American political system.

Youth from well-educated communities, however, were far less chauvinistic than those from areas with lower overall attainment. A 10 percent increase in the proportion of residents with four-year degrees dropped expressions of nationalism by 2.2 percentage points. While the children growing up in communities with lower educational attainment expressed greater nationalistic sentiment, these same adolescents were not necessarily more efficacious. Why these students believed that the U.S. system is the best even though they were not confident that the system works or that they had a voice in it is an interesting irony that we will return to later. It may make better sense that those being raised by highly educated parents express less nationalism given that they have had more exposure to the international community, more opportunities to travel abroad, and greater opportunities for interaction with diverse, foreign-born populations.

Political Orientation of Neighborhoods and Nationalism

Here we found that communities with exceptionally high turnout expressed marginally greater nationalism, suggesting some *prima facie* evidence for the connection we discussed in chapter 1 between patriotic sentiment and political participation. Highly Democratic areas produced no less nationalism among youth than Republican or more politically competitive ones.

Ethnic Diversity and the Clinton Impeachment

We sought to explain community-level influences on attitudes toward the impeachment of President Clinton mainly because we eventually wanted to assess the impact of this highly visible event on other political socialization outcomes (see chapter 8). Our main prediction for the effect of a community's demographic character on its attitudes toward the impeachment was that we expected communities with a larger black presence to be less supportive of the impeachment than others. Prominent African American elites were strongly opposed to the impeachment of President Clinton. Such a judgment may be rooted in simple partisanship, given that the vast majority of African Americans are Democrats, but we controlled for the political partisanship of these locales to parcel out the causal relationships more precisely. In fact, our results show that heavily African American and Hispanic communities were much less supportive of the impeachment than areas of Asian or predominantly white concentration. Communities with large foreign-born populations, on the other hand, were more supportive of the impeachment process.

Community Resources and the Clinton Impeachment

Community income levels did not distinguish youth responding to our questions about the impeachment of Bill Clinton. Nor were locations with better-educated residents especially opposed to the impeachment once we controlled for other variables. Higher-density urban and suburban neighborhoods were more opposed to the process than more sparsely populated rural areas. We conclude from these results that the impeachment controversy did not cleave communities by class as much as it distinguished rural from suburban and urban populations by fundamental social and moral values.

Political Orientation of Neighborhoods and the Clinton Impeachment

There was widespread consensus in the nation and in our study area that the president's conduct in the Monica Lewinsky affair did not merit his removal from office. Even so, results from our survey suggest that attitudes toward the Clinton impeachment could be predicted by at least one of the political characteristics of places that we studied: the political heterogeneity of the local environment. Our results show that a one-standard-deviation increase in the competitiveness of the vote for state and national office produced a 2 percentage point increase in support for the president's removal from office. Areas that are politically balanced may stimulate more intense discussions about political events, leading to a greater polarization of opinion on controversial matters.[11]

We certainly would not have been surprised to find the most Democratic locales producing different attitudes toward the impeachment than strongly Republican ones, but that is not what we found (table 2-1). The consensus that the impeachment process was largely a politically motivated sideshow apparently extended well into safe GOP neighborhoods.

Conclusions

If all localities looked the same way and were composed of the same interests, they would filter event-related information so similarly that there would be no place-to-place variation in opinions about politics and attitudes toward the political system. Local communities contain all of the primary agents of message transmission to youth. Because the ethnic and racial composition of a community produces specific interests that influence the way in which information is translated into opinion, political viewpoints will vary as the ethnic and racial character of neighborhoods varies. The same can be said for the capacity of income and education to provide a stimulus for amplifying certain messages and squelching others. The political character of communities also is highly variable, placing a powerful lens in the path of oncoming trans-local messages, refracting them to the point that they may look completely different from the way they did at the start.

In this chapter, we paused to see whether community characteristics structured political socialization outcomes, assuming that we had no back-

11. Zaller (1992).

ground information about our respondents other than where they lived. While our models explain rather little of the total variation in our respondents' answers, we did find several consistent results suggesting that the demographic, economic, and political composition of localities did contribute to the political socialization process. We learned that immigrant-receiving communities had low levels of political discussion and marginally lower levels of political knowledge and internal and external efficacy. In these cases, language barriers may disrupt the flow of local information, noncitizen status may give the foreign-born little incentive to invest in the acquisition of political information, and immigrants may carry beliefs about government corruption from their home country to the United States. Locations with large foreign-born populations also were doubtful about the responsiveness of local police and the justice meted out by courts. None of these characteristics of immigrant-receiving areas are conducive to the political socialization of young people living in these areas.

We were impressed with the strong influence that political party diversity had on knowledge and on internal and external efficacy. Politically diverse environments provide more stimuli than those characterized by boring, predictable, one-sided contests. Internal efficacy certainly was higher in such settings, where citizens are reminded that they have a voice when elections are hotly contested. Politically diverse settings also attract intense campaign activity, infusing the electorate with information that builds their knowledge. To the extent that public officials are more responsive to politically competitive communities than noncompetitive ones, it is no great surprise that external efficacy was higher at locations where Republicans and Democrats were present in more equal numbers. Similarly, politically competitive settings are likely to generate more positive attitudes toward local police and courts. Politically mixed environments also are likely to welcome more minorities and immigrants, especially when electoral margins are thin enough to make them a target of courtship for both parties.

By contrast, one-party dominant political settings are bad for many aspects of socialization. It is no great surprise that efficacy levels were so low in our inner-city neighborhoods. Local elections in these communities are settled so far in advance that they do not stimulate much of a sense that the individual's voice counts; lacking that sense, citizens have little reason to invest in detailed information about campaigns. Those raised in one-party Democratic settings also grow up with less confidence in the police and local court system than those in communities where the party system is more competitive or favors Republicans.

Also important was the association between voter turnout and frequency of discussion, level of knowledge, confidence in the police and the courts, and internal efficacy. Even if an area was not especially diverse in partisan terms, the model of participation presented by a high level of neighborhood turnout had a positive influence on the socialization of younger generations.

Finally, we found it interesting to note that high school students living in ethnically diverse communities were divided about the value of diversity. In the next chapter, we investigate the individual sources of these opinions to determine which adolescents expressed these views. It is possible that even black, Asian, and Hispanic youth had doubts about diversity, not just the Caucasian students. As for local law enforcement, we found that young people across the twenty-nine communities we studied uniformly complained about local law enforcement but that there were important substantive differences in the complaints. In the ethnically diverse, mostly suburban and urban communities, we were much more likely to hear stories of police nonresponse to reports of serious and violent crime, as well as stories of police corruption and brutality. In the homogeneously white suburban and rural locations, complaints were surprisingly quite voluminous, but they centered on the fact that the police had little to do but chase teenagers for minor traffic and controlled-substance violations. What this adds up to is that law enforcement authorities were subject to distrust for very different reasons as we moved from place to place. Of course it is always possible that youth in ethnically diverse communities believe that the police are less reliable and responsive, even though they are not when evaluated by some objective standard. Lacking the context provided by comparison, many citizens will come to false conclusions about government performance, particularly in areas afflicted with higher crime rates. But the fact that such views were prevalent bolsters our contention that the experience of a locality binds, structures, and colors the attitudes of adolescents, whose limited life experience inhibits their ability to think more objectively and with greater perspective about the problems that politics and government can realistically address.

3

Racial Group Membership, Neighborhood Context, and Political Socialization

In the previous chapter, we examined the influence of community characteristics on the attitudes of respondents toward government and about several important issues, working as if we had no information about our subjects' backgrounds except the locations where they lived. Limiting ourselves in this way was useful because we found that some community contexts did appear to have nontrivial effects on socialization-relevant attitudes. In this chapter, we begin to determine whether these community-level effects remain significant once the individual characteristics of respondents are taken into account.

Relying on aggregate data alone leaves too many unanswered questions. For example, in chapter 2 we found that the percentage of people of Asian ancestry settled in a place is associated with higher external efficacy, support for diversity, and nationalism. But this finding is not necessarily indicative of what Asian youth are thinking. The percentage of Asians in a neighborhood might be a very good indicator of other local characteristics, such as the size of the white population, since whites and Asians tend to live in closer proximity than Asians and other groups. When we observed in chapter 2 that Asian concentrations were associated with high external efficacy, we could not discern whether it was the Asians themselves who were supportive or the people living proximate to Asians (mainly white youth). Similarly, while we found that communities with large immigrant concentrations generally produced youth who were less nationalistic than those without immigrants, we had no way of knowing whether it was the immigrants themselves who were less nationalistic or the natives residing in immigrant-receiving areas.

In this chapter we examine these questions of context directly by adding the racial and ethnic characteristics of respondents to the work reported in chapter 2. We do this first by understanding socialization-relevant attitudes as a function of the race and immigrant parentage of respondents in addition to the racial and immigrant composition of communities. In this particular statistical framework, the race of the respondents at each school is considered to be a function of the racial makeup of communities in which the students reside. Thus community characteristics have an indirect impact on socialization outcomes by accounting for the specific selection of survey respondents at each school. But these community-level factors may still have an independent and direct effect on attitudes by creating a milieu of attitudes associated with the racial and ethnic mix of a given neighborhood. We also evaluate the effect of the respondent's gender, knowing that the previous generation of socialization research showed significant differences between the sexes in political efficacy, knowledge, and participation levels.[1]

In the second part of this chapter, we evaluate the interaction of individual racial or ethnic traits with community characteristics by using a very different model specification: a two-level model, also called a hierarchical linear model (HLM; see appendix D). Briefly, HLM is often used in social scientific data analysis when there are two (or more) levels of data; thus individuals and individual outcomes (attitudes, opinions, test scores) are subjects of observation at the first level, but these individuals are situated or "nested" within aggregate units or contexts (schools, neighborhoods, cities, counties, states) at a second level.[2] Because the individual observations are not independent of each other but are instead clustered by their confinement within a specific geographic context, the assumptions of the ordinary regression approach are violated and the standard errors of the regression estimates are untrustworthy. Hierarchical linear modeling takes into account the memberships of individuals in these second-level contextual aggregates, allowing evaluation of whether the regression parameters for the slope and intercept vary from location to location. Hence the rela-

1. Hess and Torney (1967); Jennings and Niemi (1974).
2. Raudenbush and Bryk (2002); Lee and Bryk (1989); Steenbergen and Jones (2002).

tionship between being of African American ancestry and the level of external efficacy might be entirely different in a predominantly African American community (school) than in a predominantly Caucasian one. With the information provided by the hierarchical linear model, it becomes a rather straightforward exercise to evaluate whether racial contexts matter such that individual relationships are fundamentally altered by the variable complexion of communities.

Special attention is paid to members of ethnic minority groups living in "ethnically homogeneous" neighborhoods: Asians living in neighborhoods with other Asians, Latinos in areas with substantial Latino concentrations, whites in predominantly Caucasian neighborhoods, and blacks in areas with other African Americans. This is a worthwhile focus because we anticipate that people may think and act differently in communities where they are a stronger numerical presence than in communities where they are a decisive minority. The socialization pressures on small minorities are likely to be greater than on majorities or on numerically larger minorities. The extent of an individual's immersion in a particular culture will be closely related to that person's adoption of that culture's values. An Asian in an area of Asian concentration is likely to act "more Asian" than one surrounded entirely by Caucasian neighbors. Similarly, African Americans often interact with other African Americans in ways that they do not interact with whites.

Racial integration enhances the probability of interethnic contact, potentially changing the racial composition of one's peer and friendship groups but also increasing the likelihood of greater intergroup tension, disagreement, and conflict. Disagreement and interethnic tension are not necessarily bad things if properly socialized. Disagreement, indeed conflict, can lead to greater discussion and exchange of ideas, and may be a necessary step toward greater participation and understanding. Resolutions to the most serious problems almost always involve argument, conflict, and compromise. Avoiding conflict, then, is not necessarily society's paramount goal; appropriately channeling it is.[3] We generally hypothesize that the experience of remaining embedded in a single, homogeneous racial or ethnic community inhibits many positive aspects of the political learning process and is likely to lead to poor socialization along a number of dimensions.[4] Fortunately, testing this proposition in the context of this research is relatively straightforward.

---

3. Schattschneider (1960).
4. Oliver (1999); Gimpel (1999).

The notion that individuals of different ethnic backgrounds have different socialization experiences, even within the same general setting, is so well grounded in previous research that it hardly needs to be justified. Community characteristics are important, as we pointed out in chapter 2, but experiences vary substantially within locales, particularly by race. Whether native-born African American children are socialized differently than immigrant Latino youth can be tested directly through the information we recorded about the race, ethnicity, and immigrant parentage of the students we surveyed. Including a person's race or ethnicity as a variable to explain political socialization may point to the different messages being communicated within racially homogeneous groups within local areas. Some might label these group-tailored messages "political cultures," and we have no strong objections to that term. We will avoid the term "culture," though, because of the internecine strife the concept has caused within and across several social science fields.

Patterns in the Political Socialization of Black Youth

Several earlier studies of racial differences in political socialization have found that black children have a consistently lower sense of efficacy than white children.[5] Given the pervasive fatherlessness found in black homes and neighborhoods, one is led to wonder whether racial differences in socialization are rooted in family structure or result simply from the greater economic deprivation and social discrimination experienced by African Americans. Levels of internal efficacy among African Americans have been shown to be high once socioeconomic variables have been held constant—suggesting that it is mainly economic inequality that deprives blacks of the opportunities to build their internal efficacy.[6] At the same time, feelings of *external* efficacy remain low.

In spite of the generally high levels of support for social welfare programs among African American voters, we found considerable heterogeneity of opinion about these very programs in the predominantly black high schools we visited. Our classrooms in these schools were also rife with accusations of government corruption. As one Baltimore City schoolgirl put it,

---

5. Abramson (1972); Clarke (1973); Greenberg (1970); Langton and Jennings (1968); Lyons (1970); Pierce and Carey (1971); Rodgers (1974).

6. Hughes and Demo (1989).

"City workers are lazy! They don't have to report to work on time. They don't gotta do nothin'. They don't go fix the hole in the street." At Forestville High School, situated in a lower-income neighborhood off Pennsylvania Avenue in majority-black Prince George's County, a teen whose mother was a federal employee lambasted government workers: "They [federal workers] drive down to their jobs but don't even worry about the homeless people without jobs they pass along the way."

Many African Americans doubt whether the system works for them, but according to previous research, many more remain confident that concerted action can make a difference.[7] But, to be true to our impressions, we found little confidence among the black adolescents in our study that collective action was at all relevant to their efforts to get ahead. Many African Americans coming of age in the new century view the civil rights movement as ancient history. Again and again we found that these kids had come to believe in the American individualist creed, that success is really up to them, and that poverty and other social problems stem from a lack of motivation rather than structural inequalities or discrimination. The following exchange among African American students at Forestville High exemplifies the point:

> *Question:* Has the history of slavery and discrimination made it difficult for black people to work their way out of poverty?
>
> *Raymond:* No, most blacks these days view themselves as bootstrappers.
>
> *Lashonda:* No one makes you stay in poverty. It's a choice.
>
> *Amanda:* Yeah, that argument is just an excuse for being lazy.
>
> *Darcel:* Lots of blacks have a mental slavery, not a physical slavery, and a few are lazy.
>
> *James:* That's right! It's all in their heads. We've got opportunities now.

At Dunbar High School, an all-black school in Baltimore's inner city best known for sending basketball players to the NBA, a sign above the elevator on the main floor asks, "Would you hire someone who was always late?" When we visited Dunbar, students did not rush to blame poverty on the legacy of discrimination and racism, either, but instead blamed each other:

7. Shingles (1981); Reese and Brown (1995).

Sade: The government wants women off welfare and working, but it's the men who should be out getting jobs. That would resolve the welfare problem.

Dante: Just close your legs, that would solve the welfare problem.

This hostile exchange, and many similar ones we observed in other classrooms, reflect the deterioration of gender relations in poor inner-city neighborhoods.[8] But they also are indicative of a tendency among African American youth to adopt the dominant belief system about poverty and welfare, "that the moral character of individuals, not inequities in the social and economic structure of society, is at the root of the problem."[9]

One teacher at Forestville High related a story of how the African American principal at the school was in a forum lamenting how blacks had been set back and disadvantaged by racism, and one black female student piped up and said, "Yes, but Ms. Williams, that was a very long time ago." The younger generation of black Americans has a hard time linking their experience to that of past generations and does not understand the proud history of the civil rights struggle. Especially for suburban black youth in the Baltimore-Washington area, who have grown up among a middle class population, the idea that discrimination holds them back seems less credible than it did to their parents' generation.

Once these young people gain more life experience, perhaps these impressions will change. They may eventually come to discredit the ideology of self-effort in favor of more traditional explanations for their group's socioeconomic struggles. Given that most suburbs where African Americans are concentrated remain heavily segregated, contact with members of other racial groups remains limited and so must be the experience of discrimination. Many students at the all-black high schools were amazed that we had even come to visit them because, except for police, Caucasians are seldom seen in their schools or neighborhoods.

Patterns in the Socialization of Latino and Immigrant Youth

Ethnic differences in levels of efficacy have been attributed to dominant ideologies or consistent messages communicated within particular communities. Cultures that emphasize fatalism or fatalistic beliefs and are less

8. Wilson (1996, p. 99–100).
9. Wilson (1996, p. 161).

future oriented are associated with lower personal efficacy.[10] One reason Mexican Americans are often thought to be less politically involved than Anglos, or at best an "ambivalent minority," is because of differences in value orientation.[11] The widespread nonparticipation of Latinos in politics must have its roots somewhere, and although some have questioned whether cultural differences between Anglos and Mexican Americans are of any political significance, a considerable body of evidence suggests that there is more here than negative stereotyping.[12] The Latino culture's strong emphasis on family ties may inhibit a strong sense of goal orientation in a society in which upward mobility may require separation from the family.[13] Mexican American youth are more inclined than Anglo-American youth to accept their parents' preconceived roles and commitments. The Latino family has been characterized as more authoritarian and less inclined than Anglo families to give children autonomy in decisionmaking.[14] In light of this research, it is reasonable to hypothesize that cultural values that are more future oriented and give children a sense that they can exercise control over their environment and their destiny will produce greater political efficacy than a value set that does not include these emphases. At least one study indicated that Japanese American children scored higher in political efficacy than either their Anglo- or Mexican American classmates, a finding directly attributable to the cultural stress placed on personal achievement, deference, and conformity which facilitates socioeconomic success in spite of minority status.[15]

Among immigrants and the second generation, regardless of national origin, multiple cultural identities may create ambivalence toward participation in American political life.[16] Enduring preferences for aspects of the culture of ancestry may have an isolating effect, as will residential segregation from native-born populations with highly participatory attitudes. Residential integration among the native born *alone* is not sufficient to generate a sense of efficacy among immigrants and the second generation because many native-born populations do not themselves have a strong

---

10. Gecas (1989); Kramer (1970); Ross, Mirowsky, and Cockerham (1983); Schwartz (1971).

11. Skerry (1993).

12. For a discussion of whether cultural differences between Anglos and Mexican Americans are of any political significance, see de la Garza, Falcon, and Garcia (1996).

13. Schwartz (1971).

14. Anderson and Evans (1976); Evans and Anderson (1973).

15. Stevens (1975, p. 290).

16. Garcia (1987); Lamare (1982); Stevens (1975).

sense of efficacy. For residential integration to enhance political efficacy among immigrant subgroups, it has to occur at high enough income and education levels that immigrants will be exposed to a native population whose political efficacy is high.

Finally, language barriers may prevent immigrants and their offspring from picking up socializing messages intended to assure them that their voice counts. Several studies have indicated that English proficiency is associated with greater feelings of political efficacy and higher levels of political participation.[17] Related to this finding, participatory feelings and identification with one of the two major parties are stronger among immigrants with longer residence in the country.[18]

Effect of Race and Ethnicity on Political Discussion, Knowledge, and Efficacy

Our results reported in table 3-1 demonstrate indisputably that one of the bedrock differences between white respondents and those of the ethnic minority subgroups is the frequency of political discussion with friends and family. Black youth reported the lowest volume of political discussion; specifically, African American teens engaged in 7.7 percent less discussion than white respondents. Latinos reported 6.9 percent less discussion, and Asians 6.5 percent less than Caucasian youth (see table 3-1). Interestingly, locations with larger Asian populations reported generally higher levels of discussion; however, as mentioned earlier, this was not so much due to the Asian respondents per se but instead to the fact that Asians often lived in close proximity to whites in the neighborhoods where they settled.

Levels of political knowledge exhibit noteworthy racial and ethnic differences, too. Black and Latino students were considerably less knowledgeable about politics than white students, with blacks showing an 11-point deficit and Latinos lagging 7.9 percentage points behind (see coefficients in table 3-1). Children with foreign-born parents may not engage in less political discussion than native-born whites, but they were slightly less knowledgeable than those whose parents were native born. We also see the persistence of a small gender gap, with female teens scoring about 2 points lower on the knowledge test than the males.

17. Garcia (1973); Garcia (1987); Uhlaner, Cain, and Kiewiet (1989).
18. Cain, Kiewiet, and Uhlaner (1991).

Notably, we found that areas with larger black populations also exhibited lower test scores than other locations, although we know that this has less to do with the performance of black youth, who score far lower than whites, and more to do with the fact that racially integrated areas often generate more political information than racially homogeneous ones.[19] For example, additional resources are frequently steered toward schools in racially integrated areas for curriculum enhancement purposes, the point being to boost everyone's achievement levels (although our results suggest that the nonminority students benefit most).

Some of the worst knowledge test scores were found in the heavily Latino parts of our study area. Our evidence suggests that besides the poorer performance of the Latino and immigrant youth, other aspects of predominantly Latino communities conspire to lower scores by about 9 points for every 10 percent increase in the Latino population: language barriers in Latino and immigrant communities restrict the knowledge dissemination and acquisition process.

For internal efficacy, our findings are mostly consistent with the estimates for political knowledge. Black and Latino youth trailed white youth by 5 percent, while Asians and children of immigrant parents showed no statistically significant lags. Internal efficacy was highest in areas of high Asian concentration and lowest in locations with large Hispanic and African American populations. Internal efficacy was reasonably high in immigrant-receiving communities, consistent with the findings from the previous chapter.

To summarize, the most notable neighborhood effect on political knowledge and internal efficacy was for neighborhoods with large Latino populations, where the impact was strongly negative. Among the explanations capturing individual influences on socialization, the most significant effect was for being of African American or Latino ancestry—with both of these groups exhibiting substantially lower knowledge and efficacy than Caucasian or Asian youth.

External efficacy is one's sense that the system works, and here African American youth consistently lagged behind whites, Latinos, and Asians. We find little evidence that the black youth of Generation Y have high internal efficacy but low external efficacy—something that Shingles, in a widely cited article, defined as "black consciousness."[20] On the contrary,

19. Oliver (1999).
20. Shingles (1981).

Table 3-1. *Direct Effects of Racial Context, Racial Group Membership, and Gender on Political Socialization Outcomes, Controlling for Indirect Effects of Racial Context and Direct Effects of Other Community Characteristics*[a]
Units as indicated

Explanatory variable	Frequency of political discussion	β	Level of political knowledge	β	Internal political efficacy	β	External political efficacy	β
Asian respondent	-6.528** (1.806)	-.07	-1.595 (1.360)	-.02	-1.796 (1.063)	-.03	0.786 (1.031)	.01
Black respondent	-7.716** (1.304)	-.12	-10.969** (0.982)	-.21	-4.894** (0.768)	-.13	-3.171** (0.744)	-.09
Hispanic respondent	-6.866** (1.993)	-.06	-7.876** (1.501)	-.09	-5.005** (1.174)	-.08	0.059 (1.137)	.00
Foreign-born parents	0.182 (0.644)	.01	-1.412** (0.501)	-.05	-0.121 (.391)	-.01	-0.136 (0.379)	-.01
Female	-0.621 (0.984)	-.01	-1.885** (0.741)	-.04	-3.641** (0.580)	-.11	0.549 (0.561)	.02
Percent Asian	0.471* (0.282)	.10	0.034 (0.213)	.01	-0.173 (0.167)	-.06	0.332** (0.161)	.12
Percent black	-0.046* (0.026)	-.04	-0.074** (0.019)	-.07	-0.103** (0.015)	-.13	-0.059** (0.014)	-.08
Percent Hispanic	0.148 (0.242)	.05	-0.879** (0.183)	-.35	-0.400** (0.143)	-.22	-0.363** (0.138)	-.20
Percent foreign born	-0.217 (0.222)	-.09	0.350** (0.167)	.19	0.233** (0.131)	.17	0.162 (0.128)	.12
Summary statistic								
R^2	.081		.190		.102		.094	
N	2,934		2,919		2,936		2,933	

Explanatory variable	Negativity about courts/police	β	Opposition to diversity	β	Nationalism/ chauvinism	β	Support Clinton impeachment	β
Asian respondent	2.732* (1.397)	.04	−5.359** (0.990)	−.10	−0.102 (1.267)	−.00	1.954 (1.444)	.02
Black respondent	9.024** (1.008)	.18	0.745 (0.715)	.02	−2.484** (0.915)	−.06	−9.098** (1.043)	−.18
Hispanic respondent	2.567 (1.542)	.03	−8.168** (1.093)	−.14	−0.989 (1.398)	−.01	−2.567 (1.593)	−.03
Foreign-born parents	−1.424** (0.508)	−.05	−1.635** (0.364)	−.09	−1.826** (0.466)	−.08	−0.745 (0.531)	−.03
Female	0.560 (0.761)	.01	−0.703 (0.540)	−.02	−1.837** (0.690)	−.05	−0.819 (0.787)	−.02
Percent Asian	−0.420** (0.218)	−.11	−0.089 (0.156)	−.03	0.538** (0.198)	.17	−0.317 (0.226)	−.08
Percent black	0.012 (0.020)	.01	0.048** (0.014)	.07	−0.076** (0.018)	−.09	−0.049** (0.020)	−.05
Percent Hispanic	0.270 (0.187)	.11	0.241** (0.133)	.14	0.110 (0.169)	.05	−0.551** (0.194)	−.03
Percent foreign born	−0.139 (0.172)	−.08	−0.131 (0.122)	−.10	−0.091 (0.156)	−.06	0.456** (0.178)	.25
Summary statistic								
R^2	.109		.087		.053		.066	
N	2,951		2,927		2,947		2,939	

Source: Metro Civic Values Survey, 1999–2000.

*$p \leq .10$; **$p \leq .05$.

a. Structural equations estimation. Values are regression coefficients for direct effects only with standard errors shown in parentheses. β, standardized regression coefficients. Control variables with parameters for direct effects that are not shown in this table are population density, median income, percent with four years of college, Democratic percent of the vote, political party diversity, and percent turnout.

our results suggest that black youth lag further behind whites in their assessment of their own voice (internal efficacy) than in their confidence in the system more generally (external efficacy). The black youth from our survey appeared to lack the key ingredients of racial consciousness at this point in their lives.

The children of foreign-born parents showed no clear tendency to be less externally efficacious than those of native-born parents, once we controlled for race and ethnic origin. Apparently, then, conclusions about the system being broken were not the product of a fresh immigrant background per se but rather reflected the quality of information in areas of particular ethnic concentration.

To what extent is family structure associated with decreased efficacy, knowledge, and discussion among youth? To examine the effects wrought by single- versus two-parent families, difference in means tests were conducted for each racial or ethnic subgroup for several of the political socialization outcomes, contrasting the scores of adolescents in married couple households with those from single-parent households, regardless of whether single-parenthood resulted from divorce, separation, death, or never marrying in the first place. The results from these hypothesis tests are reported in table 3-2. Negative values in these tables indicate responses in which children from married couple households ranked higher (more efficacious, more knowledgeable, more discussions) than children from single-parent homes.

For African American children, the comparisons were rather striking. Not only did the number of black children from single-parent homes exceed the number from two-parent homes, but those from single-parent homes scored significantly lower in internal efficacy, knowledge, and frequency of political discussion. There was no significant difference between black adolescents from married and single-parent households in the level of external efficacy, although children from single-parent black homes were significantly more negative toward the police and court system (see table 3-2).

The socialization of Latino and Asian youth was clearly more resistant to the negative effects of single-parenthood, although Asian youth from single-parent homes were significantly lower in their internal efficacy and higher in their negativity toward police than those from two-parent homes. White adolescents also scored much lower in political knowledge if they came from single-parent homes, and they were far more likely to be negative toward the police under these circumstances. White youth also scored

Table 3-2. *Selected Political Socialization Outcomes by Family Structure for Each Racial and Ethnic Group*[a]
Units as indicated

| | Parents are | | | | |
Dependent variables	Married (N)	Not married (N)	Mean difference	t test	Significance[b]
Political discussion					
Black respondents	303	406	−.278	−1.928	.054
Latino respondents	134	81	.091	0.365	.716
Asian respondents	224	37	−.130	−0.423	.674
White respondents	870	399	−.180	−1.522	.128
Political knowledge					
Black respondents	300	414	−.052	−3.289	.001
Latino respondents	136	82	.009	0.286	.775
Asian respondents	226	37	−.049	−1.189	.241
White respondents	870	394	−.042	−3.570	.001
Internal efficacy					
Black respondents	293	414	−.146	−2.018	.044
Latino respondents	134	82	.049	0.368	.713
Asian respondents	225	36	−.357	−2.183	.034
White respondents	868	396	−.019	−0.318	.751
External efficacy					
Black respondents	296	411	−.078	−1.018	.309
Latino respondents	134	81	.075	−0.546	.585
Asian respondents	225	37	−.231	−1.131	.264
White respondents	867	393	−.100	−1.670	.096
Negativity about police and courts					
Black respondents	300	415	.161	2.061	.040
Latino respondents	134	80	.140	1.005	.316
Asian respondents	226	37	.391	2.198	.033
White respondents	872	399	.296	4.983	.001

Source: Metro Civic Values Survey, 1999–2000.

a. Difference in means tests. Negative signs indicate that adolescents from married-couple households rank higher on the dependent variable than adolescents from non-married-couple households within each racial or ethnic group.

b. Significance tests are two-tailed.

marginally lower in external efficacy when they came from single-parent households versus two-parent households.

The effects of single-parenthood were uneven across groups, even allowing for the differences in sample size. Blacks were most hurt by variation in family structure, followed by whites. Why were the effects of single-parenthood so much harsher for black and white youth than for adolescents from Asian and Latino families? At least a couple of reasons come to mind. First, single-parenthood in the African American community is associated with far greater poverty than single-parenthood among other groups. Much of the inferiority of the single-parent household lies in its low income and low educational attainment—divorce is still the main reason women fall below the poverty line. Children growing up in households that are financially strapped, with parents who have little time to engage in political activity, much less the knowledge of how to go about it, will have fewer opportunities to learn about politics than those in better-off single-parent homes. Second, African American and white native-born communities may be devoid of the social and familial capital that can make up for the loss of a parent in the more closely knit Asian and Latino neighborhoods. Substitute parenting by grandparents, aunts, uncles, and cousins may be a real option in the locations where Latinos and Asians have chosen to settle but less available in areas where African Americans and whites concentrate and where isolated nuclear families are prevalent.

Some are likely to question why in table 3-1 we did not evaluate the effects of ethnicity and control for socioeconomic status, using family income or a similar variable that signals the level of financial well-being. Our response is twofold. First, because low socioeconomic status is so closely tied to the experience of some racial minority groups, any attempt to demonstrate that the variation across our participation-enabling outcomes is not connected to race because it can be explained by economic status would only obscure the disadvantaged position that African American and Latino students find themselves in. In other words, it is precisely the point that African Americans and Latinos do poorly on a variety of socialization indicators because their families are less educated and poorer than whites, even in the Baltimore-Washington corridor where a black middle class has thrived.

Second, our hypothesis tests clearly showed that when we did control for socioeconomic status, the effects for race and ethnicity changed very little (see tables 3-3 and 3-4 for evidence). Although many of the African American students in the study area were from middle-income homes, this higher socioeconomic status did not appreciably improve their scores on political socialization indicators relative to their lower-income counterparts. Once we controlled for economic status, for example, African American youth still lagged behind white students in their level of political knowledge. The differences between minority and white youth do not disappear when we control for poverty.

Effect of Race and Ethnicity on Attitudes toward Law Enforcement, Diversity, and Nationalism

Many social scientists have observed that race and attitudes toward law enforcement were strongly linked, such that ethnic minority populations are more likely than white populations to express hostility and suspicion toward local police and courts. Black Americans' historically negative experiences with a white-dominated police force and legal system have undoubtedly fostered a sense of alienation among members of this racial group.[21] Minorities generally are more likely to have negative police contact than whites.[22] The evidence that police discriminate against minority youth is quite strong, but it is not police action itself that matters. Rather, it is the *perception* among minority youth that police antagonize and harass them that is most relevant to understanding trust attitudes.[23] The police are widely considered by minority groups to be pro-white. Certainly these perceptions are no different in the Baltimore-Washington area than they are in other parts of the nation. In fact, certain police forces in the metropolitan area are notorious for being heavy-handed. At one Prince George's high school that is 99 percent African American, our question about whether the police were trustworthy caused the students to literally leap out of their seats with indignation.

The evidence that race influences law enforcement attitudes is quite strong, judging from the coefficients in table 3-1. Black youth were three times more critical of the police than were Asians and Latinos, although all three groups were more hostile to law enforcement than whites. Youth from immigrant households, on the other hand, were more positive about police than those with native-born parents, indicating that there is nothing about fresh immigrant ancestry per se that determines negativity toward

21. Kennedy (1997); Peek, Alston, and Lowe (1978).
22. Black and Reiss (1970); Dannefur and Schutt (1982); Parker, Onyekwuluje, and Murty (1995).
23. Hurwitz and Peffley (2001).

local authorities. Still, the results for the community-level indicators told a different story—that once we controlled for the race of our individual respondents, areas of Asian, black, and Latino concentration were *not* more likely than heavily white areas to produce negative attitudes toward police. In fact, communities with a significant Asian presence were more positive about the police and local courts than other locations. We conclude from these findings that negative attitudes toward the police *are not as context dependent* as other socialization indicators but instead are isolated among those groups that feel targeted and consider themselves victims of harassment, regardless of where they live.

Although the Asian and Latino arrivals dominating the current immigration stream are not subject to the same derogatory stereotypes as African Americans, prejudice of either a subtle symbolic or more blatant type may still be directed their way to produce an anti-immigrant effect. Latinos are routinely typecast as illegal aliens, exploiters of welfare benefits, lazy, uneducated, and associated with certain types of crime, specifically drug dealing and smuggling.[24] Asian immigrants are greeted with less hostility, due partly to their smaller numbers, their myriad nationality backgrounds, and the perception that East Asians are "model minorities." However, they are still derided as unable and unwilling to communicate, aloof and insular, avaricious, overly compliant, and in some cases, depending on the nationality and context, exploitive of government benefits, smelling bad, eating unpalatable food, and involved in certain types of crime.[25] Also, Asians are commonly lumped into a single nationality—often Chinese—by non-Asians and are perceived by African Americans to have easier access than they do to government assistance and financial capital.[26] That these stereotypes are so prevalent across settings suggests that they are not contingent upon contextual circumstances relating to interethnic proximity or economic hardship but rather have arisen from exposure to popular media portrayals.[27]

Without question, then, views of immigration-induced diversity have a strong racial component. Asians and Latinos favored diversity far more than African American youth: the African American adolescents we surveyed were about as opposed to diversity as their white counterparts. While

---

24. Cowan, Martinez, and Mendiola (1997); Feagin and Feagin (1996); Taylor, Lee, and Stern (1995); Willis-Esqueda (1997).

25. Oyserman and Sakamoto (1997).

26. Guthrie and Hutchinson (1995); Jo (1992); Ma (1998).

27. Taylor, Lee, and Stern (1995).

black *individuals* exhibit about the same level of hostility as whites, local *communities* grow more opposed to diversity as the proportion of blacks and Latinos increases. We can infer from the results in table 3-1 that it is not the Latino youth who are responsible for anti-immigrant attitudes but instead those non-Latinos living in heavily Latino neighborhoods—these would be a mix of black and white youth. This anxiety about diversity among individual native-born black and white youth living in ethnically mixed neighborhoods is probably traceable to concerns about the competition for jobs and housing posed by immigrants, although some of it may have its roots in learned prejudice picked up from cultural sources such as television, movies, and popular music.

As for the distinctiveness of Generation Y compared to previous generations, we see no absence of prejudice in the face of the record-breaking levels of immigration the nation has experienced in the last decade. At the dawn of the new century, young people certainly have far more targets for prejudice than previous generations. That there are more opportunities for contact with immigrants, though, also means a greater potential for friendship, intermarriage, and a more racially harmonious society. In this sense, it is ironic, although perhaps not surprising, that the social science literature has discovered that many of the same variables responsible for interethnic conflict are, under slightly different conditions, also responsible for improved race relations.

As for the connection between ethnicity and nationalism, we believe it is possible that chauvinistic sentiment may spur political participation and interest in politics. However, we must also reckon with the previous research showing nationalism to be associated with lower levels of interest in politics, an impoverished educational background, poor reading ability, and a narrow, parochial outlook.[28] Support for the idea that the American form of government is the best is least prominent among black youth, and this would appear to be perfectly consistent with their negativity toward police and their prevailing view that the system does not work for them. Nationalistic feeling is also more likely to be expressed by boys and those with native roots as opposed to those with foreign-born parents.

Turning to consider the direct effects of community characteristics on nationalistic sentiment, we reassessed the results from chapter 2 in light of the individual-level traits we added and found many fewer chauvinistic expressions from respondents in heavily African American communities.

28. Jennings and Niemi (1968); Kelly and Ronan (1987).

Consistent with the results from chapter 2, locations with strong Asian concentrations exhibited high levels of chauvinism, although it is now clear from the data shown in table 3-1 that these expressions were not necessarily coming from the Asian respondents themselves but from the white youth in these neighborhoods.

Effect of Race and Ethnicity on Attitudes toward the Clinton Impeachment

From the standpoint of major media stories, the Clinton impeachment qualifies as one of the most significant of the last twenty years. Few other stories during the 1990s received such intense news coverage for five months on both cable and network television. The event may have been more significant than a normal five-month political event because Americans believed that the impeachment proceedings were a culmination of months of prior investigations and rumors about the president's character.

Opinions about the Clinton impeachment are important from a socialization standpoint because socialization involves taking sides. The development of crystallized, stable opinions about important issues is likely to stimulate participation—driving people to the polls to cast votes on the basis of government policy and performance. Here we examine whether taking sides in response to the Clinton impeachment divided youth along racial and ethnic lines. If so, it suggests that race and ethnic identity are serving as a socializing influence by transforming information from major media sources into opinions favorable toward or against the president's removal.

As shown in table 3-1, racial characteristics were significantly related to judgments about the impeachment process. Black youth were about 9 percent less supportive of the president's removal from office than whites, and Latinos nearly 3 percent less supportive. Asian adolescents were, if anything, slightly more contemptuous of the president than white youth, although not to a statistically significant degree.

The similarity of Asian and white attitudes is quite possibly a reflection of the socialization of Asians by the white natives who dominate the neighborhoods and schools in the neighborhoods where Asians have settled. However, given that aspects of Asian culture are morally very conservative, it is very possible that the Asian adolescents arrived at this position quite without the peer influence of white natives. Regardless, we can at least note that on this question, the political values of Asians are far closer to those of whites than they are to other minority groups.

Effect of Community Characteristics in Interaction with Racial Background

Does it matter whether an adolescent is growing up in a neighborhood surrounded by members of his or her own racial or ethnic group? This question is addressed more directly by the results presented in tables 3-3 and 3-4, where we employed a method directly suited to evaluating whether the relationships between the ethnicity of individuals and their responses to our socialization questions vary by the racial or ethnic complexion of their communities. Specifically, the point of this analysis is to determine whether youth living among their own racial group systematically differ from those who live more proximate to other groups.

Since the concentration of ethnic minority groups (Asians, Latinos, blacks) is often associated with economic disadvantage, our general hypothesis is that youth living in segregated communities among their own are likely to exhibit lower knowledge and efficacy levels than if they were living in communities more integrated with the Caucasian population. This is not as likely to be true of the white population, however, given that its insularity from minority populations is usually a sign of privilege and exclusivity. Here we seek to determine whether a community's racial profile imprints a distinctive stamp on its more youthful members. We take the additional steps of controlling explicitly for the socioeconomic status of the respondent's family, the marital status of parents, and the interaction of Latino and black ethnicity with gender.

Discussion, Knowledge, and Political Efficacy

For Asian and Latino youth, living within their own ethnic communities did not promote political discussion. As shown in table 3-3, political discussions were less frequent in locations where students with these identities lived in close proximity to those of similar ethnic background. However, when these students resided among whites and other groups, their propensity to discuss politics with family and friends was less distinguishable from that of white adolescents. Perhaps contact with diversity, and specifically with white populations, stimulates the kind of information

Table 3-3. *Influence of Race, Gender, and Racial Context on Discussion, Knowledge, and Political Efficacy, Controlling for Family Socioeconomic Status*[a]

Units as indicated

Fixed effects	Explanatory variable	Frequency of political discussion	Level of political knowledge	Internal political efficacy	External political efficacy
School means (β_0)	Intercept	17.85** (2.25)	64.97** (1.71)	47.59** (1.40)	37.37** (0.75)
	Percent black	–0.04 (0.06)	–0.14** (0.03)	–0.04* (0.02)	0.003 (0.01)
	Percent Asian	1.06** (0.50)	–0.28 (0.33)	0.04 (0.16)	0.55** (0.07)
	Percent Hispanic	0.78** (0.31)	–0.30 (0.36)	0.01 (0.14)	0.15** (0.09)
	Percent foreign born	–0.56 (0.35)	0.22 (0.30)	0.16 (0.14)	–0.15** (0.07)
Black respondent (β_1)	Intercept	–1.05 (2.57)	–6.60** (2.09)	2.15* (1.12)	2.97** (1.32)
	Percent black	–0.05 (0.03)	0.07** (0.03)	–0.05** (0.02)	–0.03** (0.02)
	Percent foreign born	–0.01 (0.08)	–0.19** (0.07)	–0.24** (0.04)	–0.18** (0.04)
Asian respondent (β_2)	Intercept	11.32** (4.52)	2.35 (2.56)	5.37** (1.19)	5.20 (4.19)
	Percent Asian	–0.27* (0.15)	0.87** (0.22)	0.06 (0.11)	–0.12 (0.15)
	Percent foreign born	–0.45** (0.16)	–0.48** (0.18)	–0.32** (0.09)	–0.14 (0.16)
Hispanic respondent (β_3)	Intercept	–0.83 (4.62)	–2.27 (4.97)	5.15 (3.56)	–0.83 (2.36)

(continued)

exchange thought to be so valuable to good political socialization.[29] Discussion and knowledge are not identical, however. Asians living in heavily Asian communities may have high levels of political knowledge, as suggested by our results, but still not engage in much information exchange through discussion.

29. Mutz (2002a).

Table 3-3. *Influence of Race, Gender, and Racial Context on Discussion, Knowledge, and Political Efficacy, Controlling for Family Socioeconomic Status*[a] *(Continued)*

Units as indicated

Fixed effects	Explanatory variable	Frequency of political discussion	Level of political knowledge	Internal political efficacy	External political efficacy
	Percent Hispanic	−0.59*	0.14	0.06	−0.14
		(0.36)	(0.27)	(0.21)	(0.20)
	Percent foreign born	0.04	−0.16	−0.48**	0.05
		(0.25)	(0.27)	(0.17)	(0.16)
Foreign-born parents (β_4)	Intercept	−0.85	−0.73	0.53	0.72
		(1.51)	(1.22)	(0.65)	(0.70)
	Percent foreign born	0.05	−0.07	−0.02	−0.03
		(0.07)	(0.05)	(0.03)	(0.03)
Parents are married (β_5)	Intercept	0.95	4.34**	1.04	1.36**
		(1.11)	(1.05)	(0.85)	(0.52)
Female (β_6)	Intercept	−1.47	−5.02**	−5.40**	−0.10
		(1.00)	(0.93)	(0.90)	(0.53)
Black female (β_7)	Intercept	−1.28	4.10**	3.18**	−0.43
		(1.65)	(0.87)	(0.90)	(1.00)
Hispanic female (β_8)	Intercept	7.53**	−0.75	1.36	−0.03
		(3.14)	(4.08)	(2.46)	(2.05)
Socioeconomic status (β_9)	Intercept	0.22**	0.31**	0.15**	0.02
		(0.07)	(0.05)	(0.04)	(0.02)
Summary statistic					
Level-one respondents (*N*)		2,690	2,670	2,686	2,678
Percent reduction in error		4.8	9.4	6.9	2.0

Source: Metro Civic Values Survey, 1999–2000.

*$p \leq .10$; **$p \leq .05$.

a. Two-level hierarchical linear model, slopes and intercepts estimation. Values are regression coefficients with standard errors shown in parentheses. Results for reliability estimates and random effects do not appear in the table but are available from the authors upon request.

Notably, we found that Asian adolescents in immigrant-heavy neighborhoods exhibited much lower levels of knowledge and internal efficacy than those living in close proximity to the native born. Residing in newer ethnic communities could lead to information deficits as a result of fewer resources and more insularity from politically minded populations. Living in areas of immigrant presence also diminished the internal efficacy of Latinos and African American youth (see figure 3-1), even after we explicitly

Figure 3-1. *Internal Efficacy among Black, Asian, and Latino Students Living in Immigrant Neighborhoods*

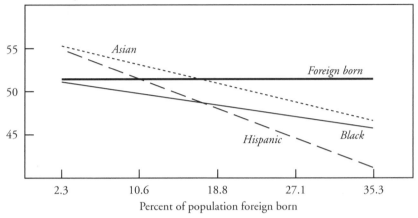

Internal efficacy score

Source: Metro Civic Values Survey, 1999–2000.

accounted for family socioeconomic status. Figure 3-1 illustrates the drop in the internal efficacy of African American youth living in areas of high immigrant concentration versus those living where there is a low immigrant presence. For Latino and Asian youth living in such neighborhoods, the drop in internal efficacy was even greater.

Why is it that living in areas of immigrant concentration often impedes the development of attitudes and dispositions consistent with good citizenship among blacks, Latinos, and Asians? For African Americans, living among immigrants who are seen to be progressing economically while blacks themselves are not, diminishes a more general sense of efficacy, which then erodes political efficacy. Latinos and *certain* Asian nationality groups who live around high concentrations of immigrants are likely to be exposed to subcultures that are inattentive to domestic politics, less likely to speak English, and are slow to naturalize. Under these environmental constraints, youth rarely encounter the kind of information that would engender participation-enabling attitudes. An older literature would have attributed the poor socialization in heavily immigrant neighborhoods to ignorance, but it is more than ignorance. Some of these populations may view the political system as if it were closed and unchangeable, reflecting attitudes toward politics held over from their experiences in their nations of origin. Thus politics and government are subjects to be avoided, and acts of participation are considered pointless.

Other results from the analysis in table 3-3 that are worth highlighting include the generally low knowledge and internal efficacy levels for adolescent girls compared with boys. Among African American youth, however, the reverse pattern held: black females were far more knowledgeable and confident in their political voice than black males. This may reflect the lower levels of personal efficacy we found among many adolescent black males. Black males are less likely than any other group, including black females, to find and maintain good employment and they have lower levels of college attendance. Many employers express preferences for hiring black women over black men in urban labor markets.[30] To the extent that personal efficacy and political efficacy are linked, it is easy for young black men to conclude that neither their efforts at work and school nor their political participation would pay off.

Notably, we also found Hispanic girls to be more talkative and marginally more internally efficacious than Hispanic boys, suggesting that African Americans are not the only minority group exhibiting gender differences in socialization. Finally, the socioeconomic status of families had an undeniably strong impact on the volume of political discussion, the amount of political knowledge, and the level of internal efficacy. Family structure was also an important influence in the socialization process, and two-parent households were usually associated with greater political knowledge and higher external efficacy among our youthful respondents.

Attitudes toward Law Enforcement, Diversity, and Nationalism

Not surprisingly, we found that among white youth who live in homogeneous Caucasian communities, there was generally solid support for law enforcement, more opposition to diversity, and more chauvinism. But table 3-4 shows that other interesting interactions also came into play. First, black respondents in ethnically mixed communities reported more unease about local police and courts. These results also indicated that the attitudes of black youth toward immigrants were not that highly context dependent: those living in the neighborhoods of highest immigrant concentration were not substantially more opposed to diversity than those containing little or no immigrant presence. Not all attitudes were context dependent, and it is as important to note the ones that were not as it is the ones that were. By

30. Wilson (1996, p. 122).

Table 3-4. *Influence of Race, Gender, and Racial Context on Attitudes about Law Enforcement, Diversity, Nationalism, and Impeachment, Controlling for Family Socioeconomic Status*[a]
Units as indicated

Fixed effects	Explanatory variable	Negativity about courts/police	Opposition to diversity	Nationalism/ chauvinism	Support Clinton impeachment
School means (β_0)	Intercept	46.54** (2.31)	53.14** (1.53)	71.08** (1.74)	54.09** (1.33)
	Percent black	0.14** (0.04)	0.01 (0.02)	−0.05** (0.02)	−0.16** (0.03)
	Percent Asian	−0.69** (0.30)	−0.18** (0.08)	0.91** (0.11)	−0.41** (0.17)
	Percent Hispanic	0.35 (0.26)	0.14** (0.09)	0.33** (0.10)	−0.59** (0.18)
	Percent foreign born	−0.09 (0.25)	−0.04 (0.09)	−0.39** (0.09)	0.33** (0.16)
Black respondent (β_1)	Intercept	12.14** (3.91)	−5.38** (1.82)	−1.09 (1.74)	−12.29** (4.10)
	Percent black	−0.16** (0.04)	0.03 (0.03)	0.02 (0.02)	0.15** (0.05)
	Percent foreign born	0.09 (0.13)	0.03 (0.07)	0.02 (0.05)	0.02 (0.11)
Asian respondent (β_2)	Intercept	4.80** (2.13)	2.65 (2.42)	−1.50 (3.97)	1.56 (2.14)
	Percent Asian	−0.09 (0.20)	−0.35** (0.10)	−0.09 (0.16)	−0.22 (0.13)
	Percent foreign born	−0.05 (0.13)	−0.13 (0.11)	0.03 (0.16)	0.08 (0.08)
Hispanic respondent (β_3)	Intercept	3.21 (4.84)	9.00 (6.51)	4.23 (3.83)	4.59 (4.12)

(continued)

contrast, both Asian and Latino respondents showed much more hostility to diversity when they were in ethnically mixed communities with whites rather than in homogeneous communities among their own.

The positions taken by black females were markedly different than those of other respondents on the diversity and law enforcement measures. Specifically, they were more positive toward local police and courts than

Table 3-4. *Influence of Race, Gender, and Racial Context on Attitudes about Law Enforcement, Diversity, Nationalism, and Impeachment, Controlling for Family Socioeconomic Status*[a] *(Continued)*
Units as indicated

Fixed effects	Explanatory variable	Negativity about courts/police	Opposition to diversity	Nationalism/ chauvinism	Support Clinton impeachment
	Percent Hispanic	0.05 (0.32)	−0.89** (0.22)	−0.42** (0.13)	0.41** (0.17)
	Percent foreign born	0.04 (0.27)	0.19 (0.26)	0.05 (0.15)	−0.65** (0.19)
Foreign-born parents (β_4)	Intercept	−2.08** (0.77)	−2.12** (0.89)	−0.76 (1.09)	−2.01** (0.74)
	Percent foreign born	0.05 (0.03)	0.02 (0.03)	−0.03 (0.05)	0.06** (0.03)
Parents are married (β_5)	Intercept	−4.65** (0.65)	−0.92** (0.38)	2.51** (0.61)	1.35* (0.78)
Female (β_6)	Intercept	2.84** (0.83)	−3.26** (0.63)	−3.33** (0.67)	−0.22 (0.59)
Black female (β_7)	Intercept	−5.01** (1.35)	4.89** (1.03)	0.55 (1.05)	−0.61 (0.87)
Hispanic female (β_8)	Intercept	−4.15 (3.29)	6.01* (3.28)	−0.49 (2.21)	4.74* (2.63)
Socioeconomic status (β_9)	Intercept	−0.06 (0.05)	−0.06 (0.04)	0.08 (0.05)	−0.04 (0.04)
Summary statistic					
Level-one respondents (*N*)		2,680	2,975	2,690	2,680
Percent reduction in error		5.3	8.0	3.6	3.2

Source: Metro Civic Values Survey, 1999–2000.

*$p \leq .10$; **$p \leq .05$.

a. Two-level hierarchical linear model; slopes and intercepts estimation. Values are regression coefficients with standard errors shown in parentheses. Results for reliability estimates and random effects do not appear in the table but are available from the authors upon request.

black males. And they were also substantially more opposed to immigration-induced diversity than young black men. One possible explanation for this finding is that African American girls anticipate eventually entering a job market in which immigrant labor will have a strong competitive presence. For black female adolescents who face the double disadvantages of race and gender discrimination, the prospective threat of immigration looms especially large.[31] Among the costs immigration may impose are adjustments to one's job search strategy, lower-paying employment, lower benefit levels, or longer periods of unemployment and welfare recipiency. Our notes from classroom discussion with the students indicated that black anxiety about immigration was especially linked to their feelings about Asians, with whom they have the most contact via Asian-owned neighborhood stores.

The statistical insignificance of several hypothesized explanations is also noteworthy because it suggests that many minority youth, especially Asians and Latinos, are ambivalent about diversity and have mixed views of local police and courts, regardless of whether they live in well integrated or more homogeneous neighborhoods. Based on our fieldwork, we believe the source of this ambivalence lies in the contradictions between the objective conditions students experience and the content of the messages they hear in schools. For example, students notice that the police are slower to respond to some calls for assistance in some neighborhoods but respond much more rapidly in others. However, in their social studies classes, they hear that our nation was founded on principles of equality and justice for all. Much of what adolescents see and experience is that American political institutions operate mainly to serve the affluent. Yet their history and government lessons extol the virtues of American democracy and the ability for everyone to achieve his or her potential. While they often feel that their opinions do not matter, they hear that it is worthwhile to go to the polls and vote. They encounter civics content that is incompatible with their life experience—incoherent lesson plans spliced together haphazardly, with a positive message that is not real to them.

Attitudes toward the Clinton Impeachment

Attitudes about the removal of the president for lying to the grand jury about his affair with Monica Lewinsky were mostly independent of racial context or neighborhood effects. Apparently, there was widespread consensus against the impeachment among African Americans, but we still found a slight tendency for black youth in predominantly black areas to support the president's removal. We are at a loss to explain this except to note that in our class discussions about the impeachment controversy, a number of black youth from inner-city Baltimore schools expressed their

31. Brown (1996); Dodoo and Kasari (1995).

resentment that the president had received special treatment that would never have been accorded average Americans, much less *black* Americans.

Another statistically significant interaction effect for attitudes toward the Clinton impeachment was for Latinos living in heavily immigrant communities: they were more strongly opposed to the impeachment than Latinos living in more ethnically integrated settings. Several explanations for this finding come to mind. First, Latinos living in immigrant neighborhoods may be familiar with widespread corruption in their countries of origin, and this background may jade them to charges of official corruption in the United States. Second, the culture of machismo may be most prevalent in Latino neighborhoods with fresh immigrant roots, leading many Latino males to conclude that the president's sexual indiscretion was nothing especially abnormal or unusual, and can even be expected of men in positions of power. Latina youth, on the other hand, were more likely to support the president's removal. Having noted these effects, we generally found race and ethnicity to be only weakly predictive of impeachment attitudes and not as heavily dependent upon neighborhood context as the other attitudes we measured.

Finally, living in a heavily immigrant community did seem to affect the attitudes of some Asian youth as they considered the impeachment issue. In this community context, youth with foreign-born parents took a dimmer view of the president's conduct than those living in nonimmigrant areas.

Conclusions

Individual race or ethnicity and the racial composition of neighborhoods both matter to most of the socialization outcomes we have been examining. Indirectly, the racial composition of neighborhoods influences political socialization by determining who is doing the communicating and by biasing the local content of opinion.[32] Because racial groups frequently stick together, developing and circulating dominant messages that communicate the group's values and beliefs about politics, the race of individuals and the race of the people among whom they live interact to produce attitudes and dispositions relevant to citizenship activity.

Generally speaking, our research suggests that living within a coethnic enclave is not conducive to a positive socialization experience, except perhaps

---

32. Huckfeldt and Sprague (1995).

for white natives whose segregation from diverse populations does not appear to tax their political efficacy. For Asians, Latinos, and blacks, however, residential integration with whites clearly stands out as an important means for building efficacy levels (see table 3-3), even after we control for the socioeconomic status of the students' households. But for residential integration to stimulate political efficacy among minority and immigrant children, it has to occur at a sufficiently high enough income and education level that immigrants and minorities will be exposed to others whose political efficacy and knowledge levels are high.

Without question, we found that being African American and living in predominantly African American communities was generally not conducive to a positive political socialization experience. This may come as a surprise given that many black youth in the study area lived in middle-class neighborhoods and attended good schools. But in spite of the economic progress African Americans have made in the Washington-Baltimore area, the black youth in our study were not a highly efficacious group, even after we controlled for the socioeconomic status of their families and communities. Black exposure to immigrant populations was associated with especially low levels of political knowledge and internal and external efficacy (see table 3-3).

Not all of our socialization-relevant attitudes were highly neighborhood dependent. Individual-level circumstances and racial characteristics assumed a certain primacy in the prediction of attitudes toward the police and courts since race predicts the probability of a police encounter. Regardless of where they lived, black youth reported high negativity toward the police and local court system, as the intercept term reveals in table 3-4. But black youth in the most heavily black communities were slightly less hostile toward the police than those living in racially mixed communities. African American responses on several socialization measures were also remarkably varied by gender, with black females reporting less hopelessness about the value of political involvement than black males as well as reporting less hostility toward local law enforcement.

On most indicators of civic engagement, Latinos ranked lower than white youth across the board, although they were mostly ahead of African Americans. Latino responses were rather invariant across neighborhoods on measures of political discussion and knowledge. Asians, on the other hand, were only slightly behind whites on the predictors of engagement, particularly when they lived in mostly Caucasian and nonimmigrant neighborhoods. Respondents with foreign-born parents were usually not that far behind the native born unless they lived in heavily immigrant communities, in which case political discussion, knowledge, and internal efficacy were sharply diminished.

To what do we attribute the generally poor political socialization of African Americans and Latinos? Differences in knowledge across racial and ethnic groups are likely to be linked to the lack of politically relevant stimuli in the communities and homes of African Americans, Latinos, and certain Asian subgroups, including the lack of family discussions about government and politics. Second, there can be little question that objective inequalities are seen and understood by the youth living within these communities as the product of an imperfect system in which opportunities for success are not distributed equally. Students we spoke to were well aware that the police responded more quickly to those calling in from suburban areas than from inner-city locations. They also exhibited an awareness of inequalities in other government services, from everyday street repair and garbage pickup to access to health care.

Black, Latino, and immigrant youth in lower income neighborhoods perceive themselves to be ill served by their municipal and state governments, and their perceptions are usually accurate. These plainly evident realities communicate a message of disadvantage and helplessness that is not sufficiently counterbalanced by messages of hope and aspiration within the communities themselves.

More often than not, in these neighborhoods there are no messages suggesting that civic engagement is worthwhile. And any positive socializing messages heard inside school are neither echoed nor reinforced by their daily experience outside school. The community's tradition of nonparticipation is perpetuated through a combination of cynicism and silence on the subject of politics. Perhaps even more damaging are the messages that are communicated within these communities that exacerbate the despair: that the political system is oppressive, deliberately manipulated to hurt certain groups, overwhelmingly biased, and closed to change except through the most extreme of means. For many African American adolescents of Generation Y, the social activism of Martin Luther King Jr. is as distant and irrelevant to their lives as ancient Greece. As far as they are concerned, what can be accomplished through political means has already been accomplished.

We were repeatedly struck by how surprised many of our African American students were that we had even come to visit specific inner-city high schools. One black teen from a Baltimore City school asked and received permission from a member of our research team to touch his (straight) hair, commenting, "I've never touched a white person's hair before." The majority of our inner-city black students had never been asked for their opinions by white people—many assumed that we were visiting their schools because we were athletic recruiters from major universities. This kind of racial segregation inevitably entails political isolation. The extent of these black adolescents' segregation from differing views of politics and lack of exposure to responsive and effective governments surprised those of us who had never experienced it before.

Despite such very unequal conditions across communities, the standard one-size-fits-all social studies curricula remain in place, usually mandated by state governments. There is little recognition that a child's environment shapes his or her psychological history and, therefore, learning experience. Thus we have found that the facts and history of the American political system, if not tailored to local conditions, may inspire some but will leave many completely unimpressed while discouraging others. This is because the standard curriculum is wrong to assume that all children come into a social studies class as blank slates, lacking a social context and personal history that will influence their absorption of and reaction to the material.

Teaching social studies with an aim of stimulating participation is a very different enterprise in African American inner-city classrooms than it is in white suburban classrooms. To complicate things a bit more, communicating this material to black children in African American neighborhoods is a different task than teaching black students living in white neighborhoods. Just how much teachers and schools can be expected to adapt standard curriculum materials to local conditions and individual needs so as to stimulate good citizenship is a question worthy of discussion. There are reasonable limits on what we can expect schools and teachers to accomplish in large classrooms—burdens and expectations are already high. But, in many communities, we can be quite certain that if the schools do not make these efforts, no other purveyor of civic values is waiting in the wings to perform the task.

4

Party Identification, Political Context, and Political Socialization

Public opinion research has consistently found major differences in political socialization outcomes across racial and ethnic groups, suggesting that the political information circulating within ethnically distinct communities varies in both quantity and content. But racial minority status is not the only minority position shaping the attitudes that enable participation and direct public opinion: political minorities also merit investigation, particularly since local settings across the nation present variable distributions of partisan leaning and policy preference.[1] In this chapter, we focus not on racial minorities but political ones to determine whether party identification and partisan context influence a variety of outcomes associated with the political socialization process.

In many big cities, Republicans are a tiny minority, constituting less than 10 percent of registered voters in many neighborhoods. In rural areas and small towns, the reverse is sometimes true, with Democrats being at a severe disadvantage. Party registration is usually more even in suburbs and smaller cities, socializing residents in an environment of intense party competition. According to insights drawn from social psychology, growing up in one kind of location cannot have the same implications for political learning as growing up in another. In one-sided settings, minority views

1. Huckfeldt and Sprague (1995); Beck and others (2002).

wind up being squelched because minorities have few politically compatible neighbors, encounter greater dissonance, and resist discussions of politics.[2] Minorities generally keep quiet, so the theory goes, because people have a sensitive "social skin" that makes them fear isolation and adopt conforming attitudes to avoid it.[3] The supply of political information within a particular jurisdiction, then, is determined by the political orientation of majority groups.[4] By supplying only certain types of information and reinforcement, local populations in one-party-dominant areas remain politically homogeneous for long periods. In politically competitive locales, however, citizens confront a more diverse supply of information, there is far less informational coercion, and political views maintain a corresponding heterogeneity.

To be sure, individuals function within several contexts, each of increasing geographical scope. The most geographically limited context is the family and friendship network, often measured by social network information supplied by group members who are queried about their relationships and communications with other associates within the network. The next would be the local macroenvironment, defined as the community or perhaps the county of residence.[5] Finally, individuals operate within political communities at the state and national level, and some may evaluate their political majority or minority status against these larger communities as well.

We are most concerned with the influence of community-level contexts, but our study areas are part of a larger region that has a sizable Democratic edge in party registration and a long history of electing Democrats to statewide office. In this sense, the external validity of our findings is open to question, and further research within one-sided GOP locales will be required to confirm the generalizability of our results.

In related research, several intriguing studies suggest that heterogeneity in one's local environment may demobilize rather than stimulate greater participation.[6] People with diverse discussion networks mostly avoid political conversations in order to minimize conflict, but over time their expo-

2. Huckfeldt and Sprague (1995, p. 155); Huckfeldt (1986).

3. Noelle-Neumann (1993).

4. Huckfeldt and Sprague (1995, p. 155); Huckfeldt, Plutzer, and Sprague (1993); Huckfeldt and Sprague (1990); Huckfeldt (1986); Berelson, Lazarsfeld, and McPhee (1954).

5. MacKuen and Brown (1987).

6. Paskeviciute and Anderson (2003); Mutz (2002a; 2002b).

sure to diverse viewpoints diminishes the kind of partisan intensity that stimulates participation. In this sense, heterogeneous friendship networks foster political tolerance but strip away much of the participatory impulse. We do not believe that there is a contradiction between these fascinating findings and our own research because political diversity in a neighborhood may not be highly related to the nature of individual friendship networks.[7] The two contexts are not one and the same. A politically heterogeneous macroenvironment stimulates participation because it increases information flow and mobilization efforts by attracting the attention of candidates and parties, not because it necessarily alters the quality of an individual's discussion network. Two individuals with similar discussion networks, one exposed to a diverse partisan context and one living within a homogeneous one, can be expected to participate at different rates.

Even in areas that do not have the benefit of a diverse partisan politics, high voter turnout generated through other means can still provide adolescents with clear and consistent examples of what good citizenship looks like. High turnout is associated with more frequent discussions of politics, suggesting that locations where people vote regularly are a much richer source of political information exchange than places where participation is taken more lightly. Since we do find locations of high participation rooted in civic-minded attitudes and not anchored in ideological heterogeneity and political conflict, we must evaluate them independently of those where partisan diversity is alive and well.[8]

While a respectable body of work now points to the important influence of local political environments on opinion formation, several researchers have expressed doubts about the extent to which social and political contexts matter. Some have argued that the effects of context are small, adding very little to our understanding of public opinion and political choice.[9] Others have suggested that geographic contrasts in political behavior amount to nothing more than differences in population characteristics such as race, class, or occupation.[10] According to these studies, once the political, social, and economic traits of those surveyed are accounted for, neighborhood or "community" effects cannot be demonstrated to exist. In other words, people in the same neighborhood act alike at the voting booth not because they talk to

7. Paskeviciute and Anderson (2003); Huckfeldt, Johnson, and Sprague (forthcoming).
8. Campbell (2002).
9. King (1996).
10. Kelley and McAllister (1985).

each other but because they share a common characteristic, such as high income, that influences their search for a neighborhood.

Prominent theories of opinion formation mostly ignore the role of local context. In his landmark book, *The Nature and Origins of Mass Opinion*, John Zaller suggests that most political information is disseminated through media elites to the masses in either two-sided or one-sided message flows.[11] Zaller's theory suggests that messages flow from elites to masses pretty much unfiltered and unaltered by local political context. An information flow downward (or outward) from national media sources will penetrate all settings to a similar degree, affecting politically aware voters in much the same way. However, the public has sources of information apart from national political elites. People rely upon their friends and neighbors for information and place value on the opinions of spouses, coworkers, and community leaders.[12] While the national political landscape may show two distinct sides, the local context may be very one sided. The bias in local environments is communicated through interactions among individuals as well as through media reports. One important study has shown that local perceptions of media bias in news stories are more influential on political behavior than actual news content.[13]

The way in which a news story is received and processed by a local population will vary directly with politically relevant population characteristics. In a community where there is broad consensus about the value of farm subsidies, for example, debates about government involvement in farming seem distant and irrelevant. Immigration may be an intensely controversial issue in California, but in many towns in the Midwest, it is still possible for natives to live out their lives without meeting *any* immigrants. The vitriolic immigration debate is alien to them, and they do not fully understand why some people feel so intensely about it. This does not make them uninformed about politics and issues; it simply means that their understanding of the issue is conditioned by the intensity of their interest in it—an intensity that is defined locally.

For adolescents and children, even more than for adults, sources of information have their origin in the local community. Depending upon where they live, they may have only the vaguest sense that there are multiple sides

11. Zaller (1992).
12. Mutz (1998; 2002a); Mutz and Mondak (1997).
13. Beck and others (2002).

on issues as controversial as welfare reform, civil rights enforcement, and immigration. Because national news stories are filtered through local agents of information and socialization, we expect the interaction of contextual and individual-level variables to exhibit a dramatic impact on both classes of socialization outcomes: those such as knowledge, efficacy, and political discussion that directly enable political participation, and those that reflect taking sides and opinion formation on policy alternatives.

It is certainly possible that once we control for the party loyalties of individuals in the community, the effects of neighborhood context will be washed away. If the party composition of neighborhoods signals nothing more than the number of survey respondents at each location who identified themselves as Republicans, independents, and Democrats, then we can expect there to be no significant effects of partisan environments on political socialization—at least once an individual's party identification is formed. But what if partisan environments are more than just a collection of individuals that happen to share the same party identity? What if they also affect the way in which these individuals communicate and learn about politics? Then there may be something added by partisan context that transcends individual psychology.

To test our hypotheses, we adopt a couple of strategies consistent with our approach in chapter 3. First, we use structural equations (see appendix D), in which party identification is understood as a function of community-level political variables (such as local partisan bias, political heterogeneity, and turnout levels). In this framework, the political context is thought to have both a direct and an indirect impact on political socialization outcomes, with effects largely, but not entirely, mediated by individual partisanship.

We then use a hierarchical linear model (see appendix D) to capture the interaction of the direct effects of individual partisanship with those of neighborhood political majority and minority status. Generally, we hypothesize that partisans living in environments where their party is a local political minority will be socialized differently than those in which their party is a strong local majority. An individual's partisanship does not have constant, fixed effects, independent of local political climates. While the two parties may be roughly even in their support on the national stage, it is the experience of the local balance of partisanship that matters most to adolescent socialization since that is the distribution of opinion adolescents experience daily.

Partisan Context and Discussion, Knowledge, and Political Efficacy

If one of the fundamental means for learning about politics is through political discussion, then it is clear that our Republican-identifying youth had a narrow advantage over Democrats and independents and a big lead over those who refused to identify with a party at all. According to the results shown in table 4-1, Republicans engaged in 11 percent more discussion than nonidentifiers; independents, about 10.5 percent more; and Democrats, about 9 percent more. If we were to rank our respondents by the extent of their political discussion on a standard grading scale from A through F, partisans and independents would rank about one letter grade higher than nonidentifiers. Party identification and reported frequency of political discussion clearly go hand in hand.

Notably, there were direct effects of neighborhood political composition independent of individual party identification, with discussion dropping about 1 percent with every 10 percentage point increase in local Democratic dominance. Conversely, Republican-dominant areas were typically characterized by greater discussion, probably because the GOP-dominant areas are still politically competitive despite the context of largely one-party, Democratic politics in Maryland. Politically balanced settings place a high premium on information, and the absence of a single dominant view generates expression of a plurality of minority opinions. Related to this effect, we found that high-turnout locales dramatically increased the amount of information conveyed through discussion, moving it up by nearly 8 percent for every 10 percentage point increase in voter turnout. While there is no question, then, that an individual's partisan identity had a direct impact on his or her level of discussion, neighborhood political factors remained undeniably important to this aspect of the socialization process.

Republican identifiers benefited from the extensive amount of political discussion they engaged in with family and friends, but these aspiring voters did not exhibit the highest levels of political knowledge. Knowledge test scores were a bit higher among Democrats, with Republicans ranking second, and independents third. The difference between Republican and Democratic identifiers was only about three points, or less than half a letter grade. Democratic identifiers ranked nearly an entire letter grade ahead of nonparty identifiers (see table 4-1).

Contextual effects on political knowledge acquisition remained strong even after controlling for an individual's partisan identification. In other words, even after a student acquired a specific political orientation, the neighborhood's political composition remained influential. Lopsided Democratic political contexts did not further knowledge-building processes, as a 10-percent increase in Democratic bias yielded an almost one-point drop in the knowledge test score. By far the most influential neighborhood effect was for turnout, where a 10-percent increase in voter participation was associated with a nearly ten-point increase in the knowledge test scores of high school students. This suggests that the best climate for generating political knowledge among adolescents is one where we find highly motivated adults taking an interest in periodic elections. Community participation levels had a powerful impact on internal and external efficacy scores, too, suggesting that adult models of participation reinforce the impression among youth that their voice matters (or will matter) and that government can be expected to respond.

Acquisition of a partisan identity was also associated with high internal efficacy. Self-identified Republican and Democratic youth scored more than seven points higher than nonpartisans in their conviction that their voice counts, with independents close behind (at 6.7 points higher). To facilitate interpretation, we might suppose that our survey was a means of grading students on their level of efficacy, just as we graded them on the knowledge test. An increase of 7.5 percent could be viewed as nearly one letter grade higher, the difference between a 90 and an 82.5. It is clear that the big difference in internal efficacy was not between partisans and independents but between independents and those who reported not knowing their party identification. Calling oneself an independent is not at all similar to having no party identification at all. This finding is consistent with research showing that many independents lean toward one of the two major parties but seem reluctant to admit it.

Finally, the influence of political context on external efficacy was remarkably robust. One-party Democratic jurisdictions seem to generate youthful cynics to an extent that politically diverse and Republican jurisdictions do not. The cash-strapped urban and suburban areas with one-party Democratic governments and low-turnout elections are very effective at producing adolescents who are negative and critical of government performance—and perhaps understandably so given the politicians and governments to which they are exposed.

Table 4-1. *Direct Effects of Political Context and Party Identification on Political Socialization, Controlling for Indirect Effects of Political Context and Direct Effects of Other Community Characteristics*[a]
Units as indicated

Explanatory variable	Frequency of political discussion	β	Level of political knowledge	β	Internal political efficacy	β	External political efficacy	β
Democratic respondent	9.144** (1.012)	.16	8.096** (0.774)	.18	7.535** (0.595)	.22	0.854 (0.582)	.03
Republican respondent	10.983** (1.272)	.15	5.055** (0.973)	.09	7.358** (0.748)	.17	1.356* (0.732)	.03
Independent respondent	10.583** (1.692)	.11	3.399** (1.295)	.04	6.722** (0.995)	.11	-1.369 (0.973)	-.02
Percent Democratic	-0.108** (0.035)	-.06	-0.073** (0.026)	-.05	0.049** (0.020)	.04	0.037* (0.020)	.04
Party diversity	-0.084* (0.044)	-.03	-0.043 (0.034)	-.02	-0.046* (0.026)	-.03	-0.067** (0.026)	-.05
Percent turnout	0.787** (0.078)	.17	0.710** (0.060)	.19	0.195** (0.046)	.07	0.088* (0.045)	.03
Summary statistic								
R^2	.123		.192		.134		.086	
N	2,938		2,919		2,936		2,933	

Explanatory variable	Negativity about courts/police	β	Opposition to diversity	β	Nationalism/chauvinism	β	Support Clinton impeachment	β
Democratic respondent	-1.439* (0.796)	-.03	-0.202 (0.571)	-.01	6.062** (0.708)	.16	-5.673** (0.789)	-.13
Republican respondent	-3.385** (1.001)	-.06	1.829** (0.719)	.05	7.288** (0.890)	.15	12.235** (0.993)	.22
Independent respondent	0.502 (1.330)	.01	-1.054 (0.955)	-.02	-0.671 (1.183)	-.01	0.951 (1.320)	.01
Percent Democratic	0.268** (0.027)	.19	-0.089** (0.019)	-.09	-0.010 (0.024)	-.01	-0.053** (0.027)	-.04
Party diversity	0.081** (0.034)	.04	-0.119** (0.025)	-.09	0.003 (0.031)	.00	0.052 (0.035)	.03
Percent turnout	-0.256** (0.062)	-.07	-0.065 (0.045)	-.03	0.094** (0.055)	.03	0.105* (0.061)	.03
Summary statistic								
R^2	.105		.051		.079		.104	
N	2,951		2,927		2,945		2,945	

Source: Metro Civic Values Survey, 1999–2000.

$*p \leq .10$; $**p \leq .05$.

a. Structural equations estimation. Values are regression coefficients for direct effects only, with standard errors in parentheses. β, standardized regression coefficients. Control variables with parameters for direct effects not shown in this model are percent black, percent Asian, percent Hispanic, population density, median income, and percent with four years college.

If one could choose where one might live in order to produce politically knowledgeable, efficacious children, the best places to move to would be jurisdictions exhibiting high turnout, regardless of whether that turnout was the result of competitive elections or simply high levels of adult engagement. If high-turnout jurisdictions were hard to find, the next best choice would be moving to Republican-leaning locations, including some small towns and certain affluent suburbs, where we found high levels of political discussion and knowledge. It is also better to socialize adolescents around other adolescents who identify with one of the two major parties or at least are independent identifiers. Placing youth among peers who have no clue where to stand politically is not a good recipe for providing an early start toward good citizenship.

The most dubious places to attempt to cultivate good citizens are one-party Democratic cities and suburbs, where we found considerably less political communication and lower knowledge scores. Moreover, big-city neighborhoods frequently report low levels of political activism among adults—clearly undermining the internal and external efficacy of youth. Political activism may have several sources, with heterogeneous local political currents being but one of them. But whatever stimulates adult political interest is almost certain to rub off on adolescents.

Partisan Context and Attitudes toward Law Enforcement, Diversity, and Nationalism

The acquisition of a partisan identity is closely associated with the development of opinions about what government should be and do. The socialization process involves not only the development of efficacious attitudes and knowledge but also the formation of viewpoints participants intend to express through their political activities. Divergent opinions about public policy largely define what it means to be a supporter of one party as opposed to another. Although opinions about issues may cause a person to prefer Democrats to Republicans—and thereby lead to the formation of a party identity—it is more likely that party identification forms during childhood, well ahead of the acquisition of views on most policy debates. We believe that partisan sympathies often come before opinions because there are entirely too many policy debates between the parties for adolescents to form opinions about them before they have acquired a more general sense of party leaning and loyalty. This is the reason why we model attitudes about law enforcement, diversity, and patriotism as a function of political party identification and partisan context rather than the other way around.

Table 4-1 shows that partisan identifiers were considerably less negative about local law enforcement than independents and nonparty identifiers. Republican-identifying youth were the most positive about local law enforcement. Neighborhood influences on trust attitudes were statistically significant: one-party Democratic jurisdictions produced less trusting attitudes, and high-turnout areas generated less skepticism and hostility toward local police than areas with lower voter turnout.

Opposition to diversity was highest among Republican youth, as we predicted, but this difference was a modest 1.8 percent. Democrats and independents were no more opposed or supportive of immigration-induced diversity than nonparty identifiers. Interestingly, neighborhood political characteristics had the most influence on views of diversity: Democrat-dominated areas and areas of close two-party competition showed the most support for diversity whereas Republican-dominated areas were the most hostile. Notably, locations exhibiting higher turnout were marginally more supportive of diversity than less participatory locations.

Why the hostility to diversity on the part of young Republican identifiers? One of the key policy attitudes defining party affiliation since the New Deal era has been that regarding redistribution of wealth and welfare, with Democratic candidates taking more activist and liberal positions, reflecting the views of their lower-income constituency, while Republicans are more restrained about using taxation to level incomes. Civil rights and race relations issues have also divided partisans, with Republicans usually showing reluctance to support affirmative action plans and other business regulations to remedy the effects of past racist and discriminatory practices, while Democrats have regularly championed such measures. Given that blacks and Latinos—who constitute much of this country's diversity—count heavily among society's economically disadvantaged, such redistributive programs and civil rights policies are often linked to them.[14] In addition, the reliance of many new immigrant groups, and their offspring, on these welfare programs has also generated a sharp partisan cleavage between Democrats and Republicans on the value of diversity induced by immigration.[15] Not coincidental to these policy stances, the constituency of the Republican Party is predominantly white, whereas

14. Gilens (1995).
15. Gimpel and Edwards (1999).

overwhelming proportions of Latinos, African Americans, and recent immigrants report Democratic sympathies.

In chapter 2 we found that partisan context measured in terms of party leaning and political heterogeneity had an undeniably strong influence on attitudes toward diversity. Politically diverse environments induced greater tolerance; lopsided Democratic environments were the most tolerant whereas heavily Republican areas were the least. And these neighborhood effects remained significant after controlling for the party identification of individuals. We also observed that adolescents growing up in heavily Republican areas would be more likely than other adolescents to take a skeptical stance toward the value of diversity and immigration (see table 4-2).

As we reviewed our data and field notes written while visiting the schools, we found that youth from two types of places consistently exhibited reservations about immigration and diversity. The first type of place could be described as "white urban fringe." Respondents growing up in these locations were living mostly around Caucasian neighbors and were marginally more Republican than Democratic in their political orientation. Frequently, the adults living in these communities had fled inner-city neighborhoods. Even so, diverse populations were perceived to be close at hand, threatening to invade the suburbs. These adolescents' views of diversity were conditioned by an atmosphere of past and anticipated future racial threat and most closely approximated traditional, or "old-fashioned," prejudice.

The second type of place could be described as "small town white." These students felt no threat from diversity and had obviously not given issues relating to immigration and race much thought. Many of them had never met an Asian person, and their views of Asians, blacks, and Latinos were mainly shaped by television programming. On more than one occasion, they approached the Asian American members of our research team with the cautious curiosity they would have reserved for space aliens. Their opposition to diversity originates mostly from a benign lack of exposure than from an active prejudice stirred up by proximity to sizable minority populations. Their parents are usually as inexperienced with diversity as they are, possibly having encountered minority populations only during military service or in college. In the remote rural settings we visited, issues of diversity had no relevance because racial conflict is not salient. Isolated rural youth grow up suspicious of the value of diversity because they have happily lived their lives without it, not because it threatens their future. Because diversity is an issue that is so seldom on their mind, they have a hard time imagining that life would be better if more immigrants moved in or if the schools were racially integrated. But this passive opposition to diversity rooted in the stable and predictable life of a small town has a very different quality to it than the kind of vocalized hostility exhibited in the suburban schools proximate to minority populations.

As we reflected on our experiences at each school site, we developed the general impression that the more Republican-leaning areas expressed greater nationalism or chauvinism than other places, and our survey results verify that nationalistic views were more likely to be expressed by Republican identifiers than by Democrats. Notably, independent identifiers and nonidentifiers were far less nationalistic than either Republicans or Democrats. Superlative assessments of the system's efficient and fair operation apparently flow from the desire to support its core institutions by becoming a party follower. Identifying with a party is itself a sign of strong support for the system, perhaps akin to the virtue of loyalty.

Just why Democrats and Republicans differ from each other in their expression of nationalistic opinions is also worth exploring. Currently, Republicans are considered more likely to express nationalistic sentiment than Democrats. Republicans are the more politically conservative of the two parties, and ideological conservatism is frequently associated with expressions of nationalistic feeling. In the closing decades of the twentieth century, Republicans fought against civil libertarians to protect and preserve important patriotic and religious symbols, such as the U.S. flag, the Bible, the pledge of allegiance, public display of nativity scenes, and the Ten Commandments, as well as historical religious phrases such as "In God We Trust." Dating to the presidential candidacies of Barry Goldwater and Richard M. Nixon in the late 1960s, Republicans have also been less tolerant than Democrats of left-wing challenges to the existing political order. Based on these considerations, we would predict that Republican youth would be stronger nationalists than Democrats.

Just as we have found that adolescents' racial views are subject to contextual forces that socialize them toward more or less tolerance, we have every expectation that expressions of nationalism are also malleable in this way. Republicans in Republican political contexts are likely to be more nationalistic because they are able to find the most consistent social support for their views. Democrats who live around Republicans would likely express strong support for the system, although perhaps not as strong as the Republican identifiers in these settings.

Apparently, however, nationalism and views of local law enforcement are issues that separate partisans from nonpartisans more than they separate

Republicans from Democrats. This is possible because the partisan attitudes of adolescents are not as ideologically constrained as those of adults.
High schools students are still in the process of learning the policy implications of partisanship. Polarization on issues is likely to be attenuated
when youth are initially exposed to party labels and partisanship and intensify as students begin to learn the policy meanings associated with the
labels. While almost any survey of adult attitudes would find political ideology and party identification to be highly associated, with only a small
number refusing to identify as a partisan or an independent, we found that
26 percent of the youth we surveyed did not express a partisan or independent affiliation. Furthermore, although the association between ideological views and party identification was significant, it was modest (tau-b
= .321).[16] By contrast, the 2000 *American National Election Study*, a com-
prehensive survey of adults, found only 12.8 percent of adults unwilling to
identify as partisans or independents, and the association between party
identification and ideology was noticeably higher (tau-b = .401).[17] We
would anticipate that if the youth from our survey were polled again in five
or ten years, there would be greater ideological constraint among the partisan identifiers.

Partisan Context and Attitudes toward the Clinton Impeachment

Given the intense partisanship of the widely covered debate among political elites about the impeachment, we had every reason to expect that adolescent opinions would cleave along party lines, particularly if they had
been attentive to the news coverage.[18] And that coverage was hard to avoid.
Information about President Clinton's travails, and the political identities
of his persecutors, was everywhere for six long months.

In our survey, we found that support for the impeachment was about
12 percent higher among Republican identifiers than among nonidentifiers
and almost 6 percent lower among Democrats than among nonidentifiers
(see table 4-1). Despite these powerful effects wrought by individual partisanship, the neighborhood effects on attitudes about the impeachment
remained quite robust. Not surprisingly, the most strongly Democratic

16. Tau-b is a measure of association ranging between 0 and 1. Higher values indicate a stronger
relationship between the two variables.

17. Burns and others (2001).

18. Zaller (1992).

neighborhoods produced attitudes hostile to the president's removal. The most politically active, high-turnout locations were the most supportive of impeachment, probably reflecting the higher levels of information circulating in these environments, including that information least favorable to the president's case.

With the power of partisanship's thick lenses, citizens block out and discount information that is hostile to or inconsistent with their partisan commitments, and they greatly magnify that information which is consistent. When moral charges were leveled against President Clinton, it was therefore easy for the most committed Democrats to be sympathetic and to dismiss the charges as part of a vast right-wing conspiracy or as a media feeding frenzy. Conversely, Republicans were quick to support prosecution and conviction—their minds were also made up well in advance. These judgments had very little to do with the substance and nature of the charges or the moral beliefs of the respondents, and the evidence mustered for or against the president was seldom considered by a public preoccupied with day-to-day tasks. Reflections on one's moral philosophy or consideration of the evidence supporting the charges was largely superfluous.

People take many of their cues from political elites, whose positions on issues like these are duly noted from consumption of the nightly news.[19] House and Senate Democrats grudgingly acknowledged that the president was guilty of misjudgment but insisted his offenses were not impeachable. While both sides discussed the articles of impeachment as if the offenses were obstruction of justice and lying to a grand jury, the public mostly understood the offense to be about sexual morality, and many doubted whether these matters were worth an impeachment trial—especially given the president's long track record of such misadventures.[20] During the final two years of his second term, the president's popularity hovered around 60 percent in spite of the fact that a solid majority of Americans believed he had lied and committed adultery. To the extent that the public was divided, the cleavage was so intensely partisan that the legitimacy of the congressional proceedings was severely undermined. The intense partisanship reflected in public attitudes on the subject was consistently reinforced by the contrary sides taken in Congress by the rival party leaders, and from the insistence of the president and his advisers that Kenneth Starr's prosecution was an illegitimate political vendetta. In the end, it was hard to

19. Zaller (1992); Ansolabehere and Iyengar (1995).
20. Andolina and Wilcox (2000).

know what a nonpartisan, truly truth-seeking process would look like, but we certainly did not have one from Bill Clinton's point of view and from the view of those who had voted for him.

Party Identification in Interaction with Partisan Context

The results so far leave a lot of room for the political characteristics of communities to have a direct causal impact on both major aspects of the socialization process: the enablement of participation through discussion, knowledge, and efficacy, and the formation of stable, crystallized opinions on issues. We have learned from the results presented in table 4-1 that neighborhood context effects are not simply reducible to the proportion of Republicans, Democrats, independents, or nonidentifiers in a place. Certainly political environments influence the party leanings of individuals, but they evidently exercise an independent impact on opinions, efficacy, and knowledge by attaching a high value to some types of information while discounting the value of other types. Generally, competitive and highly active political settings place a premium on political information, while noncompetitive and less active settings diminish its value.

Some significant social scientific evidence suggests that private political preferences are constrained by socially supplied opportunity.[21] In view of this, as well as the many theoretical concerns raised earlier in this chapter, we took the additional step of testing for interaction effects to determine whether partisans in congenial political environments develop different socialization-relevant views than those exposed to more alien political environments. Because our localities had differing distributions of party affiliation and opinion, it was quite straightforward to evaluate whether Republican and Democratic youth in environments where they were a large majority came to different conclusions than those in an environment where they were a minority or where the partisan distribution was more balanced. Partisan respondents in an environment dominated by fellow partisans could be expected to express more intensely partisan attitudes than those in a less congruent setting. Conversely, a steady bombardment of dissonance-producing information is predicted to steer adolescent respondents away from party-congruent positions. In short, the effects of partisan context that have been observed in adult populations should appear in high school students as well.

21. Huckfeldt and Sprague (1995, p. 158); Finifter (1974).

Community Effects on Discussion, Knowledge, and Political Efficacy

Table 4-2 presents results from a model where we assess the effects of the respondents' party identification in neighborhood contexts of variable turnout, partisan diversity, and political party bias. The three interactions are designed to gauge the effect of being a Democrat in a heavily Democratic context, a Republican in a Republican context, and an independent in a Republican context.[22] We also control for the effect of family socioeconomic status in this model, to eliminate the possibility that the pronounced effects we observed for neighborhood voter turnout in table 4-1 were simply a function of living in an affluent household.

Briefly, our expectation was that in each case the condition of living in an environment in which the same party was heavily favored would create attitudes opposite to those we would observe among partisans who were distinct political minorities. In other words, if Republicans were generally prone to frequent discussions of politics when they found themselves among like-minded brethren, then Republicans in Democratic environments would be more inclined to avoid such discussions—primarily because they would have fewer compatible discussion partners. At the very least, we expected that partisans who found themselves to be minorities would exhibit ambivalent results for the various socialization outcomes when compared with their fellow partisans who resided in more comfortable political climes.

The results displayed in table 4-2 conform to some of these expectations, especially for Republicans. For example, Republican-identified youth engaged in political discussion more frequently than any other group, but when they lived in politically lopsided communities, they engaged in considerably less discussion than when they resided in more diverse environments. Republicans in politically lopsided contexts also exhibited less political knowledge and a lower level of internal efficacy than GOP youth in the most politically heterogeneous areas we studied.

Because the vast majority of the one-sided neighborhoods in our study area are Democratic, not Republican, we can infer that Republicans living in these heavily Democratic neighborhoods do wind up less efficacious, less interested in discussion, and less knowledgeable as a result of being around hostile partisans. Our results for Republicans are consistent with the idea

---

22. We could have also tested for the effect of being an independent identifier in a Democratic context; the choice here was arbitrary.

Table 4-2. *Influence of Partisanship and Political Context on Discussion, Knowledge, and Efficacy, Controlling for Family Socioeconomic Status*[a]
Units as indicated

Fixed effects	Explanatory variable	Frequency of political discussion	Level of political knowledge	Internal political efficacy	External political efficacy
School means (β_0)	Intercept	5.42 (21.19)	52.42** (19.74)	51.91** (18.08)	25.60 (15.43)
	Percent turnout	0.54** (0.23)	0.35* (0.18)	−0.01 (0.11)	−0.01 (0.13)
	Party competition	−0.24* (0.14)	−0.13 (0.15)	−0.11 (0.12)	0.07 (0.09)
	Percent Democratic	−0.16** (0.07)	−0.16 (0.09)	−0.05 (0.11)	0.12* (0.07)
Democratic identifiers (β_1)	Intercept	12.82 (19.59)	9.17 (14.88)	−21.97* (12.82)	−20.30 (13.32)
	Percent turnout	0.02 (0.20)	−0.05 (0.12)	0.24* (0.13)	0.21 (0.14)
	Party competition	−0.01 (0.21)	0.07 (0.11)	0.13 (0.09)	0.10 (0.07)
	Percent Democratic	−0.09 (0.11)	−0.07 (0.06)	0.02 (0.05)	−0.05 (0.04)
Republican identifiers (β_2)	Intercept	8.80 (28.10)	−53.89 (13.52)	−38.63** (14.15)	−21.12 (14.21)
	Percent turnout	−0.45 (0.41)	0.34* (0.19)	0.34 (0.20)	0.23 (0.19)
	Party competition	0.43** (0.16)	0.47** (0.12)	0.31** (0.11)	0.12 (0.10)
	Percent Republican	−0.12 (0.09)	−0.13* (0.07)	−0.13 (0.09)	−0.09* (0.05)
Independent identifiers (β_3)	Intercept	−65.78 (33.58)	17.54 (29.51)	−28.97** (14.27)	−9.41 (13.32)
	Percent turnout	0.46 (0.34)	−0.05 (0.34)	0.22 (0.13)	0.09 (0.17)
	Party competition	0.71** (0.30)	−0.31 (0.23)	0.37** (0.15)	−0.04 (0.11)
	Percent Republican	−0.47** (0.13)	0.43** (0.16)	−0.30** (0.10)	0.13** (0.06)
Socioeconomic status (β_4)	Intercept	0.25** (0.12)	0.45** (0.08)	0.22** (0.06)	0.06 (0.04)
Summary statistic					
N		2,934	2,919	2,936	2,933
Percent reduction in error		3.4	4.7	4.1	1.2

Source: Metro Civic Values Survey, 1999–2000.

*$p \leq .10$; **$p \leq .05$.

a. Two-level hierarchical linear model; slopes and intercepts estimation. Values are regression coefficients with standard errors shown in parentheses. Results for reliability estimates and random effects do not appear in the table but are available from the authors upon request.

that political minorities are discouraged by their status, avoid discussions of politics, and have less incentive to seek more knowledge. These political minorities wind up thinking and acting very much like outnumbered racial minorities, uncertain of the value of their votes and despairing of the prospect of electing one of their own.[23] Most notably, our results held up when we controlled for an individual's socioeconomic status, indicating that even youth from well-off Republican homes are subject to the effects of their neighborhood minority or majority status.

Our results did not indicate strong neighborhood effects acting on our Democratic youth (see table 4-2). Their participation-enabling attitudes seemed largely independent of contextual political forces, except that Democratic identifiers did show greater internal efficacy in locations with higher voter turnout.

Independents appeared to benefit from living in politically heterogeneous areas in much the same way that Republican youth did. Regularity of political discussion and strength of internal efficacy increased significantly in places where the parties were evenly matched in major elections (see figure 4-1). Republican and independent youth both benefited more from local political party diversity than did Democratic identifiers (figure 4-1). This may be due to the fact that Democrats are a less powerful force in competitive areas than they are in the region more generally. Democrats are discouraged by highly competitive politics because it means they stand to lose, whereas for Republicans and for GOP-leaning independents, it indicates that they are a sizable share of the local electorate and can win at least some elections.

From this set of findings, we underscore that high-turnout neighborhoods remained influential in interaction with party identification, increasing the internal efficacy of Democratic and independent identifiers and elevating the political knowledge of Republicans (see table 4-2). The example of highly participatory adults in one's community produces a highly positive socialization experience. Partisan diversity, independent of high turnout, is also a good thing for the internal efficacy of identifiers of the minority party, and perhaps marginally so for Democrat-identified youth (figure 4-1).

The legitimate question arises as to the extent these results have any external validity. Would we find similar results in areas outside the Mid-Atlantic region, and specifically outside of the Baltimore-Washington

23. Bobo and Gilliam (1990).

Figure 4-1. *Internal Efficacy among Republican and Independent Identifiers versus Democrats in Areas of Partisan Diversity*[a]

Internal efficacy score

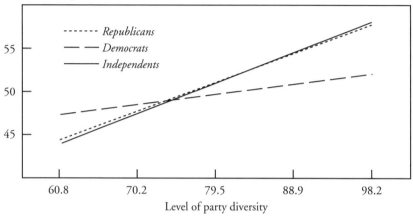

Level of party diversity

Source: Metro Civic Values Survey, 1999–2000.
a. Local party diversity formulated as 100 – [absolute(50 – percent Democratic)].

metropolitan area? Some of these findings are undoubtedly an artifact of the study's setting in a predominantly Democratic state and may not generalize to other places in the nation. We observed that Republican identifiers in this broadly one-party setting were easily discouraged and inefficacious, knowing that they rarely win statewide offices and are lucky to control a few state legislative seats. Party registration in Maryland exhibited a solid 2-to-1 Democratic edge throughout the final decade of the twentieth century and the start of the twenty-first. We suspect that Republican youth are more vulnerable to feelings of political inferiority and inefficacy in Maryland than they would be in more evenly divided states such as Ohio or Pennsylvania.

In the few places where the GOP was competitive locally, we found much less defeatism, and youthful Republicans were more confident that they had a voice. Local competition did not generate the same degree of political interest and efficacy for Democratic identifiers because Democrats are the majority party across most locales and certainly statewide—and for majority parties, fierce competition can only mean the dismal prospect of losing at the polls. Future research would do well to explore the socialization experiences of Democratic youth in majority Republican settings, perhaps in states such as Kansas, Utah, or Idaho, where one might find that politically mixed locales are a boon to the efficacy and knowledge of Democratic youth. One implication of the specific geography of our study is that the kind of strong neighborhood effects that we observe for Republicans might well be true of Democratically inclined youth in states where all prominent officeholders are Republicans and have been so for decades. Clearly, replicating our research in a different part of the country would add to our understanding of the socialization patterns of majority and minority partisans and the influence of overlapping state and local partisan contexts.

Community Effects on Attitudes toward Law Enforcement, Diversity, Nationalism, and the Clinton Impeachment

Our main expectation for the students' responses to the queries about diversity, law enforcement, and nationalism was that we would find greater attitudinal polarization among Republicans and Democrats who lived among identifiers of the same party. In fact, we did find some support for the idea that partisan intensity is lacking in individuals living among rival partisans, at least for some of these divisive issues. For example, Republicans living in Democratic settings were much less opposed to diversity than Republicans living in the most heavily GOP jurisdictions. Independents wound up expressing more hostility toward immigration-induced diversity if they lived in heavily Republican neighborhoods than if they were exposed to more Democrats (table 4-3).

Sometimes an issue will be subject to contextual pressures for some partisans but not for others. For example, opposition to diversity remained largely constant across varying political contexts among Democrat-identified youth. We also discovered that Democratic youth were generally hostile to the Clinton impeachment but were even more hostile if they lived within lopsided Democratic contexts (see table 4-3). Impeachment attitudes were not contingent on partisan context for Republican and independent identifiers.

Partisan environments incongruent with an individual's affiliation will attenuate that individual's political intensity on specific issues that are especially salient but open to the persuasion (or coercion) that accompanies social pressure.[24] Living among a cacophony of opposing voices may not change someone's mind, compelling them to switch parties, but it may create ambivalence and more disregard for one's partisanship than would be

---

24. Huckfeldt and Sprague (1995, chap. 8); Brown (1988).

Table 4-3. *Influence of Partisanship and Political Context on Attitudes toward Law Enforcement, Diversity, Nationalism, and Impeachment, Controlling for Family Socioeconomic Status*[a]

Units as indicated

Fixed effects	Explanatory variable	Negativity about courts/police	Opposition to diversity	Nationalism/ chauvinism	Support Clinton impeachment
School means (β_0)	Intercept	77.77** (27.97)	85.75** (8.39)	68.35** (16.71)	37.65** (11.59)
	Percent turnout	−0.31* (0.18)	−0.30** (0.05)	0.06 (0.13)	−0.33** (0.11)
	Party competition	−0.12 (0.19)	−0.11 (0.08)	0.02 (0.11)	0.32** (0.10)
	Percent Democratic	0.07 (0.15)	−0.10** (0.03)	−0.15** (0.17)	0.04 (0.06)
Democratic identifiers (β_1)	Intercept	−2.88 (19.38)	5.23 (13.08)	−18.45 (14.47)	1.15 (14.99)
	Percent turnout	0.10 (0.18)	0.02 (0.09)	−0.16 (0.12)	0.25 (0.16)
	Party competition	−0.09 (0.12)	−0.07 (0.10)	0.26** (0.09)	−0.20** (0.10)
	Percent Democratic	0.03 (0.09)	−0.03 (0.05)	0.22** (0.05)	−0.11* (0.06)
Republican identifiers (β_2)	Intercept	9.17 (13.35)	−12.43 (10.79)	−39.83** (12.45)	−56.37** (13.57)
	Percent turnout	−0.34* (0.18)	0.19 (0.15)	0.40** (0.16)	0.77** (0.17)
	Party competition	0.15 (0.20)	−0.10 (0.10)	0.29** (0.09)	0.15 (0.18)
	Percent Republican	−0.05 (0.16)	0.25** (0.05)	−0.19** (0.05)	0.05 (0.16)
Independent identifiers (β_3)	Intercept	44.18 (26.24)	15.20 (16.99)	1.17 (24.11)	−35.80 (16.98)
	Percent turnout	−0.73** (0.29)	−0.25** (0.11)	0.07 (0.30)	0.57** (0.25)
	Party competition	0.15 (0.29)	−0.08 (0.18)	−0.08 (0.17)	−0.03 (0.17)
	Percent Republican	−0.18 (0.25)	0.20* (0.11)	−0.04 (0.11)	−0.05 (0.14)
Socioeconomic status (β_4)		−0.23** (0.05)	−0.11* (0.06)	0.19** (0.07)	0.09 (0.07)
Summary statistic					
Level-one respondents (*N*)		2,934	2,919	2,936	2,933
Percent reduction in error		2.1	1.1	2.5	9.3

Source: Metro Civic Values Survey, 1999–2000.

*$p \leq .10$; **$p \leq .05$.

a. Two-level hierarchical linear model; slopes and intercepts estimation. Values are regression coefficients with standard errors shown in parentheses. Results for reliability estimates and random effects do not appear in the table but are available from the authors upon request.

present otherwise—a finding echoed in the work of Thad Brown on migration and partisanship.[25] Even if living among partisan opponents does not result in a conversion to their views, such politically incongruent environments produce opinions that are much harder to predict than those from partisans residing comfortably among their own.

To be sure, opinions on some issues are not always contextually dependent on the nature of local partisanship, although other aspects of the political environment may matter. For example, attitudes about law enforcement and local courts were largely impervious to local partisan composition once we controlled for family socioeconomic status. Perhaps this is because many adolescents remain unaware of political party stands on these issues, or perhaps attitudes about local law enforcement depend more on the context of neighborhood racial composition, and thus this issue is rarely discussed in terms that trigger partisan political awareness.

While evaluating the other interaction terms reported in table 4-3, we found that living in politically diverse environments generated greater nationalism among Democratic youth but less support for the Clinton impeachment. Partisan diversity had an effect akin to ideological conservatism for these adolescents. Interestingly, evenness of local party power also had the effect of making the Republican youth more nationalistic. Notably, independents were completely unaffected by the extent of local party competitiveness—perhaps a reflection of their ambivalent attitudes about government performance.

Locales with high voter turnout clearly had a strong effect on the responses of Republican and independent identifiers for a couple of issues. Highly participatory communities produced noticeably less negativity toward police and courts among these youth, while having only a modest impact on the attitudes of Democratic identifiers (see figure 4-2). High turnout was also associated with greater support for the Clinton impeachment among Republicans and independents but not among Democrats. Apparently, then, a higher level of local activism was a force for conservatism among Republicans and independents but not among Democrats, whose minds were made up regardless of the level of participation in the community. One likely explanation comes readily to mind. The level of turnout may be associated with greater intensity of local partisanship and political ideology in GOP areas and locations where many independents live, but not necessarily in locations where Democrats are

---

25. Brown (1988); Gimpel (1999).

Figure 4-2. *Student Attitudes toward Law Enforcement in Areas of High Voter Turnout*

Negativity toward law enforcement

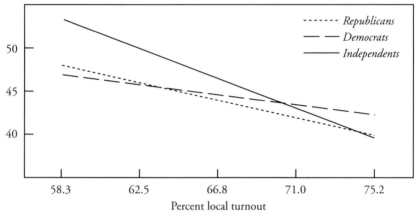

Percent local turnout

Source: Metro Civic Values Survey, 1999–2000.

concentrated. Because the Democratic Party holds a numerical and organizational advantage throughout much of the Mid-Atlantic region, activism is stimulated not by political ideology but by local political organizations aligned with the Democratic Party. These organizations are not likely to have much of a presence in the most heavily Republican or nonaligned locations.

Conclusions

The propensity to adopt a partisan stance has major implications for all of our attitudinal measures. The acquisition of partisan identity is an important step in the process of becoming a responsible, participatory citizen. Identifying with one of the two major parties predicts enhanced political discussion, greater political knowledge, and higher internal efficacy. Partisanship also facilitates the opinion formation process on policy issues, helping adolescents and young adults to understand the sides of an issue and develop consistency of thought across differing policy domains.

Political neighborhood effects remain important to the political socialization of adolescents, well after party identification is taken into account to explain these outcomes. It is not just one's own partisanship that matters to one's socialization-relevant attitudes; the partisanship of others matters, too. The main conclusion we draw from our findings is that civic engagement suffers as one's local political minority status becomes more acute. Being a persistent local political minority is demoralizing for the adherents of the minority party, causing them to turn inward. The accompanying feelings of despair and inferiority understandably undermine the feelings of efficacy that promote participation. Minority status perpetuates itself by discouraging the participation of minor party partisans in the construction of more effective party and campaign efforts.

The best place to raise politically efficacious and knowledgeable children is in an environment of high voter turnout, perhaps where such turnout is stimulated by competitive elections, but at the very least, in those locations where adult populations are most active and engaged. Partisan heterogeneity in the local neighborhood does not appear to be an important force driving adolescent efficacy, at least once we control for individual party identification and turnout levels—which are both strong correlates of political diversity. What this may indicate is that partisan heterogeneity is mostly beneficial to socialization and participation indirectly, through the acquisition of individual partisanship. Partisan diversity also may promote socialization if it occurs at multiple levels of an individual's political context: in local affairs and state government, since state government officeholders are frequently more visible than local ones. We also conclude that it is best to raise one's child around both adolescents and adults who identify with one of the two major parties. Growing up around partisans will greatly assist the inexperienced in matching their emerging self-conceptions to the social groups that are associated with the major parties.[26] Making this match between self-conception and party stance greatly facilitates later participation by simplifying the tasks of candidate evaluation and political judgment.

That individuals are members of overlapping political contexts is also important to our understanding of the results.[27] Citizens functioning under conditions where their policy interests are consistently defeated should feel less efficacious than citizens whose interests dominate.[28] Given that federal

---

26. Green, Palmquist, and Schickler (2002).
27. MacKuen and Brown (1987).
28. Weissberg (1975); Iyengar (1980).

systems permit substantial autonomy among local units of government in the conduct of elections, it is not difficult to imagine that one could be a local political minority while being a member of a statewide or national political majority. But if one is consistently marginalized in the broader political context, such as the state level, one might find a local context to be especially stimulating, even comforting. This is exactly what we found: political minorities were more sensitive to local contexts than the political majority was. Given the general Democratic orientation of the study area, strong local party diversity was especially stimulating to Republican- and independent-identified youth but had little impact on Democrats. What this means is that Democratic youth appear to have rather uniform levels of political knowledge, efficacy, and discussion, regardless of the partisan heterogeneity of the community in which they live. Again, our suggestion is that local contextual forces may play less of a role for Democratic youth since they know that they are a majority in the broader contextual setting of the study area, where the Democratic Party has a history of winning most major statewide offices. Local contexts make a much larger difference for those who are in the minority generally than those who are more safely in the majority, a conclusion that Finifter reached after studying the social interactions of Republican and Democratic workers in a factory dominated by Democrats.[29]

Finally, we found support for the idea that an individual's partisanship is muted on many divisive issues if that person must function in an incongruent or uncongenial environment. The political segregation and partisan balkanization of neighborhoods promotes a polarization of viewpoints that is intolerant of internal dissent among adherents of a particular party. Democratic respondents exhibited unified opposition to the impeachment in areas of heaviest Democratic presence, and Republican respondents were homogeneous and united in their opposition to immigration-induced diversity when they were most safely among their own. Less overwhelming party bias in the environment promotes the taking of positions conducive to ideological convergence and policy consensus.[30] We found little evidence to indicate that individuals could be consistently resocialized, so as to completely switch parties, by living entirely among those of opposite partisan stripe, but heavy social pressures certainly can create ambivalence and

29. Finifter (1974).
30. Mutz (2002b).

doubt about policy views that might be more strongly expressed in a more congenial political setting. We take from this the conclusion that neither extreme minority nor supermajority status for one's party makes for an optimal climate for political socialization. Children can be well socialized when adults are highly engaged, regardless of the level of partisan bias. But when one cannot count on high levels of activism, it helps to live in an area where one party is not overwhelmingly dominant.

5 Religion and Political Socialization

In this chapter our goal is to examine whether religious identification and practice contributes to socialization-relevant attitudes. There are good reasons for thinking that it does. Religious instruction is associated with the formation of social capital, and it communicates moral lessons directly relevant to opinion formation and the development of partisanship.[1] To be sure, families can shape a child's political socialization in ways other than religious indoctrination, such as the direct transmission of party identification and policy views, but these attitudes are also commonly influenced by forces external to the family, through peers, teachers, and other adults.[2] Religious beliefs are not as likely to come from sources outside the family and the particular community of worship selected by the family. In that sense, religious teaching is unique.

Most research shows that parents are the most important factor in shaping the religious commitments of children.[3] In turn, religion matters to public life because it is an important teacher of moral virtues such as self-sacrifice and altruism.[4] The transmission of religious beliefs to one's children can be thought of as instilling a valuable moral resource that con-

1. Leege and Welch (1989); Cohen and Kapsis (1977); Sani (1976).
2. Niemi and Jennings (1991).
3. Hoge, Petrillo, and Smith (1982); Hunsberger and Brown (1984).
4. Elshtain (2001).

tributes to participatory attitudes.[5] While our survey is not designed to capture all of the nuances of various denominational teachings within the major religions, we still believe that our simpler measures of religious affiliation and devotion can capture basic socialization-relevant differences between the religious and nonreligious.

Although the moral and political messages communicated across religious traditions do vary, our initial analysis focuses centrally on contrasts between the religious and those lacking any religious identity. To be sure, it is possible to socialize a child politically without *any* religious belief, and a religious upbringing is no guarantor of good citizenship. Nevertheless, on average, those growing up in homes with religious instruction and practice will be better socialized to contribute to society than those who do not, and a solid body of social science research can be mustered to support this contention.[6] Because religious belief and strong moral views are bound together, we should not be surprised to find that the religious see civic activity as a means for advancing moral causes.[7]

Religious identification and religious devotion do not go hand in glove. It is one thing for someone to identify themselves as Catholic, quite another for them to admit that they are committed, orthodox followers. Of the various ways of defining religious commitment, we have chosen to measure it in terms of regularity of attendance at religious services. Frequent attendance matters because children who regularly attend church are more likely to have parents who are actively socializing them than those who do not.[8] Clearly, there are other plausible measures of religious observance, such as scripture reading, but they are likely to be highly correlated with regularity of attendance at services. Attendance also taps into the most community-based aspect of religious observance and thus is most likely to affect civic engagement, whereas measures of commitment rooted in private practices such as scripture reading and prayer might not.

Our survey was performed in a sufficiently large and diverse area that we have unusually good representation of the adherents of five major religious traditions along with the nonreligious. The major categories are Protestants, Catholics (or Eastern Orthodox), Jews, Muslims, and Buddhists, Hindus, and related Eastern religious traditions. The last set of faiths we

5. Becker and Dhingra (2001); Strate and others (1989, p. 452).

6. Becker and Dhingra (2001); Houghland and Christenson (1983); Peterson (1992); Smidt (1999).

7. McVeigh and Sikkink (2001).

8. Hoge, Petrillo, and Smith (1982).

Table 5-1. *Representation of Major Religious Traditions*
among Youth Participating in the Metro Civic Values Survey
Units as indicated

Group	n	Percent
Protestant	856	36.5
Catholic or Eastern Orthodox	735	31.4
Jewish	186	7.9
Muslim	53	2.3
Buddhist, Hindu, Eastern	82	3.5
Other	40	1.7
No religion	390	16.7
Total valid responses to religion items	2,342	100.0

have grouped together because of a general similarity in worldview when compared to the Western religions. Table 5-1 shows the precise numerical breakdown of respondents into these major groups.

In general, we do not expect the effect of religious identification on socialization-related attitudes to be as highly dependent upon community composition as the racial or ethnic and partisan identities are. The fundamental teachings within a specific religious tradition are supposed to be the same, no matter where one lives or worships. Nevertheless, we are mindful of the fact that religious doctrines are highly complex and detailed. As a result, local clergy typically have considerable leeway within major religious traditions in choosing the moral and spiritual teachings they want to emphasize.[9] The implication of this selectivity in emphasis is that local contexts shape the messages that are communicated to congregants.[10]

Even clergy who find themselves supervised by a hierarchical governing structure, such as the Catholic Church, may vary widely in the messages they communicate.[11] We expect to find variation in the religious component of political socialization to be dependent upon the ethnic composition of Catholic communities. Catholics in predominantly Latino congregations may not only hear mass delivered in Spanish, they may hear a different sermon entirely from the one that is preached in predominantly

9. Johnson (1966, p. 204).
10. Jelen (1992); Wald, Owen, and Hill (1990).
11. Leege and Welch (1989).

white locales. Latino congregations may not understand linkages between religious principles and political views the way native white congregations might. Even when the same sermon is preached to Latino and Anglo congregations, church members in the Latino congregations may not pick up on subtle political cues.[12] In short, we anticipate that the impact of religious teaching on political socialization might be reduced by local ethnic culture, a possibility examined later in the chapter.

The religious homogeneity of a neighborhood may also influence the socializing messages that are communicated and how they are received. Religiously diverse communities may produce greater participation and interest in politics because in these locales values and ideas come into frequent conflict, elevating the total level of political stimulation. Like the one-party neighborhoods we discussed in chapter 4, religiously homogeneous communities may produce a consensual complacency that results in lower levels of political efficacy, knowledge, and discussion among adolescents.

In addition, there may be good reason to suggest that religiously pluralistic communities also generate more moderate or tolerant socializing messages that have less of a sectarian edge. Clergy in such areas may be more careful about communicating controversial or potentially divisive messages given that there is a relatively small pool of potential congregants and it is risky to alienate them. Conversely, clergy in religiously homogeneous areas can afford to be much more pointed in their communications, knowing that the pool of potential congregants is large and that alienating some will not come at a high cost. Furthermore, such religious homogeneity makes it likely that certain political and moral viewpoints are widely shared, giving clergy and laity more assurance that the communication of strongly worded socializing messages will not meet resistance or opposition.

Consistent with previous chapters, we model our socialization outcomes by first using a structural equations approach that treats individual religious adherence partly as a function of a community's religious composition—the selection argument we have made in previous chapters. Simply put, we are more likely to find Catholic youth among our survey respondents when the communities in which the schools are located are themselves heavily Catholic. Modeling in this manner also allows us to evaluate whether the aggregate religious composition of communities matters directly to political socialization outcomes once we control for the individual's profession of faith.

12. Jelen (1992, p. 696).

A significant obstacle in testing for the effects of community religious composition is that figures on religious adherence at the community or neighborhood level are not available.[13] As a substitute, we used the proportions aggregated from our school samples, knowing that these samples were usually large enough to provide an accurate reflection of the local population's religious distribution. Nevertheless, with this measure we do risk underestimating the proportion of the local population reporting as Catholic, since parochial schools do absorb many of these students. We may also overestimate the percentage of local residents who are nonreligious, since students who have no religious affiliation are more likely to wind up in public schools than in private church-operated schools. With those caveats in mind, however, we concluded that the school samples would be a better option than using data on religious identity available only at the county level, and would at least provide the best *available* estimate of community religious context.

Religion and ethnicity are closely associated for some populations.[14] Given that the majority of Latino immigrants are Catholic, for example, we hypothesize that there will be more professing Catholics in heavily Hispanic areas than in locations lacking this ethnic presence. And while many Asian immigrants are Christians—mostly Protestants—we naturally anticipate that we will find more Buddhist and Hindu adherents present in areas of heavy Asian concentration. Inasmuch as most of our Arab and Persian respondents usually identified themselves on the survey as being Asian in origin, we expect that adherents of Islam will also be more abundant in areas of Asian concentration. Beyond these obvious connections between religion and ethnicity, we will probe for the differences between black and white Protestants.

In addition to the multiple equation model, we also use hierarchical linear modeling (HLM; see appendix D) to examine the impact of the interaction between religious observance within the three locally dominant traditions and the concentration of religious adherents in communities. The

13. The Glenmary Research Center based in Cincinnati, Ohio, does collect data on church attendance and membership that it reports by county, but county-level figures were not adequate for our purposes given that many of our schools were situated in the same county but exhibited considerable variation on community-level variables such as race, income, and percent with a college education. For further details about this resource, see Glenmary Research Center (2001) or www.glenmary.org (June 2003).

14. Cohen and Kapsis (1977).

HLM technique permits us to contrast the effect of religious identification on political socialization in areas where one's religious belief is widely shared compared to locations where believers are more isolated among nonbelievers. Just as partisan identifiers may come to hold views that are inconsistent or only weakly consistent with their party preferences when they live among partisans of opposite stripe, the same might be predicted of religious identifiers. Even the most devout adherents of a religion may temper their views when they are not among their own.

Finally, using the hierarchical linear modeling framework, we examine the socializing impact of religious identification in communities with particular ethnic complexions. We believe that the impact of religious teaching on socialization-relevant attitudes will be stronger for Protestants in areas of high African American concentration than for Protestants in white or mixed-race communities.

Religious Identification and Discussion, Knowledge, and Political Efficacy

Even after we controlled for the religious traditions identified by individual respondents, table 5-2 shows that the religious composition of communities had a direct impact on knowledge, discussion, and efficacy levels. Particularly pronounced were the effects of living in a heavily Catholic or Muslim community. Discussion levels dropped in the most heavily Catholic communities, as did internal and external political efficacy. Youth from areas with strong Muslim representation ranked consistently lower in discussion, knowledge, and efficacy than those in other areas. These locations undoubtedly contained large immigrant populations, but we controlled for the foreign-born population of these communities, so it is doubtful that the effect of having a prominent Catholic or Muslim religious presence was simply substituting for the prevalence of a fresh immigrant influx.

Interestingly, we found that students from the communities with large Jewish populations reported having less political discussion but higher levels of knowledge and internal political efficacy. We cannot necessarily conclude that the Jewish adolescents are themselves remaining aloof from political conversation in these settings, since the results also indicated that Jewish-identified individuals ranked about 10 percentage points higher in their frequency of political discussion than nonreligious respondents (see

Table 5-2. *Direct Effects of Religion and Religious Observance on Political Socialization, Controlling for Indirect Effects of Local Context and Direct Effects of Other Community Characteristics*[a]
Units as indicated

Explanatory variable	Frequency of political discussion	β	Level of political knowledge	β	Internal political efficacy	β	External political efficacy	β
Percent Protestant	0.086 (0.054)	.03	0.131** (0.041)	.05	0.000 (0.030)	.00	-0.035 (0.031)	-.02
Percent Catholic	-0.0102** (0.044)	-.04	0.031 (0.034)	.01	-0.050* (0.032)	-.03	-0.156** (0.025)	-.11
Percent Jewish	-0.168** (0.057)	-.05	0.222** (0.044)	.09	0.129** (0.034)	.07	0.030 (0.033)	.02
Percent Buddhist or Hindu	0.248 (0.256)	.02	-0.439** (0.195)	-.04	0.449** (0.151)	.05	0.362** (0.145)	.04
Percent Muslim	-1.357** (0.243)	-.09	-1.584** (0.185)	-.14	-1.048** (0.144)	-.13	-0.199 (0.138)	-.03
Protestant	-0.052 (1.366)	-.00	-1.915* (1.043)	-.04	0.689 (0.811)	.02	1.775** (0.779)	.05
Catholic	0.005 (1.324)	.00	-2.666** (1.011)	-.05	-0.885 (0.785)	-.02	0.430 (0.755)	.01
Jewish	9.981** (2.244)	.09	1.283 (1.718)	.01	3.187** (1.333)	.05	1.712 (1.282)	.03
Buddhist or Hindu	1.991 (3.064)	.01	-2.960 (2.341)	-.02	-0.653 (1.818)	-.01	0.217 (1.747)	.00
Muslim	5.135 (3.819)	.03	-7.305** (2.916)	-.05	-3.070 (2.266)	-.03	-3.091 (2.177)	-.03
Religious observance	0.761** (0.394)	.04	0.380 (0.303)	.03	-0.205 (0.235)	-.01	-0.168 (0.226)	-.02
Summary statistic								
R^2	.169		.258		.102		.085	
N	2,120		2,098		2,119		2,115	

Explanatory variable	Negativity about courts/police	β	Opposition to diversity	β	Nationalism/ chauvinism	β	Support Clinton impeachment	β
Percent Protestant	0.042 (0.042)	.02	0.005 (0.030)	.00	0.053 (0.038)	.03	-0.227** (0.043)	-.09
Percent Catholic	-0.018 (0.035)	-.01	0.086** (0.025)	.06	-0.040 (0.031)	-.02	0.047 (0.036)	.02
Percent Jewish	0.021 (0.045)	.01	-0.218** (0.032)	-.13	-0.001 (0.040)	-.00	-0.132** (0.046)	-.05
Percent Buddhist or Hindu	-1.072** (0.198)	-.09	-0.435** (0.143)	-.05	-0.245 (0.179)	-.02	1.089** (0.205)	.09
Percent Muslim	-0.293 (0.189)	-.03	0.177 (0.135)	.02	-0.188 (0.170)	-.02	0.283 (0.194)	.03
Protestant	-1.573 (1.081)	-.04	2.212** (.762)	.07	5.617** (0.954)	.14	3.423** (1.098)	.07
Catholic	-2.204** (1.032)	-.05	2.238** (0.739)	.07	4.046** (0.926)	.10	0.821 (1.065)	.02
Jewish	-6.741** (1.751)	-.08	4.714** (1.254)	.08	7.379** (1.570)	.10	1.675 (1.808)	.02
Buddhist or Hindu	-5.693** (2.389)	-.05	-2.119 (1.711)	-.02	-2.315 (2.144)	-.02	1.112 (2.465)	.01
Muslim	1.887 (2.980)	.01	-0.121 (2.133)	-.00	0.265 (2.673)	.00	-3.252 (3.072)	-.02
Religious observance	-0.308 (0.309)	-.02	-0.806** (0.221)	-.08	-0.234 (0.277)	-.02	1.136** (0.319)	.08
Summary statistic								
R^2	.113		.116		.081		.097	
N	2,114		2,109		2,123		2,123	

Source: Metro Civic Values Survey, 1999–2000.

$*p \leq .10; **p \leq .05$.

a. Structural equations estimation. Values are regression coefficients for direct effects only, with standard errors shown in parentheses. β, standardized regression coefficients. Control variables with parameters for direct and indirect effects not shown in this model are percent black, percent Asian, percent Hispanic, population density, median income, percent with four years of college, percent Democratic, political party diversity, and percent turnout.

table 5-2). These seemingly contrary results indicate that it was the non-Jewish youth who resided in areas of Jewish concentration who were less likely to discuss politics than their Jewish peers.

Given the basic religious categories we have examined, it is clear that Jewish youth engaged in the most political discussion and expressed the most uniformly efficacious feelings about their voice in government (see table 5-2). Notably, youthful members of the other major religious traditions showed no statistically significant tendency to engage in more discussion than the nonreligious respondents.

Our indicator for religious observance suggests that more devoted followers, regardless of religious tradition, are more inclined to discuss politics than the nonobservant. Specifically, those who attended services every week ranked almost 4 percent higher in their frequency of discussion than those who never attended at all. Observance aside, we found that Protestants, Catholics, and Muslims were significantly less knowledgeable about political matters than the nonreligious, with Jews showing no less political knowledge than the nonreligious. Muslim youth ranked as the least knowledgeable of all, scoring almost a letter grade behind the nonreligious; but in spite of this deficit in their learning, they did not report significantly less internal efficacy than the nonreligious (see table 5-2).

Religious Identification and Attitudes toward Law Enforcement, Diversity, and Nationalism

Because of its moral content, religious identification is a potentially important influence on policy views, including attitudes toward law enforcement, diversity, and nationalism. We were somewhat surprised to find that Jews were the most nationalistic, with Protestants and Catholics trailing in second and third place. The youthful adherents to the non-Western religions were least nationalistic. For Protestants, at least, high levels of nationalism are understandable in light of previous research. There is a close association between allegiance to the "American way of life" and evangelical and fundamentalist Protestant theological doctrines.[15] Even outside of Protestantism, however, it appears that religious identifiers are more nationalistic than the nonreligious, perhaps because the religious are more likely to believe that the government is subject to a higher authority that ordains its existence and provides a moral standard for judging its actions.

15. McClosky and Chong (1985).

For some among the religious, American political institutions are the very expression of Judeo-Christian values. From this point of view, liberal democracy in its American embodiment cannot hope to survive without the disciplining force of religion. Belief in religious practice and the strong support for the design of liberal democratic political institutions are therefore closely associated in American identity.[16]

Religious belief is usually associated with a more general respect for authority. Christians are commonly taught that governing authorities are God-ordained, and the New Testament epistle to the Romans describes policemen as "ministers of God."[17] While religious activism may lead to protest and promote an active distrust of legal authority, as in the case of civil rights or antiabortion protests, we believe that religion's role is mostly compatible with support for and positive evaluations of government institutions, even if the most orthodox may feel that their values are sometimes threatened by state power.[18]

Our findings ran somewhat contrary to these expectations, revealing that only Protestants were significantly more externally efficacious—that is, positive about government's efficient and fair operation—than the nonreligious. Moreover, regular church attendance was expected to increase adolescent respect for local law enforcement, but it did not according to our findings in table 5-2. However, we did discover that Jews, Catholics, and Buddhist-Hindu youth expressed less hostility toward the police and local courts than the nonreligious.

The study of the connection between religion and racial prejudice has been stormy and contentious: some insist that religion gives refuge to racism and ethnocentrism, while others assert that the religious are less prejudiced than the nonreligious.[19] While few religions explicitly teach racial intolerance, the conceptual leap from devout religious adherence to intolerance is not such a large one given that many religions proclaim their moral superiority over other faiths, some espouse proselytizing, and most seek to insulate their adherents from forces that might compromise their convictions.

Other theories suggesting that the religious are more tolerant than the nonreligious focus on the minority status of specific religions within the

16. Citrin, Reingold, and Green (1990).

17. Rom. 13.

18. Rozell and Wilcox (1997); McVeigh and Sikkink (2001).

19. For an example of the former, see Griffin and others (1987). For the latter viewpoint, see Johnson (1977).

broader society. The exceptionally strong Jewish support for politically lib-eral policies has usually been explained this way. Nearly every religion has had a history of minority status and persecution somewhere, but some have more consistently found themselves a persecuted minority than others. American Jewish liberalism on issues of tolerance is the result of religious marginality in a dominant non-Jewish culture.[20] Given that political liber-alism is often a response to the threat of persecution, those religious groups who have had the most extensive history of insecure minority status can be expected to be the most liberal leaning.[21] On this basis, we might also expect the adherents of other religions that are marginal in the area, espe-cially Buddhists, Hindus, and Moslems, to express more tolerant views.

On attitudes toward immigration-induced diversity, we found the most opposition to immigration among Jews, followed by Catholics and Protes-tants. This came as a great surprise to us given the long-standing Jewish reputation for tolerance.[22] Two possibilities come to mind: the younger generation of Jewish youth are not nearly as tolerant of diversity as their parents and grandparents were, or perhaps our result does not generalize outside the geographic area in which the research was conducted. Most of the Jewish students we surveyed were from affluent families living in Mont-gomery County, Maryland (Rockville, Potomac, Silver Spring, and vicin-ity). This population clearly has no reputation for ideological conservatism, though. It is possible that what has traditionally passed for Jewish tolerance is really affluent insularity at work, such that once neighborhood and fam-ily economic status is taken into account, Jews are substantially more hos-tile toward diversity than the nonreligious.

Another intriguing explanation of this result is that the Jewish popula-tion is tolerant of diversity as an abstraction, in principle, but not under concrete conditions where they are faced with it. Our survey questions on diversity accented ethnic pluralism resulting specifically from Latino and Asian immigration, something that is clearly present throughout the Balti-more-Washington metropolitan area. In addition, the Jewish youth were surveyed in schools where there were large Asian populations who might be viewed as possible competitors in the college admissions game. In this con-text, the Jewish responses could be a reflection of intense local anxiety about diversity, even though Jews are highly supportive of immigration

20. Levey (1996, p. 386).
21. Levey (1996); Medding (1977).
22. Ginsberg (1993); Levey (1996).

and diversity as a general rule. Supporting diversity as an abstraction is very different than supporting diversity in practice.

Does orthodoxy make any difference in attitudes toward diversity? Several studies of the influence of religious observance on prejudice have found that ethnocentrism is higher among those of marginal religious belief than among the nonreligious or the most regular churchgoers.[23] Apparently, the marginal believers are not well integrated into those aspects of church life that underscore the values of justice, equality, and compassion, but they do not feel especially comfortable with those outside the church either. They have just enough religion to be suspicious of nonbelievers, but because their involvement is superficial, their views do not express the deeper social and moral teachings of the church.[24] On this basis, we might expect to find less tolerance for diversity among those who nominally affiliate with a religion, but greater tolerance among the most devout.

What the results in table 5-2 show is that regular religious observance was associated with greater tolerance of diversity. Those who attended church services every week ranked about 4 percent higher on the tolerance scale than those who never attended church at all. Viewed in total, the results for diversity confirmed the findings of previous researchers that it is those of nominal-to-middling religious commitment among Protestants, Catholics, and Jews, not the most observant, who are the least accepting of immigration.[25] The relationship between intolerance and religious observance in our survey data is depicted in figure 5-1. This graph shows that the relationship between religious practice and intolerance is shaped like an inverted U: the nonreligious and the very religious are the most likely to welcome diversity while the nominally religious are the least likely to accept it.

Religious Identification and Attitudes toward the Clinton Impeachment

Since religious beliefs inform people's moral judgments, including their attitudes on adultery, sexual promiscuity, and sex before marriage, we should expect to find religion impinging upon impeachment attitudes. But even religious youth in our study often expressed opposition to the impeachment process on the now familiar ground that one's private life and

23. Allport and Ross (1967); Chalfant and Peek (1983).
24. Eisinga, Felling, and Peters (1990).
25. Allport and Ross (1967); Chalfant and Peek (1983).

Figure 5-1. *Opposition to Diversity among the Least and Most Observant*[a]

Level of opposition

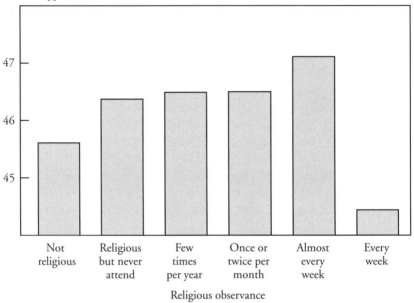

Religious observance

Source: Metro Civic Values Survey, 1999–2000.
a. ANOVA F test = 4.8; $p \leq 0.02$.

official "business" duties are separable. Many insisted that the president could be effective in office even though he had made a wreck of his personal life. Our impressions suggested that these views were more prominent in our most affluent suburban schools than they were in poorer ones. On balance, religion seemed to have a remarkably small role to play in influencing judgments about the impeachment.

Regular observance did matter, however. Regular church attendance is an indicator of religious devotion, and like conservative political ideology, is closely associated with respect for traditional values and conventional behavior.[26] The orthodox believe in a God-directed world and a timeless, absolute morality, whereas secularists contend that morality should be

26. Davis and Robinson (1996); Hunter (1991); Layman (1997); Layman (2001); Wuthnow (1988).

accommodated to the times and circumstances. Mainstream religions, not just Protestantism, look down upon sexual promiscuity before marriage and openly condemn adultery along with killing, stealing, lying, disrespect of elders, and covetousness. Buddhism, Hinduism, and Confucianism all share with Western religious traditions a belief in an afterlife in which there are sanctions for immoral behavior.[27] Our expectation, then, is that those favoring the president's conviction and removal would be among the more orthodox and religious, that is, regular church attendees, rather than among the nonreligious and nonorthodox.

Opinions on the impeachment issue are partly based in religion and moral beliefs, especially among those who are regular worshipers. Regularity of practice was associated with support for the impeachment, as was Protestant religious affiliation. Those who attended religious services every week were about 6 percent more supportive of impeachment than those who never attended services at all. The most obvious explanation for this result is that religious orthodoxy, across all faiths represented here, is a powerful indicator of moral conservatism. Unless they were observant, then, Catholics, Jews, and those professing adherence to non-Western religious faiths were no different than the nonreligious in their views of the impeachment.

Racial and Ethnic Distinctions within Protestant and Catholic Traditions

We have already observed in chapter 3 that race and ethnicity are important influences on both the participation-enabling aspects of political socialization as well as the position-taking aspects that reflect what has been learned about the political world. There is an impressive literature on black churches as agents of socialization, emphasizing that African American Protestant churches typically go above and beyond white Protestant churches in educating congregants about politics and activating them to participate in the electoral process.[28] Previous research also suggests that we should find differences between Latino and white Catholics, although these may be less attributable to the congregations they attend and more to language characteristics and immigrant status or to nonreligious aspects of what is often labeled "culture."

27. Shapiro (1976).
28. Allen, Dawson, and Brown (1989); Harris (1994); Reese and Brown (1995).

Table 5-3. *Difference in Means Tests for Political Socialization Outcomes by Religion and Racial or Ethnic Group*[a]
Units as indicated

Dependent variable	Latino (N)	White non-Hispanic (N)	Mean difference	t test	Significance[b]
Catholic respondents					
Political discussion	126	398	–.020	–0.105	.916
Political knowledge	126	387	–.140	–6.093	.001
Internal efficacy	124	397	–.065	–0.695	.488
Nationalism/chauvinism	124	397	–.385	–4.305	.001
Opposition to diversity	124	393	–.752	–7.726	.001
Negativity about police and courts	124	397	.235	2.368	.019

Dependent variable	Black (N)	White non-Hispanic (N)	Mean difference	t test	Significance
Protestant respondents					
Political discussion	271	402	–.640	–4.452	.001
Political knowledge	271	395	–.129	–8.158	.001
Internal efficacy	267	402	–.340	–4.384	.001
Nationalism/chauvinism	269	403	–.296	–3.956	.001
Opposition to diversity	268	401	–.015	–0.209	.835
Negativity about police and courts	270	404	.619	8.388	.001

Source: Metro Civic Values Survey, 1999–2000.

a. Negative signs indicate that white Catholic or white Protestant adolescents rank higher on the dependent variable than Latino Catholic or black Protestant adolescents, respectively.

b. Significance tests are two-tailed.

There were differences between Latino and white Catholic adolescents for several of our socialization outcomes, including political knowledge, attitudes toward diversity, attitudes toward the criminal justice system, and nationalistic sentiment (see table 5-3). Latino and white Catholics were similar in their level of internal efficacy and in the amount of political discussion they reported. The differences between the two groups of Catholic youth could be traceable to a variety of factors and may be rooted in religious devotion to church teachings. But a more likely explanation is that they are based on immigration-related traits, language, and nonreligious aspects of family life and ethnic history.

We also found gaping differences between black and white Protestants on nearly all of our socialization measures, suggesting that a common Protestant religious tradition does nothing to eradicate the previously noted racial differences in political discussion, knowledge, internal efficacy, nationalism, or attitudes toward police and courts (see table 5-3). The one similarity we did find common to both African American and white Protestants was an opposition to immigration-induced diversity, although that may not be attributable solely to their religious beliefs.

If devotion or church attendance could account for differences in the socialization experiences of youth within the same broad religious tradition but differing in racial or ethnic background, we would expect frequency of church attendance to vary across racial or ethnic subgroups. Our next step was to examine differences in church attendance between Latino and white Catholics and between black and white Protestants. Is it possible that the persistent ethnic and racial gaps we found in many of our socialization outcomes were the result of racial and ethnic differences in church attendance? The answer is no. We found no statistically significant differences between Latino and white Catholic youth in frequency of church attendance. We found small differences in religious devotion among black and white Protestant youth, with African American youth attending slightly more often than whites, but the differences were not great enough for us to conclude that racially distinct socialization outcomes are traceable to frequency of attendance at Sunday morning services. We conclude from these evaluations that race and religious observance operate rather independently of each other in the process of socialization. Perhaps if we had more detailed information about the doctrine and teachings of the myriad Protestant denominations, we could account for the distinctive socialization experiences of black and white youth in purely religious terms, but we do not have that information available to us presently.

Religion, Community, and Political Discussion, Knowledge, and Efficacy

Are the effects of religious tradition on political socialization contextually dependent on neighborhood characteristics—and if so, how? In tables 5-4 and 5-5, we evaluate the interaction of religious tradition with the racial-ethnic and religious composition of communities, using the same statistical approaches described in chapters 3 and 4. We have also taken the additional step of controlling for the individual race and ethnicity of the respondents, as well as family socioeconomic status and religious observance. We want to ensure that any contextual effects pointing to community ethnic or religious concentration are not simply signaling the socioeconomic status or race of the respondents. We have eliminated the Buddhist and Muslim identifiers from these hypotheses tests because these groups are mostly clustered in only two or three communities, making it difficult to test for contextual effects using the HLM procedure (see appendix D).

In many respects, our results mirror those in table 5-2. Jewish youth, on average, exhibited the highest levels of political discussion and internal political efficacy. Protestant identifiers showed lower levels of political discussion but reasonably high knowledge levels. But our main point here was to determine whether some of these relationships were altered by racial and religious context. For example, we found that both Jews and Catholics engaged in less political discussion and showed lower internal efficacy levels when they resided among their own than when they were found in religiously diverse communities. Similarly, Protestant youth exhibited lower knowledge levels when they were in locations where Protestants predominated. Religiously homogeneous contexts, then, are less participation enabling than religiously pluralistic contexts, a finding that parallels our results in the previous chapter regarding partisan diversity (see table 5-4).

Once we controlled for the race and ethnicity of the individual respondents, racial and ethnic context made no dramatic difference in the relationships between religious identification and discussion, knowledge, and efficacy levels. To be sure, black youth generally ranked lower on all of these measures than whites, Latinos, or Asians, but we saw no tendency for Protestant identifiers in African American settings to exhibit higher or lower knowledge or efficacy scores. One might suspect that Catholic youth learn less about politics if they live in predominantly Latino communities, but we found that the relationship between Catholic identity and knowledge was unaltered by the percentage of Hispanics in an area.

The main conclusion we draw is that the role of religion in promoting participatory attitudes among young people is more contingent upon context than we expected it to be. However, the context that matters is religious context, not racial or ethnic context. To be sure, race and ethnicity matters, but church congregations are so highly segregated by race that it is not the race or ethnic composition of the community that matters nearly so much as the race and ethnicity of the individual adherents.

Table 5-4. *Influence of Racial or Ethnic Context and Local Religious Concentration on Discussion, Knowledge, and Efficacy, Controlling for Family Socioeconomic Status and Individual Race or Ethnicity*[a]
Units as indicated

Fixed effects	Explanatory variable	Frequency of political discussion	Level of political knowledge	Internal political efficacy	External political efficacy
School means (β_0)	Intercept	21.79** (2.21)	65.48** (1.82)	47.44** (0.81)	41.81** (0.64)
	Percent black	–0.08 (0.06)	–0.06* (0.03)	–0.04** (0.01)	–0.04** (0.02)
	Percent Hispanic	0.07 (0.11)	–0.07 (0.12)	0.08 (0.07)	–0.08 (0.06)
Jewish respondent (β_1)	Intercept	6.72** (2.49)	1.04 (2.72)	5.60** (1.62)	2.09 (1.87)
	Percent Jewish	–0.41** (0.09)	–0.06 (0.11)	–0.25** (0.08)	–0.02 (0.07)
Protestant respondent (β_2)	Intercept	–4.76** (1.55)	2.79* (1.46)	2.23 (1.79)	0.90 (1.38)
	Percent Protestant	0.04 (0.03)	–0.10** (0.05)	–0.03 (0.06)	–0.03 (0.05)
	Percent black	0.07 (0.05)	0.02 (0.02)	–0.02 (0.01)	0.02 (0.02)
Catholic respondent (β_3)	Intercept	–0.61 (2.14)	0.33 (1.79)	2.10 (1.31)	2.21** (0.88)
	Percent Catholic	–0.12* (0.08)	–0.02 (0.05)	–0.10** (0.06)	–0.12** (0.04)
	Percent Hispanic	–0.12 (0.08)	–0.06 (0.05)	–0.05 (0.05)	0.07 (0.04)
Regular attendance (β_4)	Intercept	0.65** (0.31)	–0.02 (0.27)	–0.12 (0.20)	–0.14 (0.26)
Black respondent (β_5)	Intercept	–4.06** (1.19)	–6.72** (1.25)	–2.70** (0.63)	–1.80** (0.67)
Asian respondent (β_6)	Intercept	–1.98 (2.14)	–2.44* (1.43)	–0.97 (1.12)	2.20* (1.14)
Hispanic respondent (β_7)	Intercept	–1.74 (2.27)	–4.77** (1.79)	–2.43 (1.53)	0.12 (0.81)
Socioeconomic status (β_8)	Intercept	0.23** (0.07)	0.35** (0.06)	0.16** (0.04)	0.04 (0.02)
Summary statistic					
Level-one respondents (*N*)		2,120	2,098	2,119	2,115
Percent reduction in error		3.2	5.1	3.2	2.1

Source: Metro Civic Values Survey, 1999–2000.
*$p \leq .10$; **$p \leq .05$.

a. Two-level hierarchical linear model; slopes and intercepts estimation. Values are regression coefficients with standard errors shown in parentheses. Results for reliability estimates and random effects do not appear in the table but are available from the authors upon request.

But our most noteworthy finding is that religiously pluralistic environments produce greater discussion, knowledge, and efficacy levels, which presumably predict an increase in the likelihood of participation. Religiously one-sided environs are bad for political socialization in the same way that politically one-sided areas are: too much agreement or consensus strips people of the important participatory impulse that is rooted in value conflict and the competition of ideas. To the extent that religious pluralism strengthens religious and political commitments, it also promotes political learning, discussion, and efficacy.

Religion, Community, and Political Attitudes

Not all political attitudes are contextually conditioned by the prevailing religious climate. Jewish adherents were less negative toward the police than other religious identifiers, but this relationship between Judaism and views of law enforcement was not altered by context. In general, religion's role in generating attitudes toward the police and courts was not strongly dependent upon the religious context of communities (see table 5-5).

Neighborhood contexts did influence the relationship between religious identification and nationalistic sentiment, as well as attitudes toward the impeachment. Two aspects of context altered the relationship between individual religious identity and these socialization-relevant attitudes. First, the diversity of Protestant churches and their congregation-specific political views was reflected in the fact that Protestant youth from African American areas expressed considerably more opposition to the impeachment and far less nationalism than Protestant youth living in white neighborhoods.

The same was true for Catholic youth in the most Hispanic areas, where adolescents were less nationalistic than they were when living elsewhere. On controversial issues, such as the impeachment of the president, youth may be exposed to church teaching that is consistent with the experiences and political values of their local communities, not counter to them. If so, then religious training simply amplifies the effect of prevailing local viewpoints that contribute to the socialization experience and does little or nothing to alter these values or redirect them.

Most observers of the American religious scene would be quick to point out that the myriad Protestant denominations present in African American communities are of a rather different mix than those in all-white communities. Aren't we comparing apples to oranges? But the question remains:

Table 5-5. *Influence of Racial or Ethnic Context and Local Religious Concentration on Attitudes toward Law Enforcement, Diversity, Nationalism, and Impeachment, Controlling for Family Socioeconomic Status and Individual Race or Ethnicity*[a]

Units as indicated

Fixed effects	Explanatory variable	Negativity about courts/police	Opposition to diversity	Nationalism/ chauvinism	Support Clinton impeachment
School means (β_0)	Intercept	42.55** (1.84)	48.46** (1.39)	71.94** (1.93)	48.94** (1.26)
	Percent black	0.16** (0.04)	0.08** (0.01)	−0.06* (0.03)	−0.06** (0.03)
	Percent Hispanic	0.10 (0.09)	−0.02 (0.05)	−0.20** (0.06)	−0.21** (0.05)
Jewish respondent (β_1)	Intercept	−5.38** (2.37)	1.74 (1.08)	6.19** (2.15)	−0.91 (1.69)
	Percent Jewish	0.13 (0.10)	0.09* (0.05)	−0.04 (0.08)	0.03 (0.10)
Protestant respondent (β_2)	Intercept	0.04 (1.91)	1.32 (1.05)	2.23 (1.53)	5.98** (1.28)
	Percent Protestant	0.01 (0.05)	−0.02 (0.01)	0.05 (0.05)	−0.05 (0.04)
	Percent black	−0.03* (0.02)	0.03 (0.05)	−0.03** (0.01)	−0.08** (0.02)
Catholic respondent (β_3)	Intercept	0.56 (2.18)	1.26 (1.02)	1.67** (0.70)	−1.21 (1.32)
	Percent Catholic	−0.03 (0.08)	0.06 (0.06)	0.09** (0.04)	0.04 (0.06)
	Percent Hispanic	0.14 (0.09)	0.03 (0.04)	−0.11** (0.04)	0.05 (0.05)
Regular attendance (β_4)	Intercept	−0.37 (0.32)	−0.34* (0.18)	0.11 (0.28)	1.38** (0.34)
Black respondent (β_5)	Intercept	6.48** (1.84)	−1.78 (1.17)	−1.14 (0.75)	−8.74** (1.59)
Asian respondent (β_6)	Intercept	0.64 (1.19)	−7.57** (1.41)	−1.89* (1.04	−1.39 (0.99)
Hispanic respondent (β_7)	Intercept	0.07 (1.71)	−14.82** (3.48)	−0.80 (1.10)	−5.64** (2.09)
Socioeconomic status (β_8)	Intercept	−0.12** (0.04)	−0.11** (0.04)	0.09* (0.05)	−0.04 (0.04)
Summary statistic					
Level-one respondents (*N*)		2,115	2,111	2,117	2,110
Percent reduction in error		3.1	5.4	2.0	4.9

Source: Metro Civic Values Survey, 1999–2000.

*$p \leq .10$; **$p \leq .05$.

a. Two-level hierarchical linear model; slopes and intercepts estimation. Values are regression coefficients with standard errors shown in parentheses. Results for reliability estimates and random effects do not appear in the table but are available from the authors upon request.

why do certain denominations and religious teachings take root in the black community (apples) while rather different ones crop up in white communities (oranges)? The reasons go directly to the politics and value orientation of local communities. Churches and church leaders depend upon local populations for their financial well being. If they do not cater to the preexisting values and dispositions of those communities, they risk going under. Protestant identifiers in black and white areas take rather different positions on the impeachment not just because they are attending different churches but also because the politics and policy views of these highly segregated communities guide church teaching and doctrine.

Conclusions

Without question, our results indicated that Judaism carried with it substantial political capital and promoted uniformly better citizenship among its adherents than any of the other major religious traditions. And even when the Jewish respondents did not, themselves, show superior scores on indicators of future civic engagement, these scores were often higher in areas of high Jewish concentration—suggesting that Jewish youth are advantaged by having families who settle in neighborhoods that exhibit high efficacy and an activist orientation, even if their small numbers contribute rather little to that overall atmosphere.

The extent of religious observance, our measure of religious commitment, divided our respondents more than their separate religious identities. Tables 5-2 and 5-5 demonstrate that the very devout were more likely to welcome immigration-induced diversity and support the Clinton impeachment process than those who identified themselves as nominally religious. A salient political cleavage, even as early as adolescence, emerges between orthodox and nonorthodox, less so between Jews and Christians or Protestants and Catholics.

Notably, we found that religion's influence on shaping efficacy, knowledge, and discussion depended more upon the religious heterogeneity of the local population than its ethnic composition. Jewish- and Catholic-identified youth were more efficacious when they were living in settings of religious pluralism than when they were in religiously monolithic areas. Perhaps the greater moral consensus present in locations where populations share a common religious background lessens the role of value conflict in stimulating interest in politics and ultimately driving voters to the polls. Religious diversity is likely to be a precursor to political disagreement, and it also appears to contribute to political participation in much the same way that partisan heterogeneity does (see chapter 4).

Generally, we found an inverted U-shaped relationship between acceptance of diversity and religious observance (see figure 5-1). The most devout and those with no religious identity at all were the most tolerant of immigration-related diversity, while the nominally and sporadically religious were the most hostile to diversity. Interestingly, we did not find that Jewish youth were the most tolerant of immigration, as we expected given their long history of persecution as a religious and ethnic minority. Furthermore, this opposition to diversity was modestly higher among those living amidst other Jews. In spite of their ethnocentrism, however, these respondents were not highly nationalistic when found living in neighborhoods with consequential Jewish populations. Jewish youth from such areas expressed an intriguing mix of ethnocentrism and internationalism, perhaps a reflection of the troubled politics of the interminable Israeli-Palestinian conflict.

In evaluating differences between African American and white Protestants, we found big differences for most of our socialization-related attitudes, suggesting that a common religious identity, such as being Protestant, does nothing to reconcile ethnic or racial differences across individuals, congregations, and denominations. White Baptists will be socialized very differently from black Baptists. Undoubtedly, this comes as no surprise to seasoned religious researchers accustomed to the nuances and subtleties of the innumerable Protestant denominations. Our observation from our less intricate comparisons is simple and yet still profound: religious observance is not a force for homogenizing otherwise disparate populations. Political differences between racial groups do not completely disappear simply because the two groups adhere to a common religious tradition. Rather, the segregation of congregations by racial and cultural heritage exacerbates political differences that sustain entirely different adolescent socialization experiences. Hence political distinctions between Caucasian and Latino Catholics are also not wiped away by a common Catholic identity but instead are reinforced by their insular communities of worship.

Religion acts more as a reinforcer of community values than as a transformer of them. Follow-up discussions with many of our youth indicated that they rarely heard controversial policy issues raised from the pulpit, although they did hear exhortations to participate. Even those clergy who do use the pulpit for political purposes rarely urge their congregations to take positions that are inconsistent with those already widely held within the local community.

Regularity of religious observance appears to be important in shaping attitudes about immigration-induced diversity and the Clinton impeachment, although those inclined to attend church regularly may already be inclined to take conservative positions on such issues. Still, regular religious observance might stimulate youth to take even stronger positions on these matters—crystallizing attitudes and contributing to ideological polarization.

How does religious identity stack up as a politically socializing force when compared to race, partisan identification, and socioeconomic status? Based on our research, religion would take a back seat to race and partisanship, although it could rank higher for certain subgroups of the population, such as African American youth. Across the entire youthful population, however, religion was not as consistently important to the formation of socialization-relevant attitudes as were party identification and race or ethnicity.

A more detailed study of the impact of religion on the socialization process would evaluate religious devotion and orthodoxy with more detailed questions about doctrine and beliefs within these dominant religious traditions. Such a study was beyond what we could accomplish within the scope of this project, given its multiple aims. What we can say is that politics, race, and the variability of religious devotion undoubtedly pose a serious threat to cohesion within any major religious tradition. Because there is usually much more to a person's life than their religious commitment, we find that racial group memberships and various community characteristics steer adherents of the very same religion toward radically different viewpoints. The splintering of Protestantism into a myriad of irreconcilable sects and traditions has been but one result. Just as King Henry VIII created his own church in the interest of a convenient divorce and remarriage, many other splits within the major Western and non-Western religious traditions have been stimulated by political and economic interest, and later whitewashed with doctrinal hairsplitting. This bowing of religious devotion to secular forces has produced religious traditions that are much less dominant in the lives of believers than they would be otherwise. Religious tradition as it is manifested in the daily lives of individual adherents winds up being more shaped by local congregations of believers than it acts independently to shape them.

6

Schools, Civic Education, and Political Socialization

W hy do some schools produce better citizens than others across a broad socioeconomic distribution of students? Schools are one of the critical links between education and citizenship.[1] They are supposed to prepare students for life in the "real" world, including the political aspects of the world that concern us in this book. In previous chapters, we examined the effects of growing up in communities with specific racial, political, and religious characteristics. This chapter focuses on how civics instruction—specifically, exposure to social studies coursework about government and politics and students' appreciation of these courses—influences the socialization-relevant attitudes examined throughout this study.

Because all schools are organized hierarchically, with clear governing structures, rules, and enforcers of those rules, there are ample reasons for believing that a child's first encounter with authority outside the family is in school. From their earliest years in elementary school, students see who wields power and whose judgments count most. Moreover, the concept of "attitude toward authority" possesses generality, such that evaluations of a variety of institutional authorities—teachers, police, judges—are positively associated.[2] Adolescent evaluations of the fairness and justice of school

---

1. Niemi and Junn (1998, p. 3).
2. Rigby (1988a; 1988b).

authorities generalize to other power figures, influencing the extent to which young adults exhibit "diffuse support" for the political system.[3]

Because students' evaluations of school authority relate to how they regard political authority, it is worth our effort to understand their attitudes about the fairness of their schools and teachers. We examine, for example, whether students believe they are evaluated fairly by school authorities, specifically with respect to the way in which grades are assigned.[4]

At the outset, we should point out that we are not focused on traditional "school variables," such as school demographic composition, per pupil expenditures, or teacher salaries. Because we look at public, neighborhood schools, the school's composition and resources closely mirror the community's composition and resources. Wealthy locales finance their schools well—there is nothing surprising about that. Rather, what we are concerned about is how our political socialization outcomes are conditioned by the students' assessments of school fairness and their experiences with the social studies curriculum. Later, we take up the issue of whether those who dislike studying government and have unhappy school experiences might still be efficacious participants if they live in stimulating, politically competitive environments where alternative socializing influences are in generous supply.

One significant aspect of a school's climate that we measured was the perception by students that they are evaluated fairly when assigned grades for academic performance. Although a school's climate comprises more than the perceived fairness of its authorities, a survey question touching this topic permits a direct examination in this chapter.[5] To a great extent, teachers can influence how congruent efforts and rewards are—for example, by cracking down on cheating and by applying standards of evaluation impersonally and rigorously.

A student's perception of fairness within a school influences his or her perception of fairness within the larger world.[6] In conducting related research, one scholar found that a "single experience with extreme police brutality, for example, may have more consequence for support of the sys-

3. Easton and Dennis (1969); Weissberg (1972a, 1972b); Rodgers and Taylor (1971).
4. Schumann and others (1985).
5. We asked only one "climate" question because the research had multiple aims and we wanted to keep the survey to a manageable length.
6. Easton and Dennis (1969); Weissberg (1972a).

tem than broader, more important decisions made in Washington."[7] Similarly, if a student feels fairly treated by school authorities, then that individual is more likely to trust other authorities and, most important for our argument, feel less alienated from governing authorities in general.

To isolate the effects of curriculum on socialization outcomes, we introduced a control for the frequency of television news viewing as a source of political information outside the classroom. We also controlled for a child's educational aspirations by asking about their plans and goals after high school graduation. Intention to go to a (four-year) college is a measure of a student's general abilities, as well as an indicator of that child's incentive to retain what has been learned.[8] Many students who plan to go directly to work after high school will conclude that learning in school is a waste of time. Adolescents intending to go to college, however, need good grades and more intense academic preparation in order to achieve their goals. Including college aspirations is also an important means for separating out a general motivation to achieve from a student's specific interest in social studies courses.

In evaluating these hypotheses, we apply methods consistent with what we have used previously. First, we take a structural equations approach, in which socialization outcomes are understood as a function of community-level political variables as well as an individual's exposure to civics coursework, appreciation of his or her social studies courses, and judgment about the fairness of school authorities. We control for post–high school aspirations and media exposure. In this framework, the social and political context is thought to have both a direct and an indirect impact on socialization-related attitudes, with effects largely, but not entirely, mediated through exposure to civics coursework and assessments of school authorities. Later in the chapter, a second set of hypothesis tests evaluates the direct effects of local context and civics coursework, combined with interactions capturing the effect of competitive political environments, on those who dislike civics and those who have no plans for formal education past high school. One of our themes throughout this book is that the experience of formal schooling, while important, is not everything. Adolescents living in environments where there are vigorous political stimuli may become good citizens in spite of the fact that they may dislike civics coursework, have no plans for higher

7. Weissberg (1972a, p. 806).
8. Niemi and Junn (1998).

education, and may express doubts about the justice and fairness of the school system.

School Environments and Discussion, Knowledge, and Efficacy

In the examination of school effects on socialization outcomes, other researchers have mostly focused on the role of civics courses in the production of political knowledge. This seems entirely logical, as knowledge about the government would seem to come from formal instruction in this subject, much like knowledge about the three "Rs" comes from classes in "reading, 'riting, and 'rithmetic." Yet, in spite of the reasonableness of the connection, early research on the impact of civics coursework on political knowledge showed that classroom instruction was largely irrelevant.[9] Family background and "intelligence" or cognitive ability had more of an impact on later civic engagement than anything taught in high school.[10]

More recent literature, however, contradicts this view and shows that civics courses have a significant positive impact on political knowledge, particularly among certain subgroups of the population. Niemi and Junn looked at various indicators of political knowledge and found that with more exposure to government-related courses, students' political knowledge increased.[11] Knowledge gains from civics coursework were especially impressive among disadvantaged minorities, who apparently entered these classes with fewer resources outside school from which they could learn civic values. Additional civics coursework made less of a difference for those who were already from politically active communities and families. Such students are likely to emerge into adulthood as participants in the political system independent of their high school curriculum. Regardless, there are those for whom classroom instruction will be their only introduction to the political world.

Government-related course requirements have disappeared from many school systems in recent years. However, all schools continue to require, or at least offer, other social studies courses that have content bearing on citizenship education. Because students have limited choices in high school, though, some are likely to be forced to study subject matter for which they

---

9. Beck (1977); Corbett (1991); Dawson, Prewitt, and Dawson (1977); Langton and Jennings (1968); Morrison and McIntyre (1971); Torney, Oppenheim, and Farnen (1975).

10. Coleman (1966); Luskin (1990); Jencks (1972).

11. Niemi and Junn (1998); see also Westholm, Lindquist, and Niemi (1990); Denver and Hands (1990); Nie and Hillygus (2001).

have developed no prior appreciation. Moreover, their liking for government-related courses may not increase with exposure. While we expect that students with more social studies courses will exhibit increased knowledge, higher efficacy levels, and engage in more frequent political discussions, how students evaluate the government-related subject matter is likely to be more important than simple exposure alone.

Niemi and Junn point out that "students who regarded civics as one of their favorite subjects reported spending considerably more time on homework and achieved markedly better grades in civics classes than those who did not."[12] The connection between liking the subject matter and high achievement is no surprise. Adults who are more interested in politics are more likely to participate and have higher levels of knowledge.[13] Likewise, students who enjoy civics are also more likely to take greater interest in politics outside the classroom, through participation in school-related government activities as well as in watching television news. Assessing a student's enjoyment of civics is important as a control variable to avoid falsely attributing individual student interest to the school or classroom.[14] It is possible, however, that such interest is more than an individual characteristic: it may also say something about the schools or the classrooms in which students learn. Good teachers and pedagogical techniques preferred by students have a significantly positive influence on a student's attitudes toward a subject.[15] We expect to find that the more students enjoy civics courses, the more knowledgeable and politically efficacious they will be.

Our survey indicated that exposure to civics courses was associated with significant increases in the amount of political discussion reported, the level of factual political knowledge, and internal political efficacy. When compared to a complete lack of government-related coursework, having more than a year of exposure to such material generated a 5 percent increase in the amount of weekly discussion, a 3 percent jump in the level of political knowledge, and a 2 percent increase in internal efficacy. Interestingly, exposure to civics decreased our measure of external efficacy by about the same amount that it increased political knowledge, suggesting that learning more about government in school and concluding that it is effective and responsive are not necessarily related (see Table 6-1).

12. Niemi and Junn (1998, p. 99).
13. Delli Carpini and Keeter (1996); Luskin (1990); Zaller (1992).
14. Niemi and Junn (1998, p. 124).
15. Wilen and White (1991); Torney, Oppenheim, and Farnen (1975).

Table 6-1. *Direct Effects of Television News Exposure and Attitudes toward School Authorities and Civics-Related Courses on Political Socialization, Controlling for Indirect Effects of Local Context and the Direct Effects of Other Community Characteristics*[a]
Units as indicated

Explanatory variable	Frequency of political discussion	β	Level of political knowledge	β	Internal political efficacy	β	External political efficacy	β
Amount of civics courses	1.003** (0.341)	.05	0.576** (0.267)	.03	0.384* (0.201)	.03	−0.652** (0.199)	−0.06
Dislike studying government	−7.654** (1.323)	−.10	−6.688** (1.040)	−.10	−8.623** (0.779)	−.19	−6.825** (0.770)	−.15
Plan to attend four-year college	8.730** (1.094)	.14	6.385** (0.855)	.12	4.436** (0.644)	.12	1.658** (0.637)	.05
No plans to attend college	3.912** (1.249)	.05	0.153 (0.977)	.00	0.462 (0.735)	.01	0.328 (0.726)	.01
Grade level	0.157 (0.487)	.01	1.953** (0.381)	.08	1.284** (0.287)	.07	0.598** (0.283)	.03
I always deserve the grades I receive	3.313** (1.241)	.04	2.921** (0.971)	.05	1.820** (0.732)	.04	3.867** (0.721)	.09
I never deserve the grades I receive	1.697 (2.793)	.01	−4.755** (2.185)	−.03	−0.226 (1.647)	−.01	−6.492** (1.624)	−.07
Frequency of TV news viewing	2.748** (0.207)	.22	0.350** (0.162)	.03	1.266** (0.122)	.17	−0.034 (0.121)	−.01
Summary statistic								
R^2	.183		.264		.204		.234	
N	2,851		2,835		2,838		2,836	

Explanatory variable	Negativity about courts/police	β	Opposition to diversity	β	Nationalism/ chauvinism	β	Support Clinton impeachment	β
Amount of civics courses	0.021 (0.272)	.00	0.029 (0.199)	.00	0.090 (0.245)	.01	0.019 (0.287)	.00
Dislike studying government	7.211** (1.055)	.11	1.978** (0.772)	.05	-7.111** (0.953)	-.13	-5.355** (1.111)	-.09
Plan to attend four-year college	-2.023** (0.872)	-.04	-0.576 (0.638)	-.02	3.379* (0.787)	.08	1.073 (0.919)	.02
No plans to attend college	-0.035 (0.994)	-.00	0.077 (0.728)	.00	-0.383 (0.898)	-.00	0.634 (1.049)	.01
Grade level	0.847** (0.388)	.04	0.268 (0.284)	.02	1.136** (0.351)	.05	0.089 (.174)	.00
I always deserve the grades I receive	-6.253** (0.988)	-.10	-1.315* (0.723)	-.03	1.345 (0.893)	.03	2.473** (1.041)	.04
I never deserve the grades I receive	11.488** (2.224)	.08	5.694** (1.626)	.06	-5.424** (2.007)	-.05	-4.695** (2.342)	-.04
Frequency of TV news viewing	-0.041 (0.167)	-.00	0.242** (0.121)	.04	0.436** (0.149)	.05	0.083 (0.174)	.01
Summary statistic								
R^2	.206		0.069		.154		.069	
N	2,854		2,828		2,848		2,845	

Source: Metro Civic Values Survey, 1999–2000.

*$p \le .10$; **$p \le .05$.

a. Structural equations estimation. Values are regression coefficients for direct effects only, with standard errors in parentheses. β, standardized regression coefficients. Control variables with parameters for direct effects not shown in this model are percent black, percent Asian, percent Hispanic, population density, median income, percent with four years of college, percent Democratic, political party competitiveness, and percent turnout.

Developing an appreciation for social studies subject matter was far more critical to the political socialization process than exposure to the coursework itself. Those who reported disliking their government-related courses engaged in nearly 8 percent less political discussion, ranked more than half a letter grade lower in their political knowledge test, and were far less efficacious than those who had at least a minimum of appreciation for civics coursework. We also found that assessments of the fairness of school authorities were significantly linked to these attitudes. Students who believed they deserved the grades they received were more likely to engage in political discussion and were more knowledgeable and efficacious compared to those who believed that school authorities cheated them (see table 6-1). Our control variables indicated that knowledge and efficacy were slightly higher among upper-level students than among ninth graders. Watching television news is also associated with greater knowledge, discussion, and internal efficacy. If students were planning to attend a four-year college, the motivation to achieve, and the self-efficacy that goes along with it, had a positive impact on knowledge, discussion, and political efficacy. The effect of having plans to continue with formal education was especially pronounced for political knowledge, generating more than half a letter grade increase in the score on the fact-based exam over those who were only planning to attend a two-year college (the baseline for comparison).

From the results shown in table 6-1, we conclude that the most striking and frequently overlooked curriculum-relevant factor is the importance of liking government and politics as subject matter. Few of the variables that we examined had such a profoundly positive impact on the participation-enabling outcomes. Although it is probably unreasonable to expect all teenagers to develop a liking for social studies subject matter, much more can be done by way of curriculum development and staffing to ensure that these courses are stimulating and engaging rather than monotonous and boring. In many schools the social studies curriculum remains much too dependent upon textbooks. And in the schools we visited, social studies instruction was frequently the province of sports coaches for whom citizenship education was an afterthought.[16] To be sure, not all social studies courses are staffed with coaches whose principal interests lie elsewhere, but the proportion of social studies teaching positions filled by individuals who are in school mainly to coach a sports team is far higher than what we found in the science or mathematics curriculum.

---

16. Caliendo (2000); Fouts (1989).

School Environments and Political Attitudes

We also expected that exposure to classroom instruction about government and politics, and an appreciation for it, would not only be important for political knowledge and efficacy but also be critical to the propensity for children to hold opinions about political issues. Education provides training in critical thinking and deductive reasoning, which allows individuals to construct consistent belief systems.[17] Therefore, education level is the single best predictor of a respondent's likelihood of answering "no opinion" or "don't know" to a survey question, even controlling for question wording and content. Opinion holding, then, is very strongly a function of experience with classroom learning.[18]

It is less obvious how social studies instruction affects the *direction* of opinions. Do students that take government courses have more disdain for the police? Are they more tolerant of diversity? How did government courses influence attitudes about President Clinton's impeachment? Does exposure to government-related coursework produce "super patriots" who are dismissive of foreign nations and cultures? The civics curriculum has undergone some changes since the 1950s. Our review of contemporary instructional materials indicates a substantial curricular emphasis on pluralism and group involvement in American politics. The civil rights movement and the nation's rich history of immigration are nearly always portrayed in a positive light. In both civics courses and foreign language classes, students are taught, at the very least, a nominal appreciation for other cultures. While we do not believe that the social studies curriculum is nearly as uncritical of American political institutions as it might have been in the 1950s, the accent remains, as it did then, on good citizenship in the form of loyalty and participation.[19] We anticipate that exposure to civics courses is likely to increase nationalistic sentiment, foster respect for law enforcement, and encourage tolerance for diversity.

In our observations of over 120 social studies classrooms, we noticed one decisive area in which social studies courses fall short—they fail to develop in students an appreciation for the importance of the conflictual aspects of American political history. Students often come to view disagreement and

17. See Prothro and Grigg (1960); Almond and Verba (1963); Jackman (1972); Sarat (1975).

18. Likewise, those with "constrained" belief systems—that is, those who have stable, consistent opinions across different issues—are also among the most educated. See Converse (1964) and Zaller (1992).

19. Langton and Jennings (1968).

conflict as negative, as something to be avoided, and that no good can come of it. They fail to grasp the importance that ideological differences have played in our political history. The debates between the Federalists and the anti-Federalists are played down or ignored entirely. American history classes teach about the Civil War but generally fail to illuminate how other conflicts were resolved without war. This gives students the false impression that contemporary politics consists of pointless bickering and endless posturing, and that there are no disagreements worth fighting for. We are not saying schools should foster an appreciation for violent conflict. In fact, helping students develop an appreciation for civil disagreements founded on basic principles and illuminating how our political system has peacefully resolved many conflicts are two of the best ways to foster respect for governmental and political processes.

The results from our research indicated that an appreciation for civics coursework was not only critical as a stimulus to civic engagement but also was associated with taking sides—that is, the development of stable and consistent opinions on issues. The bottom section of table 6-1 reports the effects of several independent variables on negativity toward police, opposition to diversity, extent of nationalistic feeling, and support for the impeachment of the president. Most notably, dislike for civics was associated with substantially greater disdain for police and law enforcement and considerably less nationalistic sentiment. Those who disliked civics were significantly more opposed to diversity, too.

Our results for the school fairness measures are consistent with the idea that support for (or opposition to) the political system is diffuse—meaning that if you believe that one level of governing authority is responsive and fair, you will come to believe that about other governing authorities. A student's negative evaluation of the fairness of school authorities was clearly linked to much greater skepticism directed toward courts and the police and less enthusiasm for expressions of support for the nation (table 6-1). Conversely, when students believed that they almost always received the grades they deserved, they were also far less negative toward the courts and police.

To be sure, the causal pathway may also go in the other direction: students' perceptions of fairness within the larger world could be tainting their perceptions of fairness within school. MacLeod and Willis show that among some lower-income youth, their experience of structural boundaries to their aspirations has significantly influenced their attitudes about school.[20] Students who have bumped up against major roadblocks in the "real" world—who have been denied employment because of their address or race, or have been treated poorly by various types of authority—are much more likely to perceive their schools as being unfair places where only those who buy into society's middle-class or "white" values are given a chance at success. These considerations raise the question of whether students who conclude that their efforts are justly rewarded are only found among white middle- and upper-income populations. Are perceptions of fairness based on race and socioeconomic status?

In our sample, we did see a difference across racial and ethnic groups in the way students evaluate the fairness of grading, mostly between African Americans or biracial students (most of whom are of black-white ancestry) and whites or Asians. These comparisons appear in figure 6-1, where 68.5 percent of black students and 70 percent of biracial students reported that they "mostly" or "always" receive the grades they deserve, compared with a moderately higher 81.3 and 81.2 percent of white and Asian students, respectively. These differences are statistically significant ($p \leq .001$), although the relationship is not especially strong (Cramer's V = .09, for the complete table). Notably, black students were also slightly more likely to complain that they disliked their civics courses than either whites or Asians. Differences by socioeconomic status, while statistically significant, were not substantively overpowering. In schools where all of the students share a similar economic background, social class can have very little explanatory power. Even high school students from low-income families commonly believe that school authorities usually carry out fair evaluations.

Notably, those who believed school authorities had been unfair to them were also quite hostile toward immigration-induced diversity. Such students may resent the success and progress of others, concluding that they have been victims of discrimination while others have been allowed to jump ahead. Clearly this is the impression we received from those native-born white and African American youth in urban and suburban schools who spoke out against immigration on economic grounds. Many of the African American students expressed resentment about how immigrant entrepreneurs managed to secure financial capital after only a short time in the country, while their own communities were bereft of entrepreneurship. These less academically minded students are not only bored by their social

20. MacLeod (1995); Willis (1977).

Figure 6-1. *Students Responding That They "Always" or "Mostly" Deserve the Grades They Receive in School, by Race or Ethnic Group*[a]

Percent of total

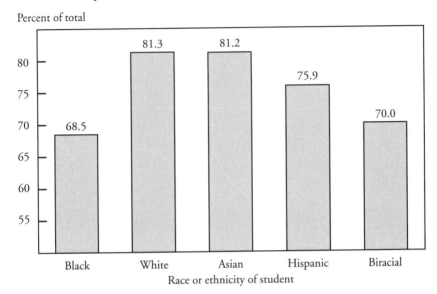

Race or ethnicity of student

Source: Metro Civic Values Survey, 1999–2000.
a. N = 2,966; χ^2 = 72.13; p = 0.001; Cramer's V = 0.09.

studies courses, they are probably uninterested in school in general. More than a few have been punished by official authority, ranging from school detentions to time in jail. Poor performance in school, and the complex of problems surrounding low achievement, diminishes students' expectations for their life chances, leading them to conclude that they might have to compete with less skilled population groups for employment in a labor market with a shrinking supply of well-paying jobs. Given that many of their competitors are likely to be recent immigrants, their opposition to ethnic diversity is completely rational.

Disliking the study of government was clearly associated with opposition to the Clinton impeachment process. This makes sense inasmuch as those less interested in politics are turned off to the subject by the perception of conflict. Students who appreciated civics subject matter were more ready to view the impeachment process as a legitimate constitutional function of government, regardless of their views of President Clinton and the Republican-controlled Congress, and regarded it less as a partisan political vendetta. These students have learned to see conflict in a more positive light, believing that a clash of viewpoints is an essential aspect of the political system and that partisan conflict is not tantamount to endless and pointless squabbling. Even after we added controls for the party identification of respondents, we still found that those who most liked studying government were significantly more supportive of the impeachment process than those who disliked it. For students who understand that American political processes are necessarily conflict ridden and disputatious, any news about national government is interesting and informative, and not necessarily indicative of a system in need of reform or repair. For those who intensely dislike studying government, it is undoubtedly intimidating to turn on the news and be barraged by intense quantities of information about something they do not comprehend.

We also noticed that students who believe they receive the grades they deserve and those who never believe they do took opposite sides on the impeachment. For the students who feel positive about the way school authorities treat them, the impeachment process was not as likely to be viewed as an illegitimate, purely partisan process, and they used their social studies classes to understand the rationale for the president's removal. Even those who favored the president's acquittal could learn to appreciate the impeachment process as a set of rules to be followed. For the better students, the impeachment may well have rescued their social studies classes from abject boredom and textbook monotony. Among adolescents, more so than among adults, evaluations of the impeachment process were not founded solely upon partisanship.

If students who are interested in government came to view the impeachment more positively than those who are not, why did so many of our youth, as well as a majority of adult Americans, come to believe that the impeachment process was an unjustified partisan attack? Probably because many did not view it through the lens of the American constitutional framework. Others with less interest in the subject may have remained ignorant about the president's offenses, while still others insisted upon a sharp distinction between a president's public and private life. Clearly, not all of the good students in our sample were Republicans who wanted to see the president removed; only a small minority took this position. Our results in table 6-1 indicate that the impeachment was opposed because most adolescents, like many adults, have no interest in government, do not like studying it, and are turned off to the conflicts that it manifests. These citizens have come to view political arguments as hopelessly intractable, apparently failing to understand how central disagreement has always been to the process of American policymaking.

For others, particularly those who are political (and perhaps racial) minorities, political argument is to be avoided because it seldom seems to pay off. American political institutions naturally favor majorities, though not always. But the perception that one's side consistently loses at political argument cannot explain the massive disengagement we see in the twenty-first century among those who are not minorities. It is for lack of knowledge and insight that major news events involving political conflict are seen in such a negative light, not because the outcomes of these conflicts are settled in advance and appear to favor only one side.

Making Up for School Failures: Discussion, Knowledge and Political Efficacy

In our second set of explorations of the survey data, we take a different approach, using a model to determine whether aspects of an adolescent's political environment can correct or mitigate the negative impact of disliking civics-related coursework or having no desire to pursue formal education after high school. We examine whether the effects of having no college plans or disliking politics are contingent upon the level of competitiveness in the political environment, the level of voter turnout, and the partisan political balance of the school's catchment area. Specifically, we are hypothesizing that highly active political environments can steer youth toward greater knowledge, discussion, and efficacy, regardless of their disposition toward their government courses or how motivated they are to achieve in order to reach future goals (such as a college education). In other words, in this section of the chapter, we are determining whether living in a politically stimulating neighborhood may generate sufficient information that the key aspects of formal education we identified earlier become less critical as means for proper socialization.

In searching for the possibly corrective effects of political environments, it is important to recall from chapter 2 that political party diversity does have a pronounced positive impact on key predictors of future participation and political involvement—most of all on the level of political knowledge. Students living in the most heterogeneous partisan neighborhoods scored much higher on the political knowledge test than those living in the least competitive environments, were far more internally efficacious, and also ranked marginally higher in external efficacy. The same was true of high-turnout areas: knowledge, internal efficacy, and discussion levels increased across the board. The effects for partisan bias were more mixed, dropping the level of political knowledge in the most heavily Democratic locales but increasing external efficacy in these same places (see chapter 2, table 2-1).

In table 6-2 the results are generally consistent with the findings from table 6-1. Exposure to more civics coursework sparked political discussion but slightly diminished external efficacy. Those who believed they always deserved the grades they received ranked consistently higher on all of the participation-enabling measures of socialization. Plans to attend a four-year college were positively and strongly associated with greater discussion, knowledge, and internal efficacy.

But what intrigues us most are the interaction effects showing the consequences of party competition and turnout for those who specifically dislike social studies courses and for those who have no plans to attend college (see table 6-2). Our estimates showed that high-turnout areas actually made political discussions less likely to occur among those who dislike the subject matter. High turnout also appeared to depress political knowledge levels among these non-college-bound youth. This is because the gap in knowledge and discussion levels between students who like government and those who do not was especially wide in areas where adults were highly active participants. These findings would appear to dampen the case for political environments as a corrective force.

On the other hand, political party competition and turnout need not occur side by side, even though they are positively related. There is clear evidence that an adolescent who dislikes social studies may still pick up greater knowledge from living in a highly competitive area, scoring as much as 9 percentage points higher on the political knowledge test in the most politically heterogeneous locations compared to those living in areas with virtually no partisan diversity. In addition, when we consider internal and external efficacy, we find that competition has a positive effect on those who dislike social studies, leading them to conclude that their voice does count and that the system does work.

There is also some evidence in table 6-2 that as we move from the least competitive area to the most politically diverse locale, partisan heterogeneity increased the level of political discussion by an amazing 17 percentage points among those with no plans to attend college. It had a similar effect on boosting the knowledge levels of those with no plans to attend college.

Table 6-2. *Effects of Competitive and High-Turnout Political Environments, Achievement, and Post–High School Aspirations on Political Discussion, Knowledge, and Efficacy*[a]

Units as indicated

Fixed effects	Explanatory variable	Frequency of political discussion	Level of political knowledge	Internal political efficacy	External political efficacy
School means (β_0)	Intercept	−33.61* (18.81)	17.84 (22.41)	4.91 (18.11)	11.76 (12.12)
	Turnout	0.44** (0.10)	0.36** (0.13)	0.03 (0.09)	0.10 (0.08)
	Party competition	−0.13 (0.11)	−0.23* (0.12)	0.01 (0.13)	0.14* (0.08)
	Percent Democratic	−0.19** (0.09)	−0.33** (0.08)	−0.06 (0.11)	0.09 (0.06)
I dislike government (β_1)	Intercept	2.24 (28.83)	−12.91 (20.18)	−63.88** (20.67)	−37.65** (10.57)
	Turnout	−0.19 (0.19)	−0.25** (0.11)	0.20 (0.12)	0.21** (0.09)
	Party competition	0.09 (0.20)	0.23* (0.13)	0.24* (0.13)	0.08 (0.11)
	Percent Democratic	0.13 (0.18)	0.07 (0.12)	0.27** (0.11)	.17** (0.05)
No college plans (β_2)	Intercept	−80.13** (26.86)	−49.62* (21.93)	−5.53 (8.33)	11.92 (7.28)
	Turnout	0.19 (0.11)	−0.11 (0.14)	−0.02 (0.07)	−0.08** (0.04)
	Party competition	0.56** (0.18)	0.42** (0.13)	0.05 (0.07)	−0.10 (0.06)
	Percent Democratic	0.41** (0.15)	0.31** (0.11)	0.04 (0.04)	0.02 (0.04)

(continued)

That competitive political environments could neutralize the negative effects of antipathy to civics coursework is perhaps the most noteworthy finding in this set of results. And competition's effect is clearly separable in some cases from the effects of high turnout. High-turnout locations depressed political discussion and political knowledge levels among those who disliked civics classes, although such environments did appear to increase levels of external efficacy in this group. Thus, when we look at levels of political knowledge and internal efficacy, the competitive political environ-

Table 6-2. *Effects of Competitive and High-Turnout Political Environments, Achievement, and Post–High School Aspirations on Political Discussion, Knowledge, and Efficacy*[a] *(Continued)*
Units as indicated

Fixed effects	Explanatory variable	Frequency of political discussion	Level of political knowledge	Internal political efficacy	External political efficacy
Civics course-work (β_3)	Intercept	1.41** (0.28)	–0.18 (0.35)	0.64** (0.21)	–0.56** (0.25)
TV news exposure (β_4)	Intercept	4.64** (0.93)	0.51** (0.18)	2.58** (0.60)	–0.02 (0.09)
I always deserve grades (β_5)	Intercept	3.64** (0.91)	2.48** (0.67)	3.09** (0.92)	2.69** (0.91)
I never deserve grades (β_6)	Intercept	–0.56 (3.36)	–5.98** (2.36)	–1.54 (1.94)	–5.36** (1.87)
Plan to attend four-year college (β_7)	Intercept	12.27** (2.34)	5.21** (1.01)	6.20** (1.42)	1.60 (1.11)
Grade level (β_8)	Intercept	1.05* (0.53)	4.77** (1.55)	2.31** (0.57)	0.45 (0.39)
Socioeconomic status (β_9)	Intercept	0.40** (0.10)	0.42** (0.08)	0.26** (0.05)	–0.01 (.02)
Summary statistic					
Level-one units (*N*)		2,417	2,417	2,417	2,417
Percent reduction in error		11.3	11.4	13.0	6.2

Source: Metro Civic Values Survey, 1999–2000.

*$p < .10$; **$p < .05$.

a. Two-level hierarchical linear model; slopes and intercepts estimation. Values are regression coefficients with standard errors shown in parentheses. Results for reliability estimates and random effects do not appear in the table but are available from the authors upon request.

ments seemed better able to counter the negative effects of disliking civics coursework than the areas of high turnout that lacked competition.

We should also note, though, that for some who dislike civics coursework and have less achievement motivation, Republican party bias in the neighborhood appeared to create a dismal environment for communicating and learning about politics. Among those who were not college bound, it was lopsided Democratic settings, not Republican ones, that stimulated discussion and knowledge gains. The fact that one-party GOP locations have this depressive effect is likely an artifact of the study area and the minority status of the Republican Party across the Baltimore and

Washington metropolitan areas. We frequently observed that Republican youth were often discouraged by the fact that their candidates so rarely won a statewide election. As we have noted elsewhere, at the time the research was conducted, Maryland had not elected a Republican governor since 1966 and had not elected a Republican U.S. Senator since 1980, a few years before most of our respondents were born. It is not just the local political context that matters, then, but also the statewide context in combination with students' party loyalties.

Having acknowledged the low efficacy of Republican-identified youth who dislike civics and are not college bound, it is not as if the students from heavily Democratic locations were especially efficacious and interested in the affairs of government. Many students in our most Democratic political environments expressed open contempt for officeholders and candidates, insisting that they were only out for themselves. They would frequently mention cases of inequality and discrimination in the provision of government service, especially law enforcement and infrastructure maintenance. Some of these accounts of bad government performance were from personal experiences of ill treatment; other times these conclusions would be drawn from observations of the poor service received by others. Most often these complaints came from African American youth in predominantly poor and black areas where turnout was exceedingly low and political diversity was nonexistent.

In our more exclusive suburban schools and in many rural locations, we encountered adolescents who often lived in homogeneous white neighborhoods. However, white racial homogeneity had completely different effects on political engagement than black homogeneity since the former had the advantage of exhibiting valuable political diversity and high levels of activism. In white suburbs, Republican and Democratic families are present in the same neighborhoods and vote regularly, even if they miss some local elections. Furthermore, unlike those politically lopsided inner-city locations, government in predominantly white suburban and rural areas reinforces citizen efficacy with its responsiveness to the reasonable but not overwhelming needs of the local population. In such areas, police brutality is not tolerated, and violent crime is rare. An attentive voting-age population ensures that white-collar corruption in government is quickly rooted out. And people generally have sufficient income to be taxed to provide for good schools and well-maintained streets. Under these circumstances, youth come to believe that government is worthy of respect because they do not see the extent of mismanagement or government irresponsibility that accompanies a one-party dominant regime afflicted with the difficult challenges of big-city governance. In these places, then, positive attitudes toward government are to be expected even when there is a lack of interest in formal schooling on the subject.

Making Up for School Failures: Political Attitudes

Highly competitive political environments also appear capable of steering adolescents who harbor an antipathy toward politics toward greater nationalism and support for diversity than they would exhibit otherwise (see table 6-3). Judging from the estimates for school means at the top of table 6-3, schools in the most politically active environments generally produced youth who exhibited less hostility toward police, more tolerance for immigration, and much greater nationalism, even after we controlled for the effects of family socioeconomic status. The role of stimulating political environments in generating tolerance for diversity is worthy of special mention. In our initial results (see table 6-1), dislike of civics had a clearly positive and statistically significant effect on opposition to diversity. But under conditions of local party diversity and high turnout, the effects of this variable are much more favorable to tolerance.

Even statistically insignificant results in table 6-3 demonstrate that when students live in a competitive setting, the effect of disliking politics on hostility to immigration-induced diversity is random as opposed to systematically positive. Exposure to divergent political views is healthy because it is instrumental to comprehending the perspectives of others. In turn, exposure to the rationales for other points of view produces greater respect and tolerance.[21]

There is at least one important positive effect of partisan diversity on the attitudes of those who have no plans to further their education after high school. This subgroup winds up less opposed to diversity than their counterparts in areas of political homogeneity. Table 6-3 illustrates the effect of exposure to local partisan diversity on both those who dislike civics coursework and those who do not plan to attend college. What this table shows is that in the presence of politically competitive environments, hostility to immigration-induced diversity dropped more steeply for those who dislike government (–11 percentage points) than for those who have some appreciation for it (–8 percentage points). Similarly, the decrease in hostility to

---

21. Mutz (2002a, p. 111-112).

Table 6-3. *Effects of Competitive and High-Turnout Political Environments, Achievement, and Post-High-School Aspirations on Attitudes toward Law Enforcement, Diversity, Nationalism, and Impeachment*[a]

Units as indicated

Fixed effects	Explanatory variable	Negativity about courts/police	Opposition to diversity	Nationalism/ chauvinism	Support Clinton impeachment
School means (β_0)	Intercept	66.54** (17.25)	75.83** (7.46)	41.76** (11.98)	44.68** (11.40)
	Turnout	−0.45** (0.11)	−0.20** (0.05)	0.15* (0.08)	−0.05 (0.08)
	Party competition	−0.11 (0.08)	−0.13** (0.06)	0.11 (0.08)	0.23** (0.08)
	Percent Democratic	0.17** (0.07)	−0.11** (0.04)	−0.02 (0.05)	−0.13** (0.07)
I dislike government (β_1)	Intercept	−6.41 (19.60)	35.13** (8.10)	47.11** (18.86)	−10.15 (21.35)
	Turnout	0.05 (0.12)	−0.11 (0.08)	−0.07 (0.17)	−0.08 (0.14)
	Party competition	0.15 (0.17)	−0.20** (0.07)	−0.37** (0.15)	−0.01 (0.14)
	Percent Democratic	−0.05 (0.12)	−0.16** (0.03)	−0.26** (0.09)	0.17** (0.08)
No college plans (β_2)	Intercept	8.01 (7.94)	48.16** (7.87)	15.12 (12.95)	28.28* (10.69)
	Turnout	0.01 (0.04)	−0.19** (0.07)	−0.08 (0.11)	−0.15 (0.13)
	Party competition	−0.02 (0.05)	−0.22** (0.04)	−0.03 (0.07)	−0.19** (0.06)
	Percent Democratic	−0.11** (0.04)	−0.24** (0.03)	−0.12** (0.05)	0.06 (0.04)

(continued)

immigration was precipitous among non-college-bound students (−15 percentage points) compared to just half that much for those who intend to go to at least a two-year college.

As for attitudes about the impeachment, we are reminded that to learn about American government is to study a history of conflict and disagreement. Politics in the United States has been popularly characterized as the socialization of conflict.[22] Liking American government coursework means,

22. Schattschneider (1960).

Table 6-3. *Effects of Competitive and High-Turnout Political Environments, Achievement, and Post-High-School Aspirations on Attitudes toward Law Enforcement, Diversity, Nationalism, and Impeachment*[a] *(Continued)*

Units as indicated

Fixed effects	Explanatory variable	Negativity about courts/police	Opposition to diversity	Nationalism/ chauvinism	Support Clinton impeachment
	Percent Democratic	−0.11** (0.04)	−0.24** (0.03)	−0.12** (0.05)	0.06 (0.04)
Civics course-work (β_3)	Intercept	0.14 (0.22)	0.46** (0.20)	−0.04 (0.22)	0.38 (0.24)
TV news exposure (β_4)	Intercept	−0.04 (0.11)	0.14 (0.09)	0.32** (0.09)	−0.10 (0.13)
I always deserve grades (β_5)	Intercept	−4.88** (0.66)	−0.81 (0.61)	0.85 (0.59)	1.49** (0.74)
I never deserve grades (β_6)	Intercept	7.96** (1.67)	3.73** (1.79)	−4.36** (1.62)	−3.82** (1.89)
Plan to attend four-year college (β_7)	Intercept	−1.02 (0.95)	0.28 (0.66)	1.73** (0.82)	−0.97 (0.96)
Grade level (β_8)	Intercept	0.96 (0.59)	0.12 (0.22)	0.84** (0.40)	−0.56 (0.37)
Socioeconomic status (β_9)	Intercept	−0.06* (0.03)	−0.05 (0.04)	0.09** (0.04)	0.001 (0.04)
Summary statistic					
Level-one units (N)		2,421	2,421	2,421	2,421
Percent reduction in error		4.0	2.8	4.3	2.2

Source: Metro Civic Values Survey, 1999–2000.

*p<.10; **p<.05.

a. Two-level hierarchical linear model; slopes and intercepts estimation. Values are regression coefficients with standard errors shown in parentheses. Results for reliability estimates and random effects do not appear in the table but are available from the authors upon request.

to some extent, developing an appreciation for the disagreements that have cleaved the nation. Competitive political settings can sometimes exacerbate the negative perception among those youth who are highly conflict averse that American politics is bogged down in hopeless gridlock. Thus students who generally disliked government coursework and those who were not college bound were significantly more hostile to the presidential impeachment proceedings if they lived in a politically competitive environment than if they lived a more homogeneous political setting (table 6-3). But our results from table 6-1 coupled with our extensive field notes indicated that regardless of party affiliation, youth who disliked government viewed the impeachment proceedings less as a legitimate government function and more as a purely partisan vendetta. While the effects of political competition and high local turnout are separable from perceptions of conflict for most youth, for others these local conditions may intensify their impression that government is bogged down in unpleasant disagreement and intractable conflict.

Conclusions

Is it necessary for high school students to have positive experiences with school authorities and their social studies courses in order to become good citizens? No, but it would certainly help. Schools can either enhance or degrade the socialization process. Not everything depends on what happens in school, but enough does that the areas of curriculum requirements, staffing, and instructional style merit continued investigation and experimentation.

Most clearly we have found a strong connection between student evaluations of government-related coursework and the attitudes that are relevant to political participation later in life. Developing an appreciation for the subjects of government and politics is much more important than just sitting through some classes. How does one go from simple exposure to an actual positive regard for the subject? We have increasingly come to the conclusion that teaching an appreciation for conflict processes is at the heart of the matter.[23] People are alienated from politics when they perceive it to be excessively disputatious and argumentative. And politics is most often perceived as pointless bickering when citizens understand neither the substance of what is being argued about nor the institutions that frame and shape the debate. The difference between the youth who like government-related coursework and those who do not lies in how the two groups understand political disagreement.

Is it contradictory to say that although many youth dislike political conflict, they nevertheless benefit from partisan and religious pluralism in the local environment? Not necessarily. Political competition and its trappings—vigorous discussion, high turnout, media coverage, and party

23. Bennett (1997).

mobilization efforts—are stimulating and can make up for deficits in schooling and motivation. But if this competition is perceived as too intense, to the point where the antagonists are seen as intransigent and uncompromising, then conflict reduces political efficacy and dampens interest. For instance, most of our respondents expressed intense disdain and contempt for negative political advertising, which they perceived to be the epitome of pointless political disputation. Of course, at just what point political contests are understood to be hopelessly conflictual is probably a matter of individual perception. It is likely that the youth who dislike civics the most are those who have the least tolerance for conflict and reach this conclusion much sooner than the others.

The role of staffing decisions in creating a stimulating atmosphere for learning about government and politics cannot be overstated—a conclusion drawn not so much from our data analysis but from our visits to dozens of classrooms. Some schools produced better citizens than others for a rather straightforward reason: they hired personnel who had an interest in the social studies subject matter and who developed novel ways of communicating the material to their students. One very effective teacher we observed handed out bonus cards as he walked around the room engaging the students in discussion. The students collected these bonus cards and exchanged them for a higher participation grade than they would have received otherwise. This was not an affluent school or a special group of students; by all appearances, they were average ninth graders. To some, this system may appear mercenary, but it worked! We observed students in a non-college-prep track tearing into civics-related subject matter as if it were on a par with rock music, professional sports, or the latest teen movie. Politically interested teachers produce politically interested students.

Our survey results certainly support the notion that diffuse support for the political system begins with experiences at school. Students who believe that their efforts in school are justly rewarded are far more likely to believe that the broader political system is responsive to them and that their voice counts. To what extent is a belief in the fairness of school authorities simply an artifact of strong academic performance? Is it only the most highly motivated students who believe that school authorities assign grades fairly? By controlling for educational aspirations after high school, we were able to isolate the effect of achievement from evaluations of fairness. What we found was that even those who were not high achievers but nevertheless believed that school authorities were fair, wound up believing that their voice counted and that their eventual political participation would be worthwhile.

What about the youth who are not interested in their civics coursework and feel like the school system has treated them unfairly? Are they destined to a life of civic disengagement and political irrelevance? We think not. Our evidence indicates that students who are growing up in politically stimulating environments will become significantly more efficacious and knowledgeable than their counterparts who are living in one-party dominant, low-turnout settings. There is strong potential, then, for political party and candidate mobilization efforts to combat otherwise high levels of disinterest and feelings of alienation. We take from this the inspiration that there are a variety of policy approaches that can address the participation deficits that prevail across the United States. Education is certainly one of these, but it is not the only tool in the toolbox. Establishment of more politically balanced electoral jurisdictions—in contradiction to the prevailing trend of creating more politically safe districts—is one policy worthy of consideration. Children raised in one-party dominant areas desperately need to hear alternative political messages that can compensate for the cynicism that is hardening by late adolescence. To this end, ways to make campaigns more competitive and to reinvigorate the role of local political parties are worth an extended discussion.

7

The Terrorist Attacks
as Politically Socializing Events

In chapter 1 we mentioned some of the more compelling studies that point to the pivotal nature of events as stimuli for political learning.[1] If events are important opportunities for political socialization, we cannot avoid speculating about the effects of the dramatic terrorist attacks of September 11, 2001 (hereafter referred to as September 11). Social scientific inquiry is limited by the fact that the attacks on the World Trade Center and the Pentagon were so unexpected. It is not as if anyone could have constructed a rigorous pre- and postevent design to precisely assess the impact on people's attitudes. At best, we have some pre-event observations and some postevent observations—and usually not of the same people. This leaves us in the imperfect but all-too-common position of having to draw some approximate inferences about the way these events influenced the socialization outcomes that interest us, trying to use statistical controls to account for the leading alternative sources of change. In this chapter we ask about the short-term impact of September 11 on adolescent attitudes thought to be relevant to the political socialization process. Later we evaluate the extent to which partisan identification and media attentiveness

1. Arterton (1974, 1975); Hershey and Hill (1975); Sears and Valentino (1997); Valentino and Sears (1998).

structure the foreign policy attitudes of young people in light of the attacks.

Arguably, no single event of the past fifty years has had as dramatic an impact on the American public as the September 11 incidents. The images of the collapsing towers of the World Trade Center will forever be seared into the minds of those who watched it on television countless times in the subsequent days and weeks. In the short term, these events appeared to change American public opinion in two ways. First, the attacks and loss of life understandably made the public more afraid. Prior to September 11, Americans viewed terrorism as an abstract or distant threat, something they did not worry about in their workaday lives.[2] Among adults, the proportion saying that they had a "great deal of confidence" in the U.S. government's ability to protect its citizens from terrorism plunged in the days after the tragedy, as people were confronted with a steady barrage of information about the immediacy and tangibility of the threat. By late October, polls of adults showed that feelings of personal security had moved back to their pre–September 11 levels, but people remained fearful, with the vast majority of Americans reporting that another terrorist attack on the United States was at least "somewhat likely." Feelings of personal security were largely restored, but fears for the nation, and for other citizens, continued to loom large and were heightened by regular reports predicting that more attacks were inevitable.

Second, surveys of adult populations also showed that the tragedy evoked a familiar "rally-round-the-flag" effect, increasing confidence in the Bush presidency and American political institutions more generally. Perhaps only Pearl Harbor compares in the extent to which it unified the American public behind a war effort and an incumbent administration. In spite of a moderate recession, the president's approval ratings remained high through the November 2002 elections, well after the Taliban regime in Afghanistan had been deposed. That the Republicans did so well in the 2002 midterm elections was widely attributed to the nation's support for a wartime leader and his party.

We should not be surprised to find the familiar rally-round-the-flag effect—expressed in greater diffuse support for American government and the incumbent administration—among the youth responding to the 2001 survey. These rally effects are said to be visible in the president's popularity ratings, as they were at the beginning of the Iranian hostage crisis during

2. Kuzma (2000, p. 92).

the Carter presidency, the Cuban missile crisis during the Kennedy presidency, and the Persian Gulf War during the first Bush presidency.[3] Beyond enhancing presidential popularity, international crises also generate a greater sense of patriotism and nationalism among Americans.[4] Particularly in cases where the nation is directly threatened, citizens are likely to respond with unconditional support as a means of helping to preserve the nation.[5] Moreover, when feeling threatened from abroad, citizens are willing to disregard economic indicators and remain more positive about the president and more trusting of government than economic conditions would ordinarily warrant.[6] Consistent with the findings of previous research, we expect students to express higher levels of external political efficacy in the wake of September 11, believing government to be more responsive than they would have allowed prior to this event.

Evidence from research on political learning provides a convincing case for the socialization process being event-driven—that is, it is the event-contingent nature of exposure to information that shapes a great many attitudes and beliefs about government and politics.[7] Big events have such socializing potential mainly due to the greater amount of information that is publicly and interpersonally exchanged in their wake.[8] Citizens of all ages have unprecedented opportunities to learn about politics from the heavy media coverage that accompanies major news stories. The more important the event, the more long-term impact it is likely to have. While elections clearly qualify as important, it is the shocking, less common events that are more likely to draw the attention of adolescents. One could argue that the Vietnam War, the Watergate scandal, the Kennedy and King assassinations, or the Great Depression were events of the latter type. The September 11 airliner attacks were not a recurrent and familiar phenomenon, like an election, but an event that was shocking, sharply focused, and of great political importance.

Of course, judgment about the long-term political impact of September 11 must be reserved for research to be conducted beyond our time horizon here. We can examine the short-term impact and perhaps speculate

3. Brody (1984, 1991); Callaghan and Virtanen (1993); Edwards and Swenson (1997); Lian and Oneal (1993); Parker (1995); Mueller (1970).

4. Mueller (1973); Kernell (1986).

5. Callaghan and Virtanen (1993, p. 762).

6. Parker (1995).

7. Beck and Jennings (1991); Sears and Valentino (1997); Valentino and Sears (1998).

8. Price and Zaller (1993).

about the durability of the effects, but grand pronouncements about generation-shaping consequences must wait until more evidence arrives. Our approach is rooted in the hypothesis that event-related messages will be received and processed differently across the adolescent population, generating variable responses. In accord with much of the other research on public opinion, we believe that event-related messages will be received variously among subgroups of the population: blacks, females, the affluent, those living in large cities, those with more political knowledge, Democrats, the nonreligious, and so forth. Political socialization is a process linked to the experiences of adolescence and young adulthood, but these experiences will differ from person to person within particular generations. Although we have focused so far on variation in socialization experiences resulting from different neighborhoods and local environments, in the investigation in this chapter, geographic context is largely invariant because the post–September 11 phase of the research was carried out in a limited number of schools.

Survey Data

We draw from two surveys conducted at the same four schools but of different students. One survey was conducted in spring 1999 (April–May), and the second was conducted six to eight weeks after the events of September 11, 2001 (October–November). This leaves a duration of two-and-a-half years in which many alternative explanations could account for whatever changes we observe between the two surveys.[9] Even if we are able to control for the main effects of having a slightly different set of respondents (for example, grade level, educational aspirations, gender) and rule out the impact of changing community characteristics (which, in the case of these schools, went mostly unchanged), that still leaves us with a basketful of alternative explanations, including the experience of socializing events such as the 2000 presidential election. Still, we may be able to discern the specific effects of the September 11 events through direct questions about terrorism and media exposure in the post–September 11 survey.

In the wake of September 11, we revisited four small-town high schools in three Maryland counties. We chose the small-town schools mainly because their populations had remained stable in the period since the original 1999 survey, and all were located outside the immediate area of the

9. Campbell and Ross (1970).

attack on the Pentagon, which could reasonably have influenced adolescents in the Washington metropolitan area differently than those outside this region. These locations allowed us to rule out rapidly changing community and school characteristics as the sources of attitude change. Approximately 351 students were surveyed in 1999, and we returned in 2001 to survey 425. Obvious differences in the two samples, such as student background characteristics, can be controlled statistically or adjusted through sample weights, and in some cases these differences were real. In the latter year, for example, we captured more black students, more ninth and tenth graders, and fewer eleventh and twelfth graders. Related to grade level differences, the earlier survey captured students with more exposure to civics or government-related coursework, although the later survey reported a higher level of educational aspiration. Also, the students in the earlier survey performed better on our seven-item political knowledge exam, the test items of which remained very much the same except for an update of the name of the current vice president (from Gore in 1999 to Cheney in 2001). The basic sample comparisons are reported in table 7-1.

Table 7-1 shows that there are differences in the traits and characteristics of the students surveyed, differences that could explain changing scores on the outcome variables of interest. Our dependent variables are the same as those from previous chapters. The details for the factor analyses are reported in appendix C, but to review briefly, there are five dependent variables formulated within the principal components framework: internal political efficacy, external political efficacy, opposition to diversity, nationalistic or "chauvinistic" feeling, and negativity toward local police and courts. In addition, two other variables from specific survey items are also treated as dependent variables in our analysis: the amount of political discussion in the last week (in number of days) and the students' scores on the seven-item factual knowledge test, expressed as the percentage of correct answers.

To counter the possible objection that the changes in scores on our dependent variables were entirely the result of background characteristics of the two sets of students, we ran a multivariate analysis of variance to check if these differences disappeared once we controlled for these competing explanations. The result of this analysis, shown in table 7-2, indicates that the differences in scores held up even after controlling for the gender, grade level, race, and post–high school ambitions of the two groups of students. Despite the fact that our post–September 11 observations are of a different group of students than those in the pre–September 11 survey,

Table 7-1. *Comparisons of 1999 and 2001 Student Populations in Four Maryland High Schools*[a]

Percent unless otherwise indicated

Sample characteristic	1999	2001
Number surveyed	351	425
White students	89.2	82.8
Black students	3.4	7.8
Female students	53.6	46.4
Male students	51.3	48.7
Grade 9	23.6	34.1
Grade 10	32.5	21.4
Grade 11	20.8	26.8
Grade 12	22.7	15.9
No television news in last week	11.8	12.2
Plans to attend a four-year college	60.1	70.4
No plans to attend college	25.9	21.4
No civics or government courses	1.7	15.3
Regular (weekly) church attendee	19.7	18.8

	Mean score	
Dependent variables	1999	2001
Average percent correct on knowledge test	71.5	61.4
Frequency of discussion	25.5	31.5
Internal efficacy	51.0	52.0
External efficacy	42.3	47.5
Negativity toward law enforcement	40.6	40.8
Opposition to diversity	51.1	52.3
Nationalism/chauvinism	76.5	75.5

Source: Metro Civic Values Survey, 1999–2000, and 2001 follow-up.

a. These marginals are unweighted percentages for all respondents.

changes in the scores are not attributable to the most obviously observable features of the respondents. Once we controlled for these background characteristics, differences in scores remained especially significant for discussion frequency, internal efficacy, external efficacy, and opposition to diversity (see table 7-2).

Our next step was to use a statistical model to control for the variable characteristics of respondents in both survey rounds, while evaluating differences across time that could be attributable to the stimulus of the Sep-

Table 7-2. *Multivariate Analysis of Variance on Dependent Variables,*
Controlling for Grade Level, Gender, Race, Civics Exposure,
and Post-High-School Aspirations[a]
Percent unless otherwise indicated

| | Mean score | | | |
Dependent variables	1999	2001	F test	p value for F
Frequency of discussion	26.3 (28.4)	32.0 (28.2)	12.57	.001
Average percent correct on knowledge test	72.0 (20.6)	62.0 (21.0)	17.13	.001
Internal efficacy	50.9 (18.4)	52.2 (16.1)	10.39	.001
External efficacy	42.6 (17.2)	46.0 (18.9)	3.83	.002
Negativity toward law enforcement	40.1 (19.6)	40.5 (22.4)	3.52	.004
Opposition to diversity	51.0 (16.7)	52.2 (18.3)	5.58	.001
Nationalism/chauvinism	77.0 (19.3)	77.0 (17.9)	2.75	.018

Source: Metro Civic Values Survey, 1999–2000, and 2001 follow-up.
a. N = 631 (unweighted). Standard deviations are shown in parentheses.

tember 11 attacks. Our "context" variables in this particular model are not
neighborhoods but the years in which the students were surveyed. We
expect those in the post–September 11 sample to differ systematically from
those in the pre–September 11 sample. Specifically, exposure to the events
of September 11 should increase the amount of political discussion, knowledge, and external efficacy—those aspects of the socialization process we
have labeled "participation enabling" due to their strong connection to later
political engagement. But the terrorist incidents may have also contributed
to socialization by inducing the taking of sides. In the post–September 11
survey, we expect many fewer students to be neutral toward immigration-
induced diversity, nationalism, and assessments of local police and courts.
And pro-nationalistic and pro-law-enforcement views should be greatly
heightened over where they were in the earlier survey.

Clearly it is possible that many commentators in the press and academic
world exaggerated the permanent and lasting effects of the September 11
crisis on public opinion. The post–September 11 round of research may have
been conducted long enough after the event that any substantial effects had

worn off. Still, this seems unlikely given the magnitude of the tragedy, the duration of the government's military and law enforcement response, and the intensity of the media coverage. Certainly among some adolescents, however, it could be the case that news fatigue had set in by October and November. A few students reported to us anecdotally that they had grown weary of the repetitious media coverage of the same themes and stories. Still others reacted as if the incidents were not quite real, rather like a television drama, finding it difficult to sympathize with victims who seemed so far away. These youth adopted the position of psychologist Lawrence Kohlberg's less mature moral reasoners, who evaluate the moral significance of actions wholly in terms of their material self-interest, apparently unable to recognize any broader implications of terrorist violence or sympathize with victims who are at a distance.[10] One suspects that few students were completely unsympathetic, and yet some of our respondents did report feeling distant from the events and largely preoccupied with their own concerns.

In addition to trying to explain socialization-relevant attitudes as a function of events, we suspect that socialization will be shaped by a variety of other factors. These variables should be included because it is possible that they are the real causes of the differences we observe in socialization outcomes between spring 1999 and fall 2001. First, we examine the effect of school-related variables, including the students' grade level, exposure to American government coursework, evaluation of social studies-related subject matter, and whether they perceive that school officials evaluate them fairly.

We also include variables designed to capture the potential for significant events to improve the standing of those who would otherwise be poorly socialized. If disliking government-related coursework is a risk factor for poor socialization, we would expect that those who dislike the subject would be positively influenced by the events of September 11, engaging in more discussion and possibly demonstrating greater knowledge and higher efficacy than those with similar attitudes toward civics who were surveyed earlier. Major news events may act as an effective substitute for formal education, since this information reaches adolescents from a myriad of sources outside the classroom. We also investigate whether the possibly detrimental effects of not attending church (see chapter 5) are at all mitigated by the experience of the terrorist attacks.

10. Kohlberg (1958, 1984, 1987).

Influence of September 11 on Discussion, Knowledge, and Efficacy

We found some evidence to support the idea that the events between the first and second surveys altered the extent of political discussion and internal and external efficacy, *even though the level of political knowledge dropped significantly* between the 1999 and 2001 survey (see tables 7-1 and 7-2). The decrease in the seven-item knowledge score was related directly to the fact that a new administration had been elected, and students were less familiar with the names of key officeholders. But in spite of the lower knowledge scores, students in the 2001 group reported having considerably higher external efficacy—nearly 6 percentage points higher, or more than half a letter grade if we were to gauge efficacy levels on a standard A–F grading scale. Internal efficacy was also higher among the 2001 students, although the difference was not statistically significant.

To be sure, many of the control variables we included were also influential in shaping these outcomes. Television news viewing heightened political discussion and internal efficacy. Grade level was influential, as high school juniors and seniors exhibited higher levels of political discussion, knowledge, and efficacy than sophomores and freshmen. Positive evaluations of the way in which one is graded in school were associated with more political discussion and higher efficacy scores (see table 7-3).

Our results also had a bearing on how the post–September 11 group of students differed from those surveyed earlier with regard to risk factors frequently associated with inferior political socialization. The interaction terms reported in table 7-3 capture the extent to which the effect of the events of September 11 compensated for alienation from school authority, rarely or never attending church, and generally disliking the subject of government and politics. And what they suggest is that these events acted as a highly positive socializing force on those who generally disliked civics subject matter. Members of this subgroup scored considerably higher on discussion, knowledge, and efficacy than their pre–September 11 counterparts, even when we controlled for related characteristics such as grade level and post–high school aspirations. The post–September 11 group of students reported a seventeen-point gain in political knowledge, a nineteen-point gain in internal efficacy, and a fourteen-point gain in external efficacy over highly similar students from the same schools who had been surveyed two years earlier! Even hardened skeptics of our research design would have

Table 7-3. *Political Socialization Outcomes Resulting from Effects of Explanatory Variables and Timing of Survey before and after September 11, 2001*[a]
Units as indicated

Explanatory variable	Frequency of political discussion	β	Level of political knowledge	β	Internal political efficacy	β	External political efficacy	β
Constant	−2.932		12.691		17.800		9.586	
Year: 0 = 1999, 1 = 2001	0.305 (0.218)	.08	−9.116** (2.559)	−.21	1.739 (2.055)	.05	5.832** (2.269)	.16
Frequency of TV news viewing	0.249** (0.032)	.30	0.599 (0.375)	.07	1.602** (0.300)	.22	−0.032 (0.332)	−.01
Amount of civics/government courses	0.082 (0.059)	.06	−1.667** (.691)	−.13	0.628 (0.553)	.06	−0.391 (0.609)	−.03
Dislike studying government	−1.244** (0.249)	−.25	−11.561** (2.920)	−.21	−11.821** (2.326)	−.27	−7.531** (2.591)	−.16
Plan to attend four-year college	0.866** (0.219)	.22	3.878 (2.535)	.09	2.409 (2.028)	.07	1.136 (2.229)	.03
No plans to attend college	0.238 (0.246)	.05	−4.203 (2.853)	−.08	−2.909 (2.274)	−.07	−0.114 (2.519)	−.02

Grade level	0.286** (0.072)	.17	5.663** (0.848)	.32	2.217** (0.680)	.15	3.256** (0.746)	.21
I always deserve the grades I receive	0.334* (0.173)	.07	1.246 (2.012)	.03	3.999** (1.604)	.10	5.604** (1.770)	.13
I never deserve the grades I receive	−0.778 (0.509)	−.07	7.003 (5.973)	.06	−4.188 (5.128)	−.04	−19.631** (5.242)	−.20
Regular church attendee	−0.446 (0.296)	−.10	5.033 (3.400)	.10	−1.609 (2.733)	−.04	−7.896** (3.022)	−.18
Never attend church	1.012** (0.369)	.22	0.188 (4.264)	.01	8.184* (3.420)	.20	5.438 (3.786)	.13
Post–September 11 x never deserve grades	0.807 (0.805)	.05	−30.946** (9.454)	−.17	10.552 (7.766)	.07	20.068** (8.301)	.13
Post–September 11 x never attend church	−1.588** (0.527)	−.23	1.371 (6.096)	.02	−10.389* (4.884)	−.18	−11.390* (5.407)	−.17
Post–September 11 x dislike studying government	2.647** (0.398)	.36	16.895** (4.625)	.21	19.021** (3.719)	.29	14.519* (4.084)	.22
Summary statistic							
Adjusted R^2	.300		.181		.204		.132	
N	526		532		523		524	

(continued)

Table 7-3. *Political Socialization Outcomes Resulting from Effects of Explanatory Variables and Timing of Survey before and after September 11, 2001*[a] *(Continued)*
Units as indicated

Explanatory variable	Negativity about courts/police	β	Opposition to diversity	β	Nationalism/ chauvinism	β
Constant	50.806		43.218		50.722	
Year: 0=1999, 1=2001	0.370 (2.733)	.01	-1.663 (2.410)	-.05	-5.545** (2.277)	-.15
Frequency of TV news viewing	-0.421 (.401)	-.05	-0.068 (0.354)	-.01	0.275 (0.334)	.04
Amount of civics/government courses	-0.320 (.737)	-.02	0.095 (0.651)	.01	-0.915 (0.614)	-.07
Dislike studying government	10.706** (3.115)	.19	-4.605† (2.749)	-.10	-6.236* (2.596)	-.14
Plan to attend 4 year college	-7.247** (2.708)	-.16	2.491 (2.418)	.07	1.372 (2.252)	.04
No plans to attend college	-6.036* (3.047)	-.12	5.894* (2.719)	.14	2.078 (2.536)	.05
Grade level	-0.258 (.905)	-.01	0.634 (0.799)	.04	2.516** (0.754)	.17

	(1)	β	(2)	β	(3)	β
I always deserve the grades I receive	−4.995* (2.146)	−.10	−1.571 (1.892)	−.04	5.883** (1.787)	.14
I never deserve the grades I receive	19.521** (6.372)	.16	7.235 (5.611)	.07	−13.563** (5.306)	−.14
Regular church attendee	5.180 (3.655)	.10	−0.088 (3.191)	−.002	6.799* (3.022)	.16
Never attend church	0.289 (4.570)	.01	−1.642 (4.012)	−.04	−8.141* (3.795)	−.19
Post–September 11 x never deserve grades	11.579 (10.323)	.06	3.270 (8.876)	.02	15.234† (8.397)	.10
Post–September 11 x never attend church	7.451 (6.531)	.10	4.322 (5.748)	.07	6.768 (5.425)	.11
Post–September 11 x dislike studying government	−18.534* (4.936)	−.23	1.533 (4.350)	.02	14.855** (4.111)	.22
Summary statistic						
Adjusted R^2	.113		.01		.089	
N	528		523		529	

Source: Metro Civic Values Survey, 1999–2000, and 2001 follow-up.

†$p \leq .10$; *$p \leq .05$; **$p \leq .01$.

a. Weighted least squares estimation. Values are regression coefficients with standard errors shown in parentheses. β, standardized regression coefficients.

difficulty arguing that *no portion* of these stunning changes can be attributed to the terrorist events and their aftermath.

The events of September 11 also appear to have affected those who never attended church, dropping their discussion and efficacy levels considerably when compared to those of students who were at least somewhat regular in their religious attendance. Most religious services addressed the subject of the tragic September 11 losses for weeks afterward, undoubtedly acting as a stimulus to discussion and perhaps providing some comfort and perspective. But for those who never attended these services, this opportunity to mentally process the events with others was missed, eroding their efficacy levels and leaving them further behind their church-attending counterparts than they would have been had the attacks not occurred.

This research design does not allow us to rule out all the alternative explanations that might challenge our hypotheses. For example, it is surely possible that the experience of the presidential election between 1999 and 2001 served to increase students' political discussion and efficacy. But if this were a major explanation, we would also have expected exposure to election coverage to bolster political knowledge, which it did not according to the direct effect reported in table 7-3. That discussion levels and efficacy increased while factual political knowledge generally decreased is suggestive of how the events of September 11 operated on public opinion: they stimulated attention to political events and bolstered trust in government and support for political institutions, but they did not necessarily build political knowledge except among those who had extremely low levels of knowledge to begin with. This leads us to question the long-term impact of the terrorist attacks. If the increased political discussion and media exposure following the terrorist incidents built political knowledge, it may have done so only among those who had the most to gain from such exposure, that is, not among the most knowledgeable nor among the most hardcore of the alienated, but among those who were attentive to the event-related information while ordinarily lacking interest in government activity and social studies coursework.[11]

Influence of September 11 on Political Attitudes

In table 7-3 we found some evidence consistent with the hypothesis that the violent attacks on the World Trade Center and Pentagon had a very positive

11. Price and Zaller (1993).

short-term impact on political discussion and internal and external efficacy and compensated for student disdain of government-related topics. We also see modest support for the idea that attitudes toward law enforcement, diversity, or nationalism were changed from one year to the next among certain student subgroups. In general, our analyses show that the most influential sources of opinion on these matters were largely independent of the September 11 attacks. Negativity toward the police among this group of adolescents was a function of post–high school educational aspirations, contempt for the subject matter of government and politics, and evaluations of school fairness. But students who reported disliking government coursework were dramatically less negative toward the police and much more nationalistic in the weeks after September 11 than they were before. Similarly, we found that those who complained that they were never evaluated fairly by school authorities scored an amazing fifteen points higher on the nationalism-chauvinism scale after September 11 than before. Apparently, the September 11 crisis compensated for adolescents' disdain for civics subject matter and mitigated the impact of their alienation from school authorities on both their patriotism and diffuse support for the system (external efficacy).

We expected the students to assume a more hostile stance toward immigrants and diversity in the 2001 survey than they had in 1999, but that is not what we found. Attitudes toward immigration-induced diversity remained mostly untouched from 1999 to 2001 according to the results shown in table 7-3. Those who were most hostile to diversity included the respondents with low educational aspirations, consistent with the results from previous chapters. President Bush's call for tolerance may have been heeded after all.

In summary, the results in table 7-3 show that in the short term, the September 11 tragedy stimulated greater political discussion and generated more positive beliefs about the responsiveness of the political system, giving our Generation Y respondents a stronger sense of their own voice. It also changed the opinions of some youthful subgroups about local law enforcement and stimulated greater nationalism in others. We have considerable evidence that information related to September 11 compensated for risk factors that are otherwise associated with negative socialization attitudes, including a dislike for civics subject matter and a conviction that school authorities are unfair, but it did not go so far as to appreciably change opinion among young people on immigration-induced diversity. The types of students who were most opposed to diversity did not find themselves any more or less opposed a few weeks after September 11.

These snapshots provide us with a concrete example of the way that shocking, once-in-a-lifetime events change and reshape attitudes, at least in the short term. For the most attentive, not much changed, although we did see an increase in external efficacy across all survey respondents in the latter year. Still others who were inattentive before the events were just as inattentive afterward, insistent that the damage was inflicted far from home and had no serious ramifications within their limited scope of awareness—in the short term or otherwise. Those who never attended church in the aftermath of September 11 were much less efficacious and less inclined to discuss politics than those who did—perhaps because these events were difficult to manage without the hope that spirituality provides. Even the inadequate answers provided by religion were better than no answers at all.

Among those for whom the events made a major impression were those who could not be reached by classroom instruction in civics. These students dislike social studies subject matter and go out of their way to avoid it. Some also believe they are ill-treated by school authorities, but that did not keep them from feeling better about their government's responsiveness and role after September 11.

Evaluating Policy Attitudes in Reaction to Terrorism

If foreign policy is a remote realm for adults, it is even more so for children. The challenge of discovering clear and consistent structure in attitudes about the terrorist attacks is complicated by the fact that we are not examining mature adult populations who have the greater experience of reacting to and forming opinions about various political issues and problems. Even if we admit that many adults operate with very little cognitive constraint in general, and even less than usual on matters of foreign policy, we surely can expect even less consistency and sophistication among adolescents ranging in age from fourteen to eighteen. Few of our Generation Y respondents, for example, had given much thought to American foreign policy toward Israel, as evidenced by their mixed or ambivalent views on the subject (see table 7-4). Their opinions on many matters of foreign policy seemed almost random, even after a crisis event had jarred many of them out of their complacency.

National polls were clear that the overwhelming majority of Americans continued to support the war in Afghanistan for months after it began in October 2001. By fall of 2002, smaller but still significant majorities even supported the expansion of the war into Iraq. We would expect that the

Table 7-4. *Responses to Policy Questions Related to September 11*[a]

Percent

Question	Strongly agree	Agree	Neither	Disagree	Strongly disagree
Assassination should be permitted	32.1	37.2[b]	15.8	12.7	2.2
Military action should be taken	51.3[b]	17.0	22.8	4.6	4.3
Strong support for Israel caused attacks	32.6[b]	25.7	25.8	10.3	5.5
Should not concern with other countries	7.1	18.4	21.3	34.7[b]	18.5
Should adopt stricter immigration laws	55.7[b]	21.3	11.8	7.7	3.5
Police should have power to read mail and e-mail	25.9[b]	21.0	23.6	17.8	11.7
Terrorism is a judgment from God for sin	12.4	11.7	35.3[b]	13.7	27.0

Source: Metro Civic Values Survey, 2001 follow-up.

a. Values show percentage of respondents answering in each category of response from weighted numbers (N = 425).

b. Modal response.

most attentive adolescents would be similarly supportive of the aggressive military, domestic, and foreign policy actions taken by the incumbent administration. Nevertheless, we were curious to know how our Generation Y adolescents perceived the attacks and reasoned about the appropriate attributions of responsibility.

Judgments about who was responsible for the attacks are important because they shape views of the government's policy response. If we were studying the adult population, we could readily offer up the hypothesis that respondents would have a number of predictable reactions. One would turn blame inward, suggesting that by pursuing misguided foreign policy, the United States government or Americans themselves were in some ways responsible for the terrorist incidents and thus were at least an accomplice to the demise of 3,000 of their countrymen. The second reaction, probably more typical, would turn blame outward, attributing responsibility to terrorist-sponsoring nations and the terrorists themselves, attributing little or no blame to the actions of American policymakers. A third group, though they might be a small minority, might maintain a strict isolationist posture, taking the view that internationalist ambitions caused the problem of terrorist resentment in the first place and that we should not be playing in the unstable international arena.

Those who turned blame inward would be most supportive of policy actions taken here at home and would oppose aggressive foreign policy action. Some of these are of liberal political mind-set and are intensely critical of U.S. support for Israel. They might also be just as reluctant to support a policy of strong domestic action, such as strengthening police power or adopting stricter immigration laws. The second group, on the other hand, would support an aggressive foreign policy of action against the terrorists, taking the hard line in support of military intervention even if more American lives were lost, and would even advocate changes in U.S. law to permit the assassination of hostile foreign leaders. This group desires to take the battle to the enemy and finds itself in consistent support of militant internationalism.[12] Internationalists and hard-liners would be among the first to rally around the flag and close ranks behind the president's decision to go to war.

The most isolationist elements of the adult American public lie among those who are least attentive to political and foreign policy matters.[13] Consistent with that conclusion, we obtained the distinct impression from some of our personal interactions with students that those among the least informed resist government action on all fronts on some underlying conviction that government is not to be trusted and that government power inevitably infringes upon personal freedoms. These respondents strongly opposed the strengthening of police power to read mail or e-mail communications and also disagreed with decisive military intervention in retaliation for the September 11 events. They opposed the adoption of tougher immigration policies and resisted the idea that the government should be involved in assassinations of hostile foreign leaders. These same respondents may fall back on the idea that the terrorist problem could be most easily resolved if we did not meddle in the affairs of other nations. Theirs is a view that government should be less active across the board, at home and abroad.

Remarkably, we do not see an overwhelming measure of consensus in the responses to the seven foreign-policy-related questions asked of students. While there was a surprising amount of variation, we found support for the first two, most dominant reactions: the one inward-looking and

12. Wittkopf (1986).
13. Wittkopf (1986, 1987).

more dovish, the other outward-looking and more hawkish. Table 7-4 shows that a majority of the adolescents we surveyed favored military action, the government-sponsored assassination of hostile foreign leaders, and the adoption of stronger immigration laws. There was less support, however, for removing ourselves from the international arena and for giving police the power to read mail and e-mail. Students were mostly against the proposition that terrorism was a judgment from God for sin. Students were in agreement with the proposition that strong U.S. support for Israel played a role in the attacks, although a significant percentage neither agreed nor disagreed with this statement and had obviously given it very little previous thought.

To analyze these responses more completely, we decided to use factor analysis to produce a single attitudinal variable that would place respondents on a single "hawk-dove" continuum. To do this, we used the questions on assassination, military action, the adoption of strict immigration laws, and giving police greater power (see appendix E for the factor analysis results for this chapter). To render the resulting variable more interpretable, we recoded it into a percentage point scale running from 0 to 100, with higher values indicating stronger support for aggressive domestic enforcement and foreign policy measures consistent with those of the Bush administration and much of the elite consensus in the immediate aftermath of the September 11 attacks.

With the questions appropriately combined and rescaled, we decided to see if support for the adoption of stricter domestic laws varied with the cognitive sophistication of our respondents. This theoretical expectation is rooted in the work of John Zaller, who, building on the work of Converse, found significant differences between the attitudes of those who were more politically attentive and those who were inattentive.[14] The most attentive were inclined to engage in "mainstreaming" on policy issues in which there was considerable elite consensus. The mainstreaming phenomenon predicts that the highly aware would come to agreement with the elite consensus on the issue, whereas the poorly informed, being unaware of the elite consensus, would be more likely to exhibit random variability in their attitudes.

Zaller's theories are highly relevant to understanding the political socialization process and to our search for structure in adolescent attitudes. After all, increasing political awareness is much of what the socialization process

14. Zaller (1992); Converse (1964).

is supposed to be about. Those who are more thoroughly socialized are more inclined to participate precisely because they know more about politics, follow political news more closely, and engage in more political discussion. Moreover, those who are better socialized are also more likely to know the opinions of elites and follow dominant elite opinion when it emerges. So it should come as no great surprise that those adolescents who exhibit more cognitive sophistication will be more likely to support enhanced police power, use of military force, and assassination of hostile foreign leaders than those who do not. We measure cognitive sophistication by the students' scores on the factual political knowledge questions, but we also control for the amount of government coursework the student has taken since ninth grade as well as the students' grade level.

We expect that those who score in the higher reaches of political knowledge will be more likely to support the prevailing elite message favoring the adoption of aggressive enforcement measures. There was a flurry of elite discussion in the weeks following September 11 about strengthening police surveillance power and cracking down on a dysfunctional or lax immigration system. While these policy proposals did not generate quite the lasting consensus that support for military action did, prominent politicians and many journalists agreed that strengthening homeland security was worth the price of some personal freedoms. To be sure, the extent of elite support for stronger police powers and stricter immigration laws was more muted than for the pursuit of military action, but few were brave enough to declare outspoken opposition to such ideas while the threat of further attacks loomed large. Support for such measures is expected to be greater among those respondents who exhibit more knowledge, again providing some evidence of mainstreaming, or socialization into agreement with a dominant elite position among the well informed. We also anticipate that those who have taken more government-related coursework will be more likely to support positions subject to broad elite consensus. Civics coursework, from this point of view, is one instrument for learning about the policy positions adopted by elites.

Evidence for Mainstreaming Effects: The Hawk-versus-Dove Continuum

Our results paint an interesting picture of how the socialization process leads those students with greater exposure to social studies coursework to support the dominant elite opinions that favor aggressive action. Table 7-5

Table 7-5. *Support among Adolescents for Aggressive Domestic and Foreign Policy in the War on Terror, October–November 2001*[a]
Units as indicated

	Model 1	Model 2
Constant	120.283 (11.674)	119.638 (11.613)
Political knowledge	0.137** (0.057)	0.114** (0.057)
Civics or government coursework	3.660** (0.863)	3.540** (0.855)
Grade level of student	–6.315** (1.251)	–6.117** (1.245)
Republican identifiers	. . .[b]	5.886** (3.034)
Democratic identifiers	. . .	–3.798 (3.175)
Independent identifiers	. . .	–2.801 (3.700)
Summary statistic		
Adjusted R^2	.082	.104
N	325	325

Source: Metro Civic Values Survey, 1999–2000, and 2001 follow-up.
**$p \le .05$.
a. Multiple regression analysis; weighted least squares estimation. Values are regression coefficients with standard errors shown in parentheses. Higher scores on the dependent variable indicate support for a more hawkish policy posture.
b. Blanks represent variables not included in model 1 that were included in model 2.

presents the results of our regression analysis of attitudes supporting stricter domestic law enforcement. Notably, those with greater political knowledge and more exposure to government classes did favor a more hawkish posture, suggesting that socialization processes may be making students aware of the widespread calls for improved homeland security (see table 7-5). Those who had taken more than a year of government-related coursework ranked eighteen points higher in support for aggressive action than those who had taken none of these courses. Student scoring a 75 percent on the knowledge test ranked nearly seven points higher in their "hawkishness" than those who had scored a 25 percent. That grade level was negatively associated with support for greater enforcement only serves to bolster the point that it is the content of civics instruction and political knowledge in particular, and not maturation processes more generally, that are responsible for the production of these policy preferences.

The pronounced effects of knowledge and formal instruction remained even after we controlled for the partisan preferences of the adolescents who participated. Note that party identification did make some difference in attitudes on aggressive action: Republicans were about 6 percentage points more supportive of these policies than either Democrats, independents, or those who reported not knowing their party stand. But even after controlling for party identification, those with greater knowledge and more civics instruction were still highly favorable toward calls for aggressive action.

Conclusions

So what have we learned? First, the events of September 11 did elevate the amount of political discussion, knowledge, and efficacy among youth who are typically contemptuous of government. While these events did not significantly increase hostile attitudes toward immigration-induced diversity, they did heighten external efficacy, bolster pride in country, and warm attitudes toward local law enforcement among many who otherwise maintain more hostile attitudes. Naturally, we are in a weak position to comment on the external validity of our findings given that we have argued throughout that geography matters and we have conducted this aspect of our study in a limited number of schools. But the thrust of this chapter has been to suggest that major events—temporal context—also matters. Among the youth we studied, the terrorist attacks had an important socializing impact because they limited the detrimental impact of antipathetic attitudes toward government and authority figures, sometimes completely countering the harmful effects of these negative viewpoints on participation-enabling attitudes. Event-related contexts can be as important to shaping socialization experiences as the spatial contexts we have focused on throughout the book.

In the longer term, other researchers should return to ask whether September 11 was as dramatic an event in the political socialization of Generation Y as some have suggested. From the perspective of our study, it is clear that events such as these are significant to some youth but not to everyone. In a study of local reaction to the Los Angeles riots of 1992, Lawrence Bobo and his colleagues found that many viewpoints about the nature of poverty and racism remained unchanged, in spite of the stunning sequence of violent events that took place in May of that year.[15] While unparalleled in its tragedy, the terrorist attacks appeared to be singular, and the ensuing wars in Afghanistan and Iraq were decisively one-sided, with the war in Afghanistan inflicting few U.S. casualties in its opening months and the later war in Iraq going almost equally well. Most polls of adults showed they had little concern about their own personal safety and security by fall 2002, although most still thought that another terrorist attack was likely, somewhere. Still, schools did not hold antiterrorism drills in the same way in which Cold War–era youth were trained to "duck and cover" in response to a nuclear attack. As people's sense of direct personal threat from terrorism subsided, maybe its socializing potential did, too.

Did our sample of youth "rally round the flag" in response to September 11? The answer is yes. They showed a positive and significant increase in their level of external efficacy, believing that government was more trustworthy and effective after the tragedy than before. And, they did support the president's aggressive foreign policy response, even agreeing that it may be necessary to assassinate hostile foreign leaders. These feelings were also associated with greater nationalistic or "chauvinistic" sentiment, as expressed by responses to questions such as "America is the best" and "I would rather live in the U.S. system than any other." Perhaps the absence of any significant change in attitudes toward immigration-induced diversity was the result of the great pains that President Bush took to avoid a domestic backlash against Arab Americans. But the absence of increased prejudice was probably due more to the fact that the least attentive youth were among those who were the most likely to express opposition to diversity anyway. Their inattentiveness to events meant that their fundamental views could hardly be changed by the terrorist attacks. And here is where we find the limits of event-driven socialization. In each generation, only those who are most attentive to event-related information are likely to be changed much by it. If this is a large group, then the potential for such information to leave a lasting imprint and distinctively shape a generation will be considerable. If the surge in information accompanying events fades quickly, however, then the group whose outlook will have been permanently changed by them will be small, and the generational impact will be muted.

15. Bobo and others (1994).

We found less structure to youthful attitudes in response to September 11 than we would expect to find in an adult population. This is not especially surprising. Foreign policy is not very well understood by many American adults, and it was clear to us that the young people we surveyed had never given it much thought. The socialization process does facilitate the crystallization of stable policy attitudes in support of mainstream or dominant views. We found that policy attitudes in reaction to September 11 were subject to mainstreaming effects as described by John Zaller: those who had more exposure to government-relevant classes and greater factual political knowledge were far more likely to support an aggressive domestic and foreign policy than those who had no related course background and less knowledge. This finding is certainly consistent with earlier research that was critical of civics education because it oriented students toward acceptance of the status quo—if by "status quo" we mean dominant elite positions.

The effects of the terrorist events of September 11 may not be as lasting as many thought they would be, but only time will tell whether the changes we have observed become a permanent and defining fixture of public opinion among Generation Y. The research we have conducted here suggests that these events have had tremendous mobilizing short-term effect, particularly on those who were marginally interested in politics and government prior to the attacks but became much more attentive afterward. Future studies would do well to examine the extent to which the effects we have documented endure for months and years. Domestic policy options such as immigration reform, border security, and greater police power will be controversial among those who perceive the international threat to personal security to be remote. Much of the socializing potential of September 11 depends upon whether this tragic event is eventually dismissed as a kind of fluke—an isolated event—or whether it is seen as something that will happen again, and does.

8   Local Contexts and the Multiple Futures of Generation Y

Who cares about this stupid election? We all know it doesn't matter who gets elected president of Carver [High School]. Do you really think it's going to change anything around here? Make one single person smarter? Or happier? Nicer? The only person it does matter to is the one that gets elected. The same pathetic charade happens every year. And everyone makes the same pathetic promises just so they can put it on their transcripts to get into college. So vote for me, because I don't even want to go to college. And I don't care. And as president, I won't do anything. The only promise I will make is that, if elected, I will immediately dismantle the student government so that none of us will ever have to sit through one of these stupid assemblies again. Or don't vote for me. Who cares? Don't vote at all![1]

These words uttered by the character Tammy Metzler in the feature film *Election* provide us with a popular vision of how political activity is viewed by many young people, to say nothing of the entertainment industry that produced and marketed the movie. *Election* aims to portray the politics of a student government election in a Nebraska high school as

1. Tammy Metzler's campaign speech for student body president from the movie *Election* (1999), based on the novel by Tom Perrotta. Tammy Metzler is played by Jessica Campbell, with direction and screenplay by Alexander Payne.

they would appear if real presidential motives and ambitions were involved. Tammy Metzler's speech, excerpted above, meets with howls of approval from the student body gathered in the gym to hear the three candidates speak. Later she quits the race, but half of the student body votes to disregard the election—"Tammy Metzler voters," the high school principal dryly observes. The other half splits almost evenly between the two remaining candidates. It is a clever film and an entertaining parody of the American electoral process.

But regardless of the ugliness of the motives at work, much more is at stake in real-life elections than in a contest for student government president. After all, officeholders shape the policies that allocate resources and regulate conduct. Politicians may not always be nice people whom we would invite over to dinner, but they do exercise real power. It may sound cute to say that elections do not matter and conclude that nothing ever changes regardless of who wins, but these judgments are naive. Politics is not everything, but it surely is not "nothing." And when large numbers of people conclude that their participation does not matter, their inaction moves from the naive to the positively detrimental. Our work is one of a number of recent contributions that are searching for ways to reverse negative trends in participation and engagement that are rooted in what students learn—or fail to learn—in adolescence.

The socialization process, as we understand it, has several fundamental elements that, if properly primed, will stimulate adolescents to be participatory, politically engaged adults. First, there is the opinion-formation aspect of political learning, where teens and young adults learn that there are debates and issues, and they begin to take sides in these debates, recognizing where their own interests lie. One might call this stage of the process "interest formation" or the rationalization of political choices. We have also referred to it simply as learning to take sides. In the work from previous chapters, we have shown that opinion formation on issues relating to diversity, nationalism, local law enforcement, and the Clinton impeachment occurs more readily in places with politically active environments, where information is plentiful.

The second step in the socialization process is learning that one's participation is not only possible but also worthwhile. This is where the concepts of internal and external efficacy become relevant. Adolescents must conclude that the government is responsive or, at the very least, that they are capable of effectuating change if they involve themselves. We have shown that politically diverse, high-turnout environments bolster assessments of efficacy while lopsided political settings discourage it, even when we control for the socioeconomic status of our respondents' families.

The link between local environments and attitudes consistent with later civic engagement is found in the way specific locales structure information exchange and impart knowledge instrumental to political involvement. Knowledge and information exchange through discussion are reciprocally related, but both undergird the extent to which adolescents take sides and the confidence with which they approach and engage the political system. Knowledge is greater and discussion is more commonly found among youth living in highly active political environments, where adolescents discover multiple viewpoints and soon perceive that information is of some value in the political decisionmaking process. One might ask if we are making a mistake by suggesting that the causal arrow runs from politically active environments to an increased participatory impulse rather than the other way around. Perhaps strong participatory inclinations are more properly considered the precursor to having a vigorous political environment. But this would be a more serious objection if we were studying the discussion, participation, and knowledge levels of the adult population, where there would surely be a strong measure of reciprocal influence. In our case, it makes more sense to suggest that children are shaped by political environments rather than to say that they are engaged in shaping them.

The contexts that shape socializing experiences can also be considered from a temporal standpoint, not just a geographic one. Events are pivotal to the socialization process, as we learned in chapter 7, because they trigger a surge in information. Major events not only attract intense media coverage but also draw more public attention to that coverage, in turn stimulating greater communication in the form of discussion with family and friends. The process of becoming a citizen, though, must begin with information exposure: communication and knowledge are the cornerstones.

In the first part of this final chapter, we examine the role of our participation-enabling and position-taking outcomes in the desire of our young respondents to vote in presidential elections. We focus on voting not because it is the only important form of participation or civic engagement, but because it is relatively easy to do. To be sure, we can find regular voters who are not highly engaged in the civic life of their communities, but we would be very hard pressed to find many nonvoters who are. Voting, or the desire to vote, can be considered a necessary but not an exclusive indicator of political interest and engagement. In the second part of the chapter, we return to the subject of contextual influences on political socialization to ask

Table 8-1. *Direct Effect of Internal and External Efficacy on Intention to Vote among Adolescents, Controlling for Direct and Indirect Effects of Political Discussion and Political Knowledge*[a]
Units as indicated

Explanatory variable	Would vote in 2000	β
Internal efficacy	−0.001 (0.001)	−.02
External efficacy	0.001** (0.0005)	.04
Political discussion	0.026** (0.005)	.11
Political knowledge	0.002** (0.0004)	.09
Date of survey	0.002** (0.0006)	.05
Summary statistic		
N	2,874	
R²	.027	

Source: Metro Civic Values Survey, 1999–2000.

**$p \leq .01$.

a. Maximum likelihood estimation of structural equations. Values are unstandardized regression coefficients with standard errors shown in parentheses. β, standardized regression coefficients. Coefficients for indirect effects are not shown. Dependent variable: 0 = would not vote; 1 = would vote.

what types of communities provide the best opportunities for promoting good citizenship.

Information, Efficacy, and Political Participation

Table 8-1 portrays the relationship between discussion, knowledge, and political efficacy and the intention to vote. We also include a control variable for the date of the survey. First, we should note that not only did discussion and knowledge shape internal efficacy, they had a powerful direct effect on our respondents' intention to vote when they turn eighteen. Every ten-point increase in the political knowledge test score increased the probability of intending to vote by 2 percent. Similarly, every additional day of the week in which an adolescent engaged in political discussion elevated the desire to vote by 3 percent. In fact, the direct effects of internal efficacy on the intention to vote were not statistically significant once we controlled for the more powerful effects of knowledge and discussion.

Assessments of governmental responsiveness, as measured by our indicator of external efficacy, have a small direct impact on intentions to vote, with a 10 percentage point gain in external efficacy producing a modest step-up in the desire to vote later. But by far the most important effects, direct or indirect, on plans to vote are produced by political knowledge and discussion. Apparently, nothing is more critical to developing an adolescent's conviction that he or she has a stake in an election outcome than communication combined with some basic factual knowledge about politics. Once again, these results reinforce our conclusion that discussion and knowledge are the foundation of political socialization, and that environments that promote knowledge and discussion—inside and outside of school—are superior to those that do not.

Position Taking and Political Participation

Just as we have seen that political discussion and knowledge shape efficacy and directly influence intentions to vote, we can also evaluate the effects of discussion and knowledge on the views adolescents come to hold about diversity, nationalism, the Clinton impeachment, and local law enforcement. Discussion and knowledge are critical because they not only generate opinions but also influence the intensity of those opinions on matters of controversy.[2] Table 8-2 demonstrates how the intention to vote increased as political discussion and knowledge shaped specific policy attitudes relevant to political socialization.

Several notable effects are present. First, nationalism and attitudes toward local law enforcement were closely associated with the level of political knowledge. Our results indicated that gains in political knowledge stimulated the conviction that the United States is superior to other nations. Knowledge exerted a similarly positive effect on attitudes toward law enforcement, where more knowledgeable respondents were far more confident of their ability to obtain a fair trial and feel protected by police than those with less knowledge. As we have seen in previous chapters, knowledge levels are highly contingent upon (or endogenous to) community context, suggesting that it is the place where knowledgeable adolescents live that conditions them toward support for American institutions and inspires their confidence in the local police and courts.

---

2. Zaller (1992).

Table 8-2. *Direct Effect of Position Taking on Intention to Vote among Adolescents, Controlling for the Direct and Indirect Effects of Political Discussion and Political Knowledge*[a]

Explanatory variable	Would vote in 2000	β
Nationalism/chauvinism	0.001 (0.0004)	.02
Opposition to immigration	0.0002 (0.0005)	.01
Negativity about police and courts	−0.001** (0.0004)	−.05
Support for Clinton impeachment	0.001** (0.0004)	.04
Political discussion	0.023** (0.004)	.10
Political knowledge	0.002** (0.0004)	.08
Date of survey	0.002** (0.0006)	.04
Summary statistic		
N	2,855	
R^2	.029	

Source: Metro Civic Values Survey, 1999–2000.

**p ≤ .01.

a. Maximum likelihood estimation of structural equations. Values are unstandardized regression coefficients with standard errors shown in parentheses. β, standardized regression coefficients. Coefficients for indirect effects are not shown. Dependent variable: 0 = would not vote; 1 = would vote.

Generally, the acquisition and retention of information about politics and government generate more positive evaluations of the latter's performance. To the extent that this knowledge originates from exposure to civics education and media sources, our findings may provide evidence of an indoctrinating effect. Certainly earlier socialization scholarship was highly critical of news media and social studies curricula for their uncritical support of American political institutions. Our findings are also consistent with the simple notion that those who learn more about politics like the subject matter, or at least do not go out of their way to avoid it. Knowledge and political discussion are rooted in communities that exhibit an appreciation of, perhaps even an affection for, politics and government, which is then communicated to the offspring who live there.

Political discussion had its most pronounced impact on shaping the direction of attitudes toward the Clinton impeachment and diversity. Daily discussants exhibited far greater support for the removal of the president than those who avoided all such discourse (see table 8-2). Teens who followed television news about the impeachment story were far more eager to discuss its progress than those who avoided the media coverage. Youth who engaged in more political discussion also were about four percent less opposed to diversity than those who completely avoided such discussions. Those who discussed politics more frequently also expressed less criticism of local law enforcement.

It is not just having a definite opinion on policy issues that matters to socialization. The direction of one's position or the specific side one takes is sometimes just as important. We found that students who were opposed to the Clinton impeachment were quite demoralized about government and expressed less of a desire to vote than those who were supportive. We found no tendency for opponents of the impeachment to want to vote out of a sense of outrage or disgust. Rather, the proceedings' negative and bitterly partisan tone simply served as a turnoff to future engagement. Cynical attitudes toward local police and courts were also associated with lower interest in future participation. The effect was not huge, but a one standard deviation increase in hostility toward local police and courts dropped intended participation by about 2 percentage points ($p \leq .01$), just slightly more than opposition to the impeachment. Unfortunately, multiple participation-depressing attitudes often accumulate within a single youthful population and then are carried over into adulthood, helping to explain why some locales vote at much lower rates than others.

Notably, the positions taken regarding immigration-induced diversity and nationalism were not prominent forces shaping future intent to vote. Apparently, attitudes about immigration and ethnicity were not politicized among the adolescent population in the same way that the presidential scandals and views of law enforcement were. Whether they opposed or supported immigration, a similar proportion of respondents indicated their intention to vote, suggesting that attitudes toward diversity have no direct bearing on participation. And chauvinistic views of the American political system did not translate into a significantly stronger desire to vote, although we did find a positive but statistically weak association once we controlled for the direct effects of political knowledge and discussion. Contrary to our expectations, instilling in students the conviction that the

American system is the best form of government and convincing them that they are better off here than anywhere else did very little to increase intentions to vote upon reaching the eligible age.

What is the impact on political efficacy of having certain specific, crystallized opinions about nationalism, impeachment, local law enforcement, and diversity? Those opposed to the impeachment and those expressing more nationalistic sentiment scored lower in internal and external efficacy (data not shown). Those who were suspicious of local police and courts were less efficacious than those who had more confidence in law enforcement authorities. These results have clear policy implications. One pathway to higher efficacy and greater future engagement could be through exposure to positive models of police work. Improving the quality, responsiveness, and fairness of local law enforcement may be one of the best ways to improve levels of civic engagement among youth in big cities. If the community policing movement has accomplished these goals, then spread the word.

As for the impeachment proceedings, we learned from our survey that this highly divisive effort did nothing to improve adolescent efficacy and stimulate the desire to participate. Undoubtedly, it was the contentious partisan character of the Clinton impeachment that embittered many of the students we interviewed, regardless of their partisan leanings. Does this mean that Congress should never again initiate the impeachment process for fear of depressing efficacy and civic engagement? Of course not, but what it does mean is that educators may need to develop in students a greater appreciation for the role of conflict and partisanship in the conduct of American constitutional processes.[3] Our visits to dozens of classrooms convinced us that many adolescents do not understand the centrality of conflict and disagreement to the operation of government in the United States. Educators have done a poor job instilling in students the understanding that conflict is an ever-present feature of our political system and that its existence does not provide sufficient reason for noninvolvement, much less despair. Instead of viewing conflict as a necessary and essential feature of liberal democratic processes, adolescents and adults come to view it as endless disputation, not realizing that one alternative commonly found elsewhere in the world is a crushing dictatorial silence.

Finally, opposition to diversity was associated with lower internal efficacy—an artifact of the low self-esteem and lower educational aspirations

3. Bennett (1997).

among those most threatened by high levels of immigration. In earlier chapters, we learned that opposition to diversity was concentrated among certain populations and closely associated with those who have no plans to attend college. The impression that immigrant competitors may threaten the livelihood of those who will work at low- to no-skill jobs is probably an accurate one in many locations, pitting the native-born against Asians and Latinos in larger cities. These natives understandably feel powerless and frustrated in the face of the immigrant influx, believing that government policy is neither representing their interests nor looking out for their future. They ultimately decide that they have no voice in what government does, and their chain of reasoning leads them to the conclusion that participation is a waste of time.

Youth "At Risk" for Nonparticipation

The findings from this study have reinforced much of the previous research that has identified poorly socialized populations. Among our respondents, those most at risk for nonparticipation were blacks, Latinos, the poor and those living in a single-parent household, the children of the foreign-born, women, those with low educational aspirations, those living in noncompetitive or low-turnout political environments, the nonreligious, those who are not attentive to news media, students who avoid or simply are not exposed to discussions of politics, and those who dislike their government-related courses and otherwise doubt that school authorities treat them fairly. For the respondents who possess more than a few of these risk factors, the likelihood of nonparticipation as an adult is exceedingly high. For the respondents who have only two or three of these traits, there is the possibility that the presence of positive forces in an adolescent's environment may neutralize or overcome the ones that diminish participatory impulses.

Imagine that each risk factor is a kind of weight that adds to the inertia holding one away from moving toward the goal of responsible citizenship.[4] Those most heavily burdened may never reach the point where they even register to vote, much less volunteer for a campaign. The most burdened citizens possess a sufficiently high number of risk factors that noninvolvement is the most likely outcome. Others may possess some of the risk factors, but positive forces in their environment, such as stimulating political

4. Plutzer (2002).

campaigns and adult models of participation, can help to overcome the factors that otherwise predict cynicism.

It is easy to argue that parents should assume more responsibility for civically educating their children, but getting from here to there is not a wide and straight path. Mitigating the sources of poor socialization may be the responsibility of parents; however, if parents were completely adequate to the task, we would not have such widespread nonparticipation among young adults in the first place. Nonparticipatory attitudes, just like those favoring civic engagement, are intergenerationally transmitted. And for children who live in communities characterized by poor citizenship, one of the only places where good citizenship can be modeled is in school.

Several of the factors affecting good citizenship are directly manipulable by education policymakers, including aspects of school climate and the social studies curriculum and its instructional methodology. We believe that excellent classroom instruction about government and politics is critical for building knowledge. But exposure to civics-related coursework is not enough to make more than a marginal difference for the vast majority of students. Far more important to predicting students' knowledge and discussion levels is whether they acquire a liking for the subject matter. Students who disliked the study of government scored as much as twenty points lower than others on our political knowledge test. If school-based reforms are directed solely at increasing students' exposure to social studies coursework without reshaping the content to make it more stimulating, they will not accomplish much.

Our research indicates that discussion about educational policy needs shift from empty curriculum requirements to development of customized curriculum content and improvement of instructional style. Experiments with curriculum reform, mentoring, guidance, and instructional method may go a long way toward revealing those techniques for teaching about politics that can compensate for living in neighborhoods with poor involvement. Hiring social studies personnel that have an interest in and knowledge related to classroom instruction is yet another means for ensuring better citizenship education. This latter recommendation may seem obvious, but we visited a surprising number of classrooms where we came away questioning the teacher's background and interest in the subject matter.

Exposure to television news and the amount of political discussion about current events may also be affected by curriculum modification. News media exposure, as we learned, stimulated political discussion but did not contribute directly to the basic factual knowledge that we evaluated. However, news sources may have contributed to information gains that we did not detect with our particular research design. Several studies have documented that citizens do learn about politics from exposure to television campaign advertising.[5] And discussion is causally linked to knowledge, so television news is not completely without value as a tool for learning via the medium of interpersonal exchange. We suspect that exposure to television news can compensate for aspects of an adolescent's environment that have a depressing effect on discussion and knowledge, such as living in a low-turnout area with little party or candidate mobilization activity.

Along with others, we have also come to view bad political socialization as part of a more general problem of adolescent development and motivation. Many students who suffer from poor school performance and low self-esteem exhibit the corresponding characteristics of low political efficacy and system support. At the same time, it is not inevitable that students with less of an academic orientation become badly socialized. The answer to the problem of low civic engagement is not necessarily to make everyone want to go on to a four-year college and become a physician or a professor. Many observers apparently believe that only people with college degrees are capable of making informed political judgments—that somehow good citizenship requires a certain requisite number of years of formal education. This makes us wonder how all of those uneducated (albeit male) masses in nineteenth century America managed to get to the polls and be so civically engaged.

V. O. Key Was Right

Although there is undeniable evidence that education and knowledge go hand in hand, and that formal education greatly facilitates political choice and decisionmaking, more years in a classroom are not the only ticket to good citizenship. Nor does that mean that whatever learning is necessary to become a good citizen is packaged in a college-prep curriculum. Legions of high school adolescents remain destined for perfectly respectable working lives as metro bus drivers, stay-at-home parents, food service workers, longshoremen, and bank tellers. If the only path to civic engagement is through formal education, we might as well give up on these citizens ever passing muster, to say nothing of those who wind up below them in society's socioeconomic strata.

---

5. Ansolabehere and Iyengar (1995).

The connection between citizenship and formal education has been overemphasized to the point where we fail to consider other avenues for achieving political literacy. Much of what needs to be learned to exercise competent political judgment can be picked up from sources outside school. If our visits to rural communities have taught us anything, they have shown us that high levels of political engagement can be found among populations that are not especially well educated or wealthy. Adolescents destined for full-time jobs after high school, and even high school drop-outs, can be politically active citizens provided that they grow up seeing models of good citizenship or experience political campaigns that remind them that their participation is worthwhile. School is important, but it is not everything.

Writing in the middle of the last century, political scientist V. O. Key pointed to the value of partisan diversity and high turnout as driving forces behind democratic governance. The habit of nonvoting resulted in a shrunken electorate in one-party states. The limited electorate, in turn, influenced the nature of factional politics within a single party "by practically eliminating from the voting population substantial blocs of citizens whose political interests and objectives, if activated, would furnish the motive power for important political movements and demands."[6] Key went on to add that a government founded on democratic principles became some other sort of regime when large proportions of its citizens were nonvoters.

Political party competition and the associated mobilization efforts by parties and candidates were seen by Key to be the instrument of democratic restoration. Notably, he made no mention in his landmark work of the need to improve formal education in schools, although he did attack the anachronistic presence of suffrage restrictions in state law, which have since been ruled unconstitutional. In the last several years, social scientists have rediscovered the problem of low turnout, alarmed by the fact that despite the elimination of suffrage restrictions and the amazing improvements in the level of education over the course of the last century, participation rates have steadily declined, currently hovering at around 51 percent. While a few observers have claimed that the drop in turnout has been exaggerated, the decline is still real and significant.[7] Gerber and Green argue persuasively that turnout has dropped because people are no longer being asked

---

6. Key (1949, p. 508).
7. See McDonald and Popkin (2001) for a challenge to the idea of significant voter decline.

to vote—and being asked face to face is really what counts.[8] Party and candidate mobilization efforts have diminished with the extinction of politically competitive elections in many areas, along with a shift toward more professionalized campaigns that rely increasingly on slick but impersonal technology rather than door-to-door canvassing.

What we have found is that adolescents' sense of political efficacy and level of political knowledge is greatly enhanced in politically active areas that exhibit partisan diversity and high turnout. While we doubt that there is a lot of door-to-door campaigning going on in the highly participatory neighborhoods we visited, what we do find are adults who are interested in discussing politics with young people and modeling good citizenship behavior by voting regularly. Thus even if a teenager's parents are not modeling participatory behavior, the adolescent can still see relatives, neighbors, and other adults in the community taking elections seriously.

Is Rural Homogeneity Better?

Were the communities in which the most efficacious students were produced always small, homogeneous towns—as might be suggested by some of the literature on civic engagement?[9] Our rural homogeneous schools did rank high, but it was not just our small towns that raised children destined for involvement. Many suburbs produced highly efficacious and knowledgeable adolescents, although the diversity of suburban communities makes it difficult to generalize to all suburban locations. Not all suburbs should be maligned as barren and devoid of meaningful examples of good citizenship; on the contrary, we found many examples of good socialization in suburban neighborhoods.

Certainly some suburbs enjoy the advantages associated with high socioeconomic status, including excellent schooling, but in the suburbs where we found the most knowledgeable and efficacious children, socioeconomic status was not the principal source. Instead, we found that the most serious political campaigns are waged in suburban locales that exhibit substantial political and racial diversity. The youth in these locations are being exposed to viewpoints other than the ones they hear at home, and this greatly enhances the learning process. Much of the development of partisan identification, for example, lies in the ability to see which social

8. Gerber and Green (2000).
9. Campbell (2002); Gamm and Putnam (1999); Putnam (2000); Skocpol, Ganz, and Munson (2000).

groups underlie the two parties; then making the match between the partisan allegiances of those social groups and their self-identification with one or more of those groups.[10] Youth are more likely to learn to defend their parties' positions, to others and to themselves, when they are in the presence of peers and adults who are of the opposite party.

Many of our suburban youth were not highly tolerant of immigration-induced diversity; it rather depended on the extent to which these youth (or their parents) felt threatened by it. But this is why we have drawn a distinction between the position-taking and the participation-enabling aspects of the socialization process. People may be highly active and participatory, and take any number of positions on policy issues. Often it is not the particular side taken that counts as much as the fact that crystallized opinions have formed, for this indicates an appreciation for politics in general as a way to socialize conflict and make it possible for people to disagree without doing harm to one another.

Multiple Outlooks for the Millennial Generation

The current generation of youth, some 76 million strong, will begin to replace the baby boom generation in the electorate by about 2010. Given that the size of these two cohorts varies from place to place across the nation, the electoral change wrought by this great generational turnover will not be uniform.[11] At some locations, the change will be virtually imperceptible, while other places could undergo a period of electoral volatility not seen since the New Deal. Saddled with the heavy burden of providing for the retiring Baby Boom generation in its old age, younger generations are likely to carry into the electorate very different attitudes about social security, the social security payroll tax, and healthcare benefits than their elders. This raises the specter of generational cleavages that may divide much of the electorate in the first half of the new century, with Generation Y activists threatening to reduce payouts to the most affluent Boomers.[12]

Yet our work suggests that it is hard to generalize to the entire population of youth in a specific generation given the persistence of contextual

10. Green, Palmquist, and Schickler (2002).
11. Gimpel, Morris and Armstrong (forthcoming).
12. Howe and Strauss (2000, p. 318).

effects. The Millennial Generation is encountering greater ethnic diversity than any in the past, but many will still grow up having never met an immigrant. Instead of a single distinctive generation, it probably makes more sense to talk about multiple generations growing up at the same time but subject to varying environmental forces. There are some unifying experiences and watershed events, such as September 11, but much of the current research suggests that reactions to these events depend on the distinctive psychological histories of individuals, which are significantly influenced by local environmental conditions.

Clearly some adolescents will confront head-on the challenges posed by ethnic and cultural pluralism and the demise of a single dominant racial group. While we saw indications among the youth we surveyed that this transition could be smooth and relatively effortless, these signs most often cropped up in affluent areas where students were comfortably college bound. Among the youth in our lower-income areas, we saw signs that acceptance of cultural change and diversity could be quite slow if it comes with economic pressure on the low-wage, low-skill labor market. Sustained high in-migration of low-skill labor from abroad threatens to exacerbate economic and racial cleavages in certain regions of the country.

On the other hand, in places more accepting of diversity, interracial marriages and multiracial children are likely to be ever more common as the nation approaches the 2020s. With fewer families able to claim that they hail from a "pure" ancestral stock, there will be social forces at work to resolve ethnic and racial tensions and dissolve cultural differences. One very positive outcome of the September 11 tragedy would be a push for greater cross-cultural and cross-racial understanding, steering a multiethnic student body toward a search for a common history out of which can be carved a common experience. This is an optimistic scenario but not necessarily the most likely one.

We detect no universal signs across our study area, much less throughout the entire country, that the students we surveyed are bound for heroic deeds or fantastically high levels of political activism, yet many of them will become highly engaged nonetheless. What do we make of the high level of cynicism present in some schools? Pessimism about what government can accomplish was present in most of the schools we visited, even those schools where a large share of the parents were *employed* by the government. And while we have repeatedly noted that more than a few people grow up failing to appreciate the conflictual aspects of our political system, some of this pessimism is a sign of a self-reliant spirit that sometimes comes across as defiance. There may be a silver lining to the variably dense clouds of cynicism we found in the places we visited.

The more enlightened of the cynics may know something that the other students do not. The budgetary and programmatic fits and starts of the last forty years have conveyed the message that the government is not a reliable long-term partner. Some who have grown up with less faith in government are not going to be content to wait for state and federal policymakers to fix a problem, and as a result, they may be more inclined to get involved to address it themselves through nongovernmental, or at least nonfederal, means. It is not inevitable that low expectations for government responsiveness (low external efficacy) should lead directly to widespread nonparticipation in the political arena. Indeed, the opposite may well be true. Efficacy levels are not only a function of how government responds but also of what we expect of it. If expectations for what government can capably manage are adjusted downward, citizens may conclude, rightly, that when restricted to an appropriate sphere of activity, government involvement is a genuinely beneficial and entirely positive force. Imagine the stellar heights political participation could reach if cynicism were reduced by appropriate expectations. The truth about what government can capably manage may eventually dawn on all of us, and maybe we should welcome the day it does.

The Effect of Place: Policy Implications

We began with the hunch that places may matter to the way young people are socialized, and we believe that our work has established the relevance of the local environment to attitudes consistent with positive political socialization. We bring our work to a conclusion by summarizing some policy recommendations that we think follow from this understanding of the role of place. We direct our recommendations to two basic areas: policies designed to enhance civics education and curriculum, and policies designed to promote political diversity and activism in local environments. Some of these recommendations are familiar, others less so. Some are vague, pointing only in a general policy direction. We do not pretend to be experts at implementation, but we do hope that some of these ideas are discussed and that it is not the most controversial ones that are highlighted at the expense of the others.

Civics Instruction and Curriculum

Our work shows that political socialization does not and should not be presumed to work the same way everywhere, independent of contextual forces or local distributions of opinion that can either mitigate or aggravate individual risk factors that predict nonparticipation. A one-size-fits-all social studies curriculum and an accompanying test will not work if socialization is really more locally contingent than we have been led to believe. Rather than adopting uniform state or national standards, standards should be locally modified to meet the challenges and needs of specific populations.

The precise standards for civics education have long been debated among political philosophers, education scholars, and policymakers. While we believe this debate is necessary, there is unlikely to ever be complete consensus. A level of basic knowledge about governmental institutions, procedures, and history is necessary for students to grow up to be competent democratic citizens, capable of political discourse and participation. But we contend that the emphasis of civics education should be less about pinpointing a precise level of necessary political knowledge and more about how to best teach students so that they remain interested in politics and government as they enter adulthood. Besides, standards have already been identified: the National Assessment of Educational Progress Civics Assessment test as well as state-level standards are clearly reasonable guides.[13]

We also believe that scores from standardized tests should not be the sole measure of performance—either for a child or a school. Value-added assessment seems to us to better incorporate local conditions in the evaluation of performance and learning. Value-added assessment measures and compares the gains in achievement, or the "value added" by a school or teacher, from one point in time to another.[14] Because it can provide a baseline at the beginning of the schooling experience, it gives some indication of what students "bring in" with them from outside of school. When used in concert with standardized tests, as well as other measures of educational progress such as dropout rates, attendance rates, and postsecondary education, value-added assessment provides a good tool to gauge student and school progress.

13. Gibson and Levine (2003, pp. 32–33).
14. For a discussion of the pros and cons of value-added assessment, see Ballou and others (2002).

The emphasis on high-stakes testing has forced policymakers to be concerned almost solely with indicators of factual political knowledge. While knowledge is important and is linked to efficacy, political efficacy does have other sources, particularly political discussion. Discussion's role in building confidence and efficacy points us toward classroom climate and instructional styles. Where students feel comfortable expressing their opinions, especially about controversial topics, their confidence in their own ability to deliberate about politics increases. A teacher's willingness to discuss controversial issues is important for a child's political learning. An inviting classroom climate will teach students to be critical citizens, capable of discussion even with others who disagree with them.[15]

Too often we found the most creative and dedicated civics instructors in the schools that least needed them, where there were ample resources outside the schools that could teach the lessons of good citizenship. Much of the focus of civic engagement research has been directed toward schools because many children are unlikely to receive instruction in civics in any other venue. To the extent that forces outside of school cannot be counted upon to properly socialize young people, schools will be expected to bear more of the responsibility for teaching the values consistent with good citizenship. This is likely to place more pressure on urban school systems to reform curriculum and experiment in search of effective instructional styles. We need a policy initiative that will appropriately compensate and reward teachers for succeeding in the most challenging environments. It is hard to fail in a classroom in which all of the students have aspirations to attend Princeton.

Immigrant youth and the children of immigrant parents are commonly at a disadvantage when it comes to learning about the American political system. In addition to existing compensatory courses for new immigrants, such as English as a Second Language, immigrant children need compensatory education in civics and social studies. They are the least likely to receive information about American government from home, and they have not been socialized with the same symbols and history lessons that children born in the United States have been.

We support programs that link the local community to the classroom. Local government should sponsor internships for high school students and encourage local businesses to do the same. Community leaders, war veter-

---

15. Torney, Oppenheim, and Farnen (1975); Niemi and Junn (1998); Torney-Purta and others (2001).

ans, and state and local politicians should be brought in as guest speakers in social studies classes to discuss their experiences and engage students in real-world decisionmaking activities. Students should be rewarded for participation in school-based, as well as community-based, civic activities. Service-learning programs can work, although obviously some settings and internship experiences will be better than others. Research has shown these programs to be successful in activating students beyond the course requirement when teachers use class time to make explicit links between course material and community service.[16]

Social studies curricula should emphasize the meaning of party labels and assist students in making the connection between the major parties and the social groups that comprise the party coalitions. Teachers need not take sides in communicating the meaning of party labels, but learning what the parties stand for, and for whom, is a critical part of learning to be an informed voter. A critical threshold in the socialization process is crossed when youth learn which sorts of "social, economic, and ideological groups affiliate with each party, while sorting out which group labels properly apply to themselves."[17]

Teachers must take seriously how they present American political institutions. Course materials that present American political institutions and leaders as hopelessly rigged and corrupt instill cynicism and negative attitudes about government. At the same time, it is not necessary to portray American history without any of its flaws and shortcomings, as this will only reinforce the confusion students experience when what they see in their daily lives does not correspond to what they learn in school. Students are likely to simply disregard civics instruction if it is wholly unlike their own life experiences. American history and government are not "all bad" or "all good," and teachers should help adolescents learn to appreciate the difficulty of making important decisions in a complex and uncertain world.

Finally, through our discussions with students at the high schools in our study, we found there was widespread disdain for conflict and political argument. Except for those students who would be interested in politics regardless of their school experience, we found most students who disliked civics and government to express open contempt for the disputatious nature of political discourse typically displayed in media coverage of Congress and the presidency, to say nothing of the interminable debates on

16. For a review of service-learning practices and results, see Mann and Patrick (2000).
17. Green, Palmquist, and Schickler (2002, p. 137).

programs such as CNN's *Crossfire*. Social studies instruction should do much more to highlight the role of conflict and disagreement in the operation of American political institutions, while showing that these disagreements are soluble and manageable.

Students must be assured that disagreement and diversity can be safe, that people need not take offense when others do not agree with them. They should be shown examples of disputes that were resolved peacefully, through compromise, and that even more persistent disagreements can be tolerated. In some schools, there are extracurricular activities, such as mock trials or the debating team, that help adolescents learn the value of principled dispute. However, relatively few students participate in these activities. Elements of debate and discussion should be incorporated into all social studies courses, and in many other areas of the curriculum, such as philosophy and history.

Bolstering Political Diversity and Encouraging Activism

We believe that our results show the importance not only of good civics education but also of growing up in a politically and socially diverse environment. While the community is certainly not as manipulable from a policy standpoint as civics curricula or assessments of educational progress, we believe there are measures that states and communities can take to create more participation-enabling environments. We want to emphasize that schools are not the only answer for elevating the level of informed participation.

Political leaders of the local minority party should target schools in the most politically insular and isolated communities for visits so that the students in that area become exposed to different ways of thinking about politics and issues. For Democratic Party leaders, this would involve sending representatives to the most rural and heavily Republican locations, where the homogeneity of pro-GOP views is most likely to squelch local Democratic voices and discourage more open classroom discussions. For Republican party leaders, this would involve dispatching speakers to the most urban school systems, where the student body is often greater than 90 percent minority and perhaps just as Democratic in their political orientation. Having a regular staff of speakers, employed as part of the political party hierarchy, who regularly visit schools where students tend to be of opposite political stripe will go a long way toward inculcating a respect for political difference and disagreement that is entirely absent in locations where only one side dominates. As part of the socialization process, students need to learn that there are legitimate reasons for holding opposing viewpoints. At the same time, they can benefit by having to defend their policy positions to others and to themselves.[18] At locations where dissonant views do not surface as a natural product of local diversity, dissonance must be introduced through other means.

In addition to party representatives, White House and congressional leaders should fund a speakers' bureau made up of high- and mid-level political appointees from major cabinet level agencies. On a rotating basis, these speakers would visit secondary schools to promote positive messages about government activity while illustrating pathways for resolving disagreement and reaching decisions in their respective issue and policy areas.

To the extent possible, election districts should be drawn so as to maximize political heterogeneity and diversity rather than to protect incumbent officeholders. District lines should be drawn on the basis of nonpolitical criteria, such as population equality and contiguity. Several states, including Arizona, Colorado, Hawaii, Iowa, Missouri, Montana, New Jersey, Ohio, Pennsylvania, and Washington have implemented independent, nonpartisan commissions to draft redistricting plans. In response to the 2000 census, Iowa was the only state where such a commission redrew the districts and gave the legislature an up-or-down vote only, with no chance for piecemeal revisions. Although all incumbents eventually won, in the 2002 elections, five of six incumbents for the U.S. House and Senate in Iowa faced serious opposition. Young people should be confronted with elections that provide a serious partisan choice. In general, youth across many one-party locations are in desperate need of exposure to political diversity, partly to demonstrate that multiple viewpoints can coexist peacefully and that disagreement is not intolerable.

One of the best instruments of positive political socialization is responsive government, or at least government that is not widely corrupt. Working to create less discriminatory policing and a more professional, serviceoriented bureaucracy are two means to this end. In addition, focusing on local rather than national government in the classroom may also help demonstrate that government can be responsive to those problems that are often most salient to people. Frequently, social studies and current events courses depend heavily upon national media sources and on national political issues. Examining local problems and local solutions can enhance the perception that government is responsive.

18. Mutz (2002a, p. 116).

Residential integration of ethnic minorities with middle- and upper-income white populations is another instrument for building a positive socialization experience. Conservatives would suggest that this goal is met by providing economic opportunity and upward mobility for those on the lower rungs. Liberals would suggest that fair housing policy and affirmative action are instruments to the integration of minorities with whites. We are agnostic on these options, believing that there is more than one way to achieve the same goal. Real-world policy problems can rarely be resolved from within a single party's ideology or dominant policy framework.

In addition to contributing to the policy discussions on these critical topics, we hope our work helps to resuscitate political socialization research in the social sciences. The time is ripe for reconsidering the findings from earlier studies. Times are changing. During the next two decades, the Depression-era generation, those who came of age during the 1930s and 1940s, will make a final exit from the electorate through mortality. The Baby Boom generation, the large post–World War II birth cohort currently in its late forties and fifties, will be entering retirement, and it too will begin to drop out of the electorate. Bracketing the other end of the population distribution is an enormous and fast-growing population under age twenty-five. These are the children—and among the youngest, the grandchildren—of the Baby Boomers.[19] While some of these young people will become good citizens, the outlook for their political engagement is far from uniform. An overall decline in the level of voter participation with the passing of the Baby Boom generation would appear to lie ahead. Unless we come to a better understanding of the local forces that create good citizens and do what we can to stimulate them in the places where they are not operating on their own, good "small-d" democrats may sometime in the future pine for the days when voter participation levels were at 51 percent.

---

19. Gimpel, Morris, and Armstrong (forthcoming).

Sample Characteristics and Description

We selected school districts with an aim to represent a variety of geographic contexts in the Baltimore-Washington metropolitan area. The goal in the beginning was to utilize multistage cluster sampling, although in the end, the exigencies associated with ensuring the cooperation of school authorities meant that we had to settle for less than a perfect random draw of adolescent respondents at the third stage. We began with clusters consisting of fourteen school districts (counties) within the greater Baltimore-Washington, D.C., metropolitan areas that represented urban, suburban, and rural contexts with varying levels of homogeneity for relevant population characteristics such as race, socioeconomic status, political partisanship, and political participation. Two of the fourteen districts where we originally sought the cooperation of school authorities turned us down, and they were replaced with two demographically and politically similar districts.

At the next stage, we selected schools out of these fourteen districts by random draw, choosing a larger number of schools (up to five) in the districts with larger student populations. Each district had a minimum of one school site selected. In accord with sampling theory, the more heterogeneous the population in each school district, the larger our sample of schools had to be. In general, then, our sample involves a large number of suburban schools exhibiting maximum heterogeneity on relevant characteristics such as race, socioeconomic status, and political viewpoint, and a smaller number of rural and inner-city schools where the student populations were much more homogeneous using these criteria.

Once the school sites were selected, we had our "sampling frame" from which student respondents could be selected. We aimed to survey between 70 and 200 students at each of the twenty-nine school sites, contingent upon the size of the school. But we could not simply wander in on a given school day and ask 150 students to drop everything and leave their classes to complete a thirty- to forty-minute survey. In the practice of social science research, is not always possible to draw a random probability sample of a population where each element has a perfectly equal chance of being selected. Although it was certainly possible to come by a list of all possible respondents at our twenty-nine school sites, the challenge was that we could not implement a method of selecting those respondents that fit the "equal chance" criteria. This was because the cooperation of school authorities was not unconditional. Teachers and educational administrators are understandably protective of their curriculum and work hard to maintain the organization and order of the school day. Calling randomly selected students out of separate classrooms to participate was judged to be entirely too disruptive.

Teachers and school officials were willing to participate so long as we added something to the social studies curriculum (by way of a fifteen-minute postsurvey presentation on our work), and we did not interrupt classrooms or disturb the course of the school day. We also met other requirements to ensure accountability to parents and maintain the privacy of adolescent respondents. Survey respondents were guaranteed anonymity and no names, social security numbers, related identifying information, or school records were collected. Meeting these various conditions meant that we surveyed classrooms of students from social studies courses (typically history, economics, government, psychology, or sociology). Fortunately, social studies is a sufficiently ubiquitous part of the high school curriculum that we were permitted a wide choice of classrooms, achievement levels, grade levels, and student populations.

As a result of these necessary adjustments to the design, we wound up requesting visits to classrooms where we could obtain a representative sample of the school's population using criteria that would best promote the representativeness of the sample, primarily achievement level and race or ethnicity of students. We were especially careful not to survey more than one "honors" level classroom containing only the most academically capable students, except at several schools where the overwhelming majority of students were tracked in the honors, college preparatory stream. Following administration of the survey, and the short presentation about our work, we usually used the remainder of the class (varying between five and thirty minutes) for a focused discussion on topics covered by the survey.

Given that our research is principally aimed at exploring relationships between socialization outcomes and underlying attitudinal, demographic, and contextual characteristics, a perfectly representative sample is probably not critical. But sometimes the sample and population characteristics match up well even when less than ideal selection strategies are employed. In spite of the potential sampling error resulting from clustering and from nonprobabilistic methods of selection at each site, our sample comes remarkably close to representing the school populations in terms of their racial and ethnic characteristics. More information about the schools included in the study can be requested directly from the authors. In the aggregate, the sample and population proportions are even more similar than they are at each individual site. (See table A-1 for total sample characteristics by race and ethnicity.)

Other characteristics of our respondents are presented in tables A-1 and A-2 by quartiles of the population density of zip codes in which the schools were located. We present density by quartiles because they approximate our initial aim to ensure a mix of urban (high density), suburban (mid- to high density), and rural (low density) areas. Using density as a measure for urbanism is also desirable because many locations otherwise classified as suburbs exhibit all of the characteristics of large inner-city neighborhoods: low socioeconomic status, high levels of social disorder, and racial homogeneity (predominantly African American). Although usually there was no student population information available on the political variables presented in table A-2, the comparisons at least exhibit the prima facie representation of the sample by exhibiting its variability and by closely approximating what is known about the traits of the adult population of the metropolitan Baltimore-Washington area from the 2000 U.S. census and recent election returns.

Finally, we also examined the distributional features of our measure of socioeconomic status for each density quartile (see appendix B for description of this measure). While this indicator for socioeconomic status is undoubtedly "noisy" as it is derived from a rank ordering of income estimates associated with students' descriptions of their parents' occupations,

Table A-1. *Demographic Characteristics of the Metro Civic Values Study*
Sample Population, by Quartiles of Population Density
Percent, except as indicated[a]

Characteristic	Lowest density quartile	Second density quartile	Third density quartile	Highest density quartile
Both parents native born	92.5	60.3	66.9	56.2
One parent foreign born	6.5	8.1	9.3	7.9
Both parents foreign born	1.0	31.5	23.8	36.0
N	709	799	782	609
African American	7.3	12.4	45.5	36.2
White	85.6	58.2	29.4	30.0
Latino	1.0	4.0	7.7	18.2
Asian	1.0	18.7	8.1	6.8
Biracial/multiracial	4.2	6.3	8.4	8.5
N	713	791	782	614
Students from married couple families	63.2	71.0	54.4	55.6
Students from divorced families	24.0	17.8	19.9	19.1
Students whose parents never married	4.5	4.3	15.3	14.0
N	451	717	804	628

Source: Metro Civic Values Survey, 1999–2000.

a. Percentages are from unweighted data.

the forty-two-point scale does exhibit the distribution we would expect in each density quartile: lower median socioeconomic status in the most rural and the most urban areas, and higher socioeconomic status in the locations of middling population density (suburban areas).

Sample weights were constructed and used in the regression analysis to correct for the unequal sizes of sample subclasses.[1] The weights are defined by the inverse probability of selection and corrected for the slight over-sampling or undersampling of populations in some districts within the study area. The weights are defined by

$$Weight_i = 1/\{N \ of \ Districts \times [(School \ n/District \ N) \times (School \ n/School \ N)]\},$$

where *Weight_i* is the sample weight for individual *i*, *N of Districts* is equal to the number of school district clusters (14), *School n* is equal to the num-

1. Kish (1987, section 4.5).

Table A-2. *Political Characteristics and Post–High School Aspirations of the Metro Civic Values Survey Sample Population, by Quartiles of Population Density*

Percent, except as indicated[a]

Characteristic	Lowest density quartile	Second density quartile	Third density quartile	Highest density quartile
Republican identifiers	29.4	20.1	14.1	14.2
Democratic identifiers	27.6	49.5	53.4	50.7
Independent identifiers	11.1	7.7	9.1	10.1
Don't know identification	32.0	22.7	23.4	25.0
N	722	770	747	613
No plans to attend college	22.2	11.2	19.8	19.8
Plans to attend two-year college	16.4	5.1	13.9	15.9
Plans to attend four-year college	66.1	85.3	71.0	68.0
N	694	798	778	621

Source: Metro Civic Values Survey, 1999–2000.

a. Percentages are from unweighted data.

ber of students sampled at the particular school in which i is a student, *District N* is equal to the number of students in the entire district in which i is a student, and *School N* is equal to the total number of students in the school in which i is a student.

The need to use these weights is debatable. Their use typically makes little difference to the magnitude of coefficients in our regression analyses, but the variances are typically increased by their use, and consequently the standard errors (and significance tests) are often changed. The fundamental conclusions of our study remained robust to specification of the models with and without the weights, so we present the results using the weighted data because they adjust for the size of population subclasses that were less perfectly captured by the raw data alone.

Survey Items, Coding, and Descriptive Statistics

To avoid repetition in the following table, we provide the description, range of coding, and means and standard deviations of only the new variables that are introduced in each chapter.

Units as indicated

Survey items	Range of values or coding scheme	Mean	Standard deviation
Dependent variables			
Political knowledge (test score based on the following seven items)[a]	0–100	70.44	21.50
How many senators?		61.80	48.99
Who is elected to preside in the U.S. House?		75.60	42.93
Where can you find the Bill of Rights?		74.20	43.76
Presidential elections held four years?		89.20	30.99
Power divided in a federal system?		61.00	48.77
Who is the current vice president?		94.00	23.82
Who is the current chief justice?		62.80	48.35

Survey items	Range of values or coding scheme	Mean	Standard deviation
Internal efficacy	0–4[b]		
I have a good understanding of issues		1.81	1.02
I'm as well informed as others		1.87	1.02
Government is too complicated		1.72	1.09
Other people understand issues better than I do		1.98	1.04
External efficacy	0–4[b]		
I don't have any say in government		2.18	1.17
Wealthy have more influence than others		1.21	1.09
Public officials don't care what I think		1.69	0.99
Problem is we don't give equal voice		1.74	1.10
Public officials don't listen		1.47	0.91
People in government waste money		1.25	0.95
Political discussion	0–100[c]		
Talking about politics with family and friends		25.37	27.58
Opposition to diversity	0–4[b]		
Immigrants speak English ASAP		0.97	0.95
Better for race/ethnic to live apart		3.30	0.94
Slavery has made it difficult/blacks		1.96	1.21
Fewer problems if less immigrants		2.42	1.16
Hispanic immigration will contribute ideas/customs		1.93	0.93
Better place if more immigrants moved in		2.38	0.86
Support for Clinton impeachment	0–4[b]		
President Clinton should be removed		2.42	1.33
Impeachment has turned me off		2.05	1.10
Negativity toward police	0–4[b]		
I could get a fair trial		1.66	1.01
I can trust the police to protect me from crime		1.90	1.14
Nationalism	0–4[b]		
U.S. system is better than others		0.84	0.90

(continued)

Survey items	Range of values or coding scheme	Mean	Standard deviation
American form of government is the best		1.27	0.90
Chapter 2, independent variables			
Population density (per square mile)	24.05–11,275.94	2,931.22	2,979.68
Percent Asian or Pacific Islander	0.23–19.2	7.02	5.99
Percent non–Hispanic black	0.12–88.9	22.27	22.04
Percent Hispanic white	0.26–37.11	8.00	9.09
Percent who are foreign born	0.15–32.28	8.00	9.09
Median income (in dollars)	34,517 – 147,113	68,141	25,551
Percent whose parents have four-year college degree	3.47–31.71	19.39	8.52
Percent Democratic[d]	28.67–92.37	61.57	15.23
Political party competition within area[e]	57.63–98.9	84.45	11.13
Percent turnout	54.3–78.3	69.07	6.19
Magnet program participant	0–1[f]	0.10	0.30
Chapter 3, independent variables			
Asian respondent	0–1[f]	0.09	0.28
Black respondent	0–1[f]	0.25	0.43
Hispanic respondent	0–1[f]	0.07	0.26
Foreign–born parents	0–2[g]	0.53	0.84
Female	0–1[f]	0.51	0.50
Black female	0–1[f]	0.13	0.34
Hispanic female	0–1[f]	0.04	0.18
Marital status of parents	0–3[h]	0.67	1.00
Socioeconomic status[i]	1–42	24.05	7.58
Chapter 4, independent variables			
Democratic respondent	0–1[f]	0.43	0.50
Republican respondent	0–1[f]	0.19	0.39
Independent respondent	0–1[f]	0.09	0.29
Chapter 5, independent variables			
Percent Protestant	10.2–46.34	27.96	9.16
Percent Catholic	1.18–45.26	24.00	11.28
Percent Jewish	0–30.56	6.07	9.37
Percent Buddhist/Hindu	0–6.67	2.68	1.94
Percent Muslim	0–8.65	1.73	2.06

(continued)

Survey items	Range of values or coding scheme	Mean	Standard deviation
Protestant respondent	0–1[f]	0.37	0.48
Catholic respondent	0–1[f]	0.32	0.46
Jewish respondent	0–1[f]	0.08	0.27
Buddhist/Hindu respondent	0–1[f]	0.04	0.18
Muslim respondent	0–1[f]	0.02	0.15
Religious observance (frequency of attendance)	0–4[j]	1.96	1.48
Chapter 6, independent variables			
Amount of civics courses	0–5[k]	3.7	1.4
Dislike studying government	0–1[f]	0.15	0.36
Plan to attend a four-year college	0–1[f]	0.73	0.45
Grade level of respondent	9–12	10.65	0.97
I always deserve the grades I receive	0–1[f]	0.59	0.49
I never deserve the grades I receive	0–1[f]	0.03	0.17
Days you watched TV news past week	0–7[l]	3.67	2.3
Chapter 7, dependent variables, 2001 data for four schools	0–4[b]		
Permit assassination of hostile foreign leaders		1.16	1.06
Should take military action, even if lives lost		0.93	1.14
Strong support for Israel led to attacks		1.37	1.21
U.S. should not concern itself with other countries		2.30	1.21
U.S. should adopt stricter immigration laws		0.82	1.10
Police should have power to read mail and e-mail		1.73	1.33
Terrorism is a judgment from God for sin		2.32	1.30
1999 sample, four schools in survey			
Political knowledge (test score based on the following seven items)[a]	0–100	71.51	20.97
How many senators?		63.25	48.28
Who is elected to preside in the U.S. House?		81.48	38.90

(continued)

Survey items	Range of values or coding scheme	Mean	Standard deviation
Where can you find the Bill of Rights?		74.36	43.73
Presidential elections held four years?		93.73	24.27
Power divided in a federal system?		66.57	47.24
Who is the current vice president?		93.16	25.28
Who is the current chief justice?		28.49	45.20
Internal efficacy	0–4[b]		
I have a good understanding of issues		1.72	0.95
I'm as well informed as others		1.79	1.00
Government is too complicated		1.77	1.10
Other people understand issues better than I do		2.00	1.01
External efficacy	0–4[b]		
I don't have any say in government		2.26	1.19
Wealthy have more influence than others		1.29	1.05
Public officials don't care what I think		1.72	1.02
Problem is we don't give equal voice		1.92	1.19
Public officials don't listen		1.50	0.92
People in government waste money		1.10	0.90
Political discussion	0–100[c]		
Talking about politics with family and friends		25.52	28.01
Opposition to diversity	0–4[b]		
Immigrants speak English ASAP		0.95	0.98
Better for race/ethnic to live apart		3.15	1.02
Slavery has made it difficult/blacks		2.21	1.19
Fewer problems if less immigrants		2.03	1.16
Hispanic immigration will contribute ideas/customs		2.12	0.88
Better place if more immigrants moved in		2.55	0.87
Support for Clinton impeachment	0–4[b]		
President Clinton should be removed		1.91	1.33
Impeachment has turned me off		2.06	1.03

(continued)

Survey items	Range of values or coding scheme	Mean	Standard deviation
Negativity toward police	0–4[b]		
I could get a fair trial		1.44	0.92
I can trust the police		1.83	1.07
Nationalism	0–4[b]		
U.S. system is better than others		0.70	0.92
American form of government is the best		1.16	0.90
2001 sample, four schools in survey			
Political knowledge (test score based on the following seven items)[a]	0–100	61.44	21.49
How many senators?		59.29	49.18
Who is elected to preside in the U.S. House?		29.41	45.62
Where can you find the Bill of Rights?		70.59	45.62
Presidential elections held four years?		90.59	29.24
Power divided in a federal system?		64.24	47.99
Who is the current vice president?		82.12	38.37
Who is the current chief justice?		33.88	47.39
Internal efficacy	0–4[b]		
I have a good understanding of issues		1.29	0.80
I'm as well informed as others		1.69	0.99
Government is too complicated		1.75	1.05
Other people understand issues better than I do		1.96	1.05
External efficacy	0–4[b]		
I don't have any say in government		1.68	1.15
Wealthy have more influence than others		1.18	1.01
Public officials don't care what I think		1.65	1.02
Problem is we don't give equal voice		1.68	1.14
Public officials don't listen		1.93	1.04
People in government waste money		1.90	1.05
Political discussion	0–100[c]		
Talking about politics with family and friends		31.46	28.47

(continued)

Survey items	Range of values or coding scheme	Mean	Standard deviation
Opposition to diversity	0–4[b]		
Immigrants speak English ASAP.		0.97	0.94
Better for race/ethnic to live apart		3.06	1.08
Slavery has made it difficult/blacks		2.08	1.16
Fewer problems if less immigrants		1.84	1.23
Hispanic immigration will con-tribute ideas/customs		2.05	1.00
Better place if more immigrants moved in		2.65	1.02
Support for Clinton impeachment	0–4[b]		
President Clinton should be removed.		1.91	1.33
Impeachment has turned me off		2.06	1.03
Negativity toward police	0–4[b]		
I could get a fair trial		1.52	1.08
I can trust the police		1.74	1.14
Nationalism	0–4[b]		
U.S. system is better than others		1.05	0.93
American form of government is the best		0.91	0.79
Chapter 7, independent variables, 2001 data, four schools in survey			
Dislike studying government	0–1[f]	0.15	0.36
Never attends church	0–1[f]	0.23	0.42
Never deserves grades	0–1[f]	0.03	0.17
Grade level	9–12	10.43	1.08
Days you watched TV news past week	0–7[l]	3.34	2.35
Amount of civics courses	0–5[k]	3.25	1.40
I always deserve the grades I receive	0–1[f]	0.20	0.40
No plans to attend college	0–1[f]	0.21	0.42
Plan to attend a four-year college	0–1[f]	0.70	0.46
Regular church attendee	0–1[f]	0.20	0.40
Socioeconomic status	2–36	22.44	7.23
Chapter 7, independent variables, 1999 data, four schools in survey			
Dislike studying government	0–1[f]	0.18	0.38
Never attends church	0–1[f]	0.21	0.41

(continued)

Survey items	Range of values or coding scheme	Mean	Standard deviation
Never deserves grades	0–1[f]	0.02	0.14
Grade level	9–12	10.25	1.09
Days you watched TV news past week	0–7[l]	3.43	2.20
Amount of civics courses	0–5[k]	2.39	1.70
I always deserve the grades I receive	0–1[f]	0.24	0.43
No plans to attend college	0–1[f]	0.27	0.44
Plan to attend a four-year college	0–1[f]	0.62	0.49
Regular church attendee	0–1[f]	0.25	0.43
Socioeconomic status	7–41	23.44	5.17
Chapter 8, dependent variable			
Intention to vote in 2000, if age 18	0–1[f]	0.69	0.46

a. Students were given a multiple choice of four possible answers.

b. Strongly agree–strongly disagree.

c. Rescaled, days per week.

d. Consists of percent of Democratic vote for state legislature (1998), governor (1998), and president (1996).

e. Formulated as 100 – [absolute(50 – percent Democratic)].

f. No, Yes.

g. Both born in U.S., one born abroad, both born abroad.

h. Married, divorced, never married.

i. Formulated as a ranking from 1 to 42 based on the mean income of each occupational category listed.

j. Never, a few times per year, once or twice a month, almost every week, every week.

k. 0, <0.5, 0.5, 0.5–1, 1, 1+ years.

l. 0 to 7 days.

Factor Analysis
of Dependent Variables

Six of the eight dependent variables in the analysis presented in chapters 2 through 6 are constructed as "factor scores," using a statistical technique called principal components. The measures for internal efficacy, external efficacy, attitudes toward law enforcement, opposition to diversity, nationalism, and support for the impeachment of the president are all derived from principal components, sometimes described as a type of factor analysis, although factor analysis has several variants. Principal components and factor analysis are frequently used in connection with attitude and opinion surveys when complex attitudes cannot be adequately measured by single questions. A detailed explication of the method can be found in specialized but still accessible texts.[1]

As explained by Kline, the goal of factor analysis is to take a matrix of correlations among related variables (in our case, responses to survey items) and explain them in terms of a single or small number of underlying factors. A factor is a dimension or construct that is a condensed statement of the relationships among a set of variables.[2] Simply put, factors account for variance and explain correlations among multiple survey items. Principal components is a particular type of factor analysis used to identify (or

1. Kline (1994); Maruyama (1998, chap. 7).
2. Kline (1994, p. 5).

Figure C-1. *Depiction of the Measurement Overlap of Three Survey Items That Generates the Factor or Component Score in Factor Analysis*

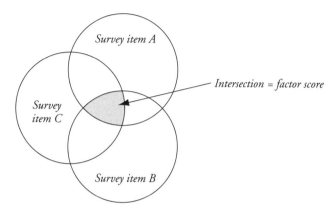

"extract") these factors. The first factor (technically called a "component" in principal components analysis) always explains the most variance in the correlation matrix of survey items. If more than one factor is extracted, the factors are ordered from highest to lowest in terms of the amount of variance they explain.

Using student responses to four of several possible survey questions to measure internal efficacy, for example, factor analysis allowed us to capture the extent of overlap in these individual items by mathematically identifying their interrelationship or common correlation (see figure C-1). We found that our four survey items pointed to an underlying structure, allowing us to reduce multiple items to just one, identifying that single factor as the construct "internal efficacy." In this manner, factor analysis allowed us to take a large set of indicators for a single theoretical construct (such as internal efficacy or opposition to diversity) and determine if one or a few more basic variables ("factors" or "components") are at their foundation.

When several items are found to indicate a single underlying factor, the principal components procedure produces a "factor score" derived from the weighted combination of the individual survey items that are highly associated with (or "load highly on") that factor. Factor loadings are simply the correlations of each individual survey item with the factor. In most cases the number of survey items we used produced a small matrix and only a single factor was extracted that explained a large proportion of the

Table C-1. *Factor Analysis for Internal Efficacy*
Units as indicated

	Initial eigenvalues		
	Total	Percent of variance	Cumulative percent
Component 1	2.05	51.20	51.20
Component 2	0.86	21.42	100.00
Component matrix: variables	*Component 1*		
Other people understand better	0.73		
I have a good understanding	−0.70		
I'm as well informed as others	−0.72		
Government is too complicated	0.72		
Correlation matrix	*Other people...*	*I have a good...*	*I'm informed...*	*Govern- ment...*
Other people understand better	1.00	−0.28	−0.32	0.47
I have a good understanding	−0.28	1.00	0.44	−0.29
I'm as well informed as others	−0.32	0.44	1.00	−0.30
Government is too complicated	0.47	−0.29	−0.30	1.00

variance. Consistent with social science convention, we do not present results from factors with eigenvalues less than 1. In cases where more than one factor was extracted by this criterion, we ordinarily found that the first factor (and its derivative score) was the best measure of the more complex construct. This new measure was then used in subsequent regression analysis.

In addition to internal efficacy, we took multiple survey items to derive our factor score measures for nationalism, external efficacy, support for impeachment, opposition to diversity, and attitudes toward law enforcement. The survey items and their respective factor loadings and inter-item correlations for chapters 2 through 6 are reported in tables C-1 through C-6.

Table C-2. *Factor Analysis for External Efficacy*
Units as indicated

	Initial eigenvalues		
	Total	Percent of variance	Cumulative percent
Component 1	2.17	36.16	36.16
Component 2	0.92	15.41	51.56
Component 3	0.85	14.09	65.65
Component 4	0.82	13.71	79.35
Component 5	0.70	11.58	90.93
Component 6	0.54	9.07	100.00

Component matrix: variables

	Component 1
People in government waste money	0.30
Wealthy have more influence	0.16
Problem is no equal voice	0.40
Public officials don't care	0.48
Public officials don't listen	0.45
I have no say in government	0.39

Correlation matrix

	People waste...	Wealthy have...	...no equal voice	...don't care	...don't listen	I have no say...
People in government waste money	1.00	0.15	0.18	0.27	0.24	0.20
Wealthy have more influence	0.15	1.00	0.11	0.16	0.16	0.15
Problem is no equal voice	0.18	0.11	1.00	0.25	0.37	0.29
Public officials don't care	0.27	0.16	0.24	1.00	0.33	0.38
Public officials don't listen	0.24	0.16	0.37	0.33	1.00	0.20
I have no say in government	0.20	0.15	0.29	0.36	0.20	1.00

Table C-3. *Factor Analysis for Negativity toward Local Police and Courts*
Units as indicated

	Initial eigenvalues		
	Total	Percent of variance	Cumulative percent
Component 1	1.32	65.89	65.89
Component 2	0.68	34.11	100.00
Component matrix: variables	*Component 1*		
I can trust the police	0.81		
I could get a fair trial	0.81		
Correlation matrix	*Fair trial*		*Trust police*
Fair trial	1.00		0.32
Trust police	0.32		1.00

Table C-4. *Factor Analysis for Opposition to Immigration-Induced Diversity*
Units as indicated

	Initial eigenvalues		
	Total	Percent of variance	Cumulative percent
Component 1	2.50	41.70	41.70
Component 2	1.02	17.00	58.70
Component 3	0.91	15.18	73.88
Component 4	0.65	10.77	84.65
Component 5	0.52	8.72	93.36
Component 6	0.40	6.64	100.00

Component matrix: variables	Component 1	Component 2
Asian immigration contributes	0.72	0.45
Hispanic immigration contributes	0.77	0.36
Better place if more immigrants	0.73	0.01
Fewer problems if less immigrants	-0.72	0.31
Better for race/ethnic to live apart	-0.43	0.29
Immigrants speak English ASAP	-0.38	0.71

Correlation matrix	Asian...	Hispanic...	Better place...	Fewer problems...	...live apart	...speak English
Asian immigration contributes	1.00	0.60	0.39	-0.32	-0.15	-0.10
Hispanic immigration contributes	0.60	1.00	0.44	-0.37	-0.21	-0.14
Better place if more immigrants	0.39	0.44	1.00	-0.44	-0.19	-0.21
Fewer problems if less immigrants	-0.32	-0.37	-0.44	1.00	0.30	0.29
Better for race/ethnic to live apart	-0.15	-0.21	-0.19	0.30	1.00	0.08
Immigrants speak English ASAP	-0.10	-0.14	-0.21	0.29	0.08	1.00

Table C-5. *Factor Analysis for Nationalism-Chauvinism*
Units as indicated

| | Initial eigenvalues | | |
	Total	Percent of variance	Cumulative percent
Component 1	1.48	74.10	74.10
Component 2	0.52	25.90	100.00

Component matrix: variables	Component 1
American government is best	0.86
U.S. system is better	0.86

Correlation matrix	American government...	U.S. system...
American government is best	1.00	0.48
U.S. system is better	0.48	1.00

Table C-6. *Factor Analysis for Support for the Clinton Impeachment*
Units as indicated

| | Initial eigenvalues | | |
	Total	Percent of variance	Cumulative percent
Component 1	1.09	54.48	54.48
Component 2	0.91	45.52	100.00

Component matrix: variables	Component 1
Impeachment turned me off	0.74
President should have been removed	−0.74

Correlation matrix	Impeachment...	President should...
Impeachment turned me off	1.00	−0.09
President should have been removed	−0.09	1.00

Description of Structural Equation Modeling and Hierarchical Linear Modeling

Social scientists and statisticians have developed a number of regression-related methods specifically tailored to the analysis of multilevel data. These innovations have been pursued because of the special statistical challenges of data analysis when individual observations are clustered within schools, geographic jurisdictions, or distinct temporal periods, rather than independently distributed in time or across space.

In this book, we work principally with two levels of data: individual level responses from students at level one, and community or neighborhood characteristics at level two. Our goal is to evaluate the impact of the individual level characteristics (for instance, party identification) on individual attitudes (such as internal efficacy) while evaluating the influence of community characteristics (for example, percent Democratic). Standard regression approaches assume that observations are independent of each other in space, clearly a faulty assumption in our case because students in particular schools and neighborhoods interact with each other and share the same conditioning environment. Given our theory of the spatially contingent nature of the socialization process, a student in "Big City High School" is, on average, going to look more like another student in Big City High School than she will look like a student in "Remote Rural High School," 120 miles away. The spatial clustering of students at school sites and in communities necessitated methods that would not require the strong assumption that the survey observations be independently distributed in space.

In the first sections of chapters 3 though 6, and in chapter 8, we use structural equation modeling (SEM) to estimate the effects of community and individual characteristics on socialization-relevant attitudes. At the end of chapters 3 through 6, we also use hierarchical linear modeling (HLM) to examine these relationships and test for the influence of interactions between community and individual characteristics (for example, being a Republican in a Republican neighborhood as opposed to being a Republican in a politically balanced or Democratic neighborhood).

Structural Equation Modeling

A clearly written and accessible introduction to SEM for social science research can be found in Maruyama.[1] Maruyama explains that SEM is an approach where the relationships between variables are defined by a series of equations that describe hypothesized structures of relationships.[2] In our model for chapter 4, for example, the party identification of the respondent is a function of the partisan composition of the community (figure D-1). But both the party of the respondent and the partisan composition of the community may play a role in explaining the respondent's level of, say, internal efficacy.

In figure D-1, path A captures the direct effect of party identification on internal efficacy; path B captures the direct effect of percent Democratic identifiers in the community on the party identification of the respondent; and the third path, C, captures the direct effect that the partisan composition of the community has on internal efficacy. Paths A and C capture the primary relationships of interest to us throughout the book. Path B is a necessary control because it helps determine, in this case, how the party identification of survey respondents is usually connected to the partisan bias of the community in which they live. The partisan composition of the community not only helps us understand the selection of student respondents in particular communities but also arguably has a substantive impact on their choice of partisan identities as they come of age. The choice of party identity, in our view, is not strictly determined by environmental circumstances, but the range of choices, and the likelihood of adopting one

1. Maruyama (1998).
2. Maruyama (1998, p. 10).

Figure D-1. *Effect of Individual Party Identification on Internal Efficacy, Controlling for the Influence of Partisan Environments on Party Identification and Internal Efficacy*

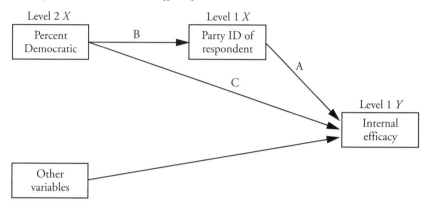

viewpoint rather than another, can certainly be influenced by a person's collection of experiences at a certain place.

In figure D-1, then, the party identification of the respondent is considered "endogenous to" (caused by) percent Democratic, and internal efficacy is considered endogenous to the party identification of the respondent, percent Democratic, and "other variables." Indirect effects are also present in this model because percent Democratic influences the party identification of the respondent, which in turn influences internal efficacy. To preserve economy in the tabular presentation of the results and focus on the key relationships of interest, we usually do not present all of the direct and indirect effects in this book, but complete results for all SEM models are available upon request from the authors. The results we report for SEM models include the unstandardized regression coefficients and standard errors, along with standardized regression coefficients.

Hierarchical Linear Modeling

HLM is employed in the second part of chapters 3 through 6. It is covered extensively in a recent book by Raudenbush and Bryk.[3] Given the substantive aims of this book, we will only lay a foundation for an intuitive understanding of the method here.

---

3. Raudenbush and Bryk (2002). See also Lee and Bryk (1989); Steenbergen and Jones (2002).

Briefly, we use HLM to evaluate hypotheses about how our community level variables influence relationships at the individual level. So, for example, if we hypothesize that Democratic identifiers will come to think differently about the impeachment of President Clinton if they live in a Democratic neighborhood rather than a Republican one, HLM is a tool designed explicitly to test such hypotheses.

If we were studying adolescents at a single school site, HLM would not be necessary because the neighborhood or "environment" would not vary. Ordinary regression techniques could be employed in assessing the outcomes of interest. If we were working with data drawn from multiple school sites, but we had no theoretical expectation that neighborhood characteristics would matter to the individual level relationships, then HLM would not be necessary either. Because our theory suggests that neighborhood characteristics may matter and because we are working with data drawn from twenty-nine distinct neighborhoods, we concluded that HLM was a method we could not do without, regardless of whatever advantages the SEM approach also provides.

Specifically, HLM provides us with the powerful advantage of testing for the variability of individual relationships across environments. Consider the possibility that the amount of social studies coursework is more positively related to internal political efficacy at some locations than at others, according to the three plots in figure D-2. In this case, it is clear that semesters of social studies are most clearly associated with rising internal efficacy at the first location and least associated at the second. The individual relationship between social studies exposure and internal efficacy is not invariant across contexts. The question is, what accounts for this variability in the slopes and intercepts? HLM is designed to address this very question.

Since it is not practical to use scatter plot diagrams to summarize the relationship between social studies exposure and internal efficacy for a large number of schools, HLM provides a model by which we can estimate the variability of the regression coefficients (slopes and intercepts) across communities.[4] We use the slopes-and-intercepts estimation technique to ask what characteristics of communities allow us to predict, for instance, why some neighborhoods produce children with higher internal efficacy than others, and why exposure to social studies education has a greater effect on internal efficacy in some places than in others. Suppose that we were inter-

4. Raudenbush and Bryk (2002, p. 27).

Figure D-2. *Variation in the Relationship between Social Studies Coursework and Internal Political Efficacy, by Location of School*

Internal efficacy score

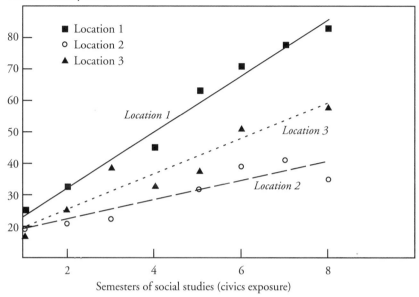

Semesters of social studies (civics exposure)

ested in modeling the relationships in figure D-2, hypothesizing that the extent of political party diversity in local communities explains the variability of the relationship between efficacy and civics exposure at level one. The level-one model for internal efficacy can be written as follows:

$$Y_{ij} \; \textit{(Internal Efficacy)} = \beta_{0j} + \beta_{1j} \; \textit{(Civics Exposure)} + r_{ij} ,$$

where a student's internal efficacy (Y_{ij}) is characterized simply by two standard parameters: an intercept (β_{0j}) and a slope (β_{1j}) for civics exposure, and a normally behaved error term (r_{ij}). The $_{ij}$ subscript for the dependent variable indicates that each level-one unit, i, is nested in a level-two unit, j. The regression parameters differ from a standard ordinary least squares (OLS) regression model because they vary across the level-two units.[5] In HLM the intercept and slope in the above equation are themselves modeled as a function of level-two predictors, in our case, a single predictor: partisan

5. Steenbergen and Jones (2002).

political diversity. The level-two model incorporating the community effect of partisan political diversity can be written as

$$\beta_{0j} = \gamma_{00} + \gamma_{01} \, (\textit{Partisan Diversity}) + \mu_{0j}$$

and

$$\beta_{1j} = \gamma_{10} + \gamma_{11} \, (\textit{Partisan Diversity}) + \mu_{1j} \, .$$

The combined HLM model is written as

$$Y_{ij} = \gamma_{00} + \gamma_{01} \, (\textit{Partisan Diversity}) + \gamma_{10} \, (\textit{Civics Exposure})$$
$$+ \gamma_{11} \, (\textit{Partisan Diversity} \times \textit{Exposure}) + \mu_{0j} + \mu_{1j} + r_{ij} \, .$$

In this model, internal efficacy can be understood as a function of the overall intercept (γ_{00}), the main effect of partisan diversity (γ_{01}), the main effect of exposure to social studies (γ_{10}), the cross-level interaction of exposure to social studies x partisan diversity (γ_{11}), the error terms for modeling both the slope and intercept parameters at level one with the level-two units (μ_{0j} and μ_{1j}), and a final term to capture level-one prediction error (r_{ij}).

Interpreting the results of the estimation of this model is more involved than interpreting output from a straightforward OLS regression because of the larger number of parameter estimates reported. The hypothetical output for this example appears below in table D-1. The results presented in this table show that partisan diversity among the level-two units does not significantly predict the intercept, but it does predict the within-neighborhood slopes for the relationship between civics exposure and internal efficacy. There is a tendency for neighborhoods with greater partisan diversity to have a stronger positive (upward sloping) relationship between civics exposure and internal efficacy than those with less ($\gamma_{11} = .04$; $p < .05$). The addition of this particular level-two predictor may not explain all of the variability in the civics exposure-efficacy relationship that we pictured in figure D-2, but it does account for some variation across contexts.

The bottom part of the table under the heading "random effects" provides information about the variation and covariation of the intercepts and civics exposure slopes across schools. The value 12.22 is the estimated variance of the intercept and the figure 0.67 is the estimated variance of the slope. The significance levels evaluate whether these variances are larger or

Table D-1. *Effect of Partisan Diversity in Neighborhoods on the Relationship between Civics Coursework and Internal Efficacy, Two-Level Model*

Units as indicated

	Hierarchical linear model[a]
Fixed effects	
Community means	
Intercept γ_{00}	37.61**
	(8.76)
Partisan diversity γ_{01}	0.09
	(0.06)
Civics coursework	
Intercept γ_{10}	2.19
	(2.25)
Partisan diversity γ_{11}	0.04*
	(0.02)

	Variance component	χ^2 *significance*
Random effects		
Intercept	12.22	.20
Civics coursework	0.67	.04
Level-one R^b	249.01	. . .

Source: Metro Civic Values Survey, 1999–2000.

* $p \leq .10$; ** $p \leq .05$.

a. Slopes and intercepts estimation cell entries are regression coefficients; standard errors are shown in parentheses.

b. Number of level-one units = 2,802; deviance = 24,141.6.

smaller than if partisan diversity had not been added to the model at level two. The chi-square significance test is used to evaluate the null hypothesis that no variation in the slopes and intercepts remains. With respect to the intercept, the insignificance indicates that the null hypothesis is accepted and that no significant variation in the intercept remains. However, the significance of the variance component for the slope for civics exposure indicates that variation in the slopes remains unexplained even after controlling for partisan diversity. In the process of data analysis and exploration, we might want to examine other theoretically relevant level-two predictors to determine their additional explanatory power.

A large variety of other specification and fit tests can be performed in the HLM context. We do not spend time on these here since our primary interest is in the substantive and statistical significance of slopes and intercepts after adding level-two variables. To economize on the presentation of results, given the sheer number of HLM models we estimate, we omit the bottom portion of the tables describing the variance components and ordinarily do not discuss model fit. Not surprisingly, every one of our models shows a statistically significant chi-square test when appropriate likelihood ratio tests are performed. Complete results are available upon request from the authors.

Factor Analysis Results from Chapter 7

For our abbreviated treatment of factor analysis, see appendix C. In the latter portion of chapter 7, we use a factor score to place students on a single "hawk-dove" continuum according to their policy views on the government's proper response to the September 11 terrorist attacks. Positive values on the factor score indicated approval of a more aggressive (hawkish) posture.

This factor score resulted from a principal components analysis using four survey items to gauge students' reaction to public policy proposals that were widely discussed by elites following the attacks. The results from this analysis are presented here in table E-1. This survey was conducted between six and eight weeks after September 11, 2001, in four Maryland high schools.

Table E-1. *Factor Analysis for Taking Aggressive Policy Action after September 11, 2001*

Units as indicated

	Initial eigenvalues		
	Total	Percent of variance	Cumulative percent
Component 1	2.17	54.16	54.16

Component matrix: variables	Component 1
Assassinate hostile foreign leaders	0.569
Military should take action, lives lost	0.778
Police should have power to read mail	0.766
Should adopt strict immigration laws	0.806

Correlation matrix	Assassinate	Military action	Police power	Adopt strict laws
Assassinate hostile foreign leaders	1.00	0.27	0.22	0.35
Military should take action, lives lost	0.27	1.00	0.49	0.47
Police should have power read mail	0.22	0.49	1.00	0.48
Should adopt strict immigration laws	0.35	0.47	0.48	1.00

References

Abramson, Paul R. 1972. "Political Efficacy and Political Trust among Black Schoolchildren: Two Explanations." *Journal of Politics* 34 (4): 1243–75.

Abramson, Paul R., and John H. Aldrich. 1982. "The Decline of Electoral Participation in America." *American Political Science Review* 76 (3): 502–21.

Allen, Richard, Michael Dawson, and Ronald Brown. 1989. "A Schema-Based Approach to Modeling an African American Racial Belief System." *American Political Science Review* 83 (2): 421–41.

Allport, Gordon W., and J. M. Ross. 1967. "Personal Religious Orientation and Prejudice." *Journal of Personality and Social Psychology* 5 (3): 432–43.

Almond, Gabriel A., and James S. Coleman, eds. 1960. *The Politics of the Developing Areas.* Princeton University Press.

Almond, Gabriel A., and Sidney Verba. 1963. *The Civic Culture.* Princeton University Press.

Alwin, Duane F., and Jon Krosnick. 1991. "Aging, Cohorts, and the Stability of Sociopolitical Orientations over the Life Span." *American Journal of Sociology* 97 (1): 169–96.

Anderson, James G., and Francis B. Evans. 1976. "Family Socialization and Educational Achievement in Two Cultures: Mexican-American and Anglo-American." *Sociometry* 39 (3): 209–22.

Andolina, Molly W., and Clyde Wilcox. 2000. "Public Opinion: The Paradoxes of Clinton's Popularity." In *The Clinton Scandal and the Future of American Government,* edited by Mark J. Rozell and Clyde Wilcox, 171–95. Georgetown University Press.

Ansolabehere, Stephen, and Shanto Iyengar. 1995. *Going Negative: How Political Advertisements Shrink and Polarize the Electorate.* Free Press.

Arterton, F. Christopher. 1974. "The Impact of Watergate on Children's Attitudes toward Political Authority." *Political Science Quarterly* 89 (2): 269–88.

———. 1975. "Watergate and Children's Attitudes toward Political Authority Revisited." *Political Science Quarterly* 90 (3): 477–96.

Atkin, Charles K. 1978. "Broadcast News Programming and the Child Audience." *Journal of Broadcasting* 22: 47–61.

Atkin, Charles K., and Walter Gantz. 1978. "Television News and the Child Audience." *Public Opinion Quarterly* 42 (2): 183–98.

Baldassare, Mark, ed. 1994. *The Los Angeles Riots: Lessons for the Urban Future.* Westview Press.

Ballou, Dale, and others. 2002. "Forum on Accountability Gains: Will Value-Added Analysis Make Performance-Based Evaluations a Viable Tool for School Improvement?" *Education Next* 2: 9–23.

Bandura, Albert. 1977. "Self-Efficacy: Toward a Unifying Theory of Behavioral Change." *Psychological Review* 84 (2):191–215.

Bartels, Larry M. 1996. "Uninformed Votes: Information Effects in Presidential Elections." *American Journal of Political Science* 40 (1): 194–230.

Beck, Paul Allen. 1977. "The Role of Agents in Political Socialization." In *Handbook of Political Socialization*, edited by Stanley Allen Renshon, 115–41. Free Press.

Beck, Paul Allen, and M. Kent Jennings. 1982. "Pathways to Participation." *American Political Science Review* 76 (1): 94-108.

———. 1991. "Family Traditions, Political Periods, and the Development of Partisan Orientations." *Journal of Politics* 53 (4): 742–63.

Beck, Paul Allen, and others. 2002. "The Social Calculus of Voting: Interpersonal, Media, and Organizational Influences on Presidential Choices." *American Political Science Review* 96 (1): 57–73.

Becker, Penny Edgell, and Pawan H. Dhingra. 2001. "Religious Involvement and Volunteering: Implications for Civil Society." *Sociology of Religion* 62 (3): 315–35.

Bennett, Stephen E. 1997. "Why Young Americans Hate Politics, and What We Should Do about It." *P.S.: Political Science and Politics* 30 (1): 47–52.

Berelson, Bernard R., Paul F. Lazarsfeld, and William N. McPhee. 1954. *Voting: A Study of Opinion Formation in a Presidential Campaign.* University of Chicago Press.

Berman, David R., and John A. Stookey. 1980. "Adolescents, Television, and Support for Government." *Public Opinion Quarterly* 44 (3): 330–40.

Black, Donald J., and Albert J. Reiss Jr. 1970. "Police Control of Juveniles." *American Sociological Review* 35 (1): 63-77.

Bobo, Lawrence, and Franklin D. Gilliam Jr. 1990. "Race, Sociopolitical Participation, and Black Empowerment." *American Political Science Review* 84 (2): 377–93.

Bobo, Lawrence, and others. 1994. "Public Opinion before and after a Spring of Discontent." In *The Los Angeles Riots: Lessons for the Urban Future,* edited by Mark Baldassare, 103–34. Westview Press.

Brewer, Marilynn B. 1999. "The Psychology of Prejudice: Ingroup Love or Outgroup Hate?" *Journal of Social Issues* 55 (4): 429–44.

Brewer, Paul R., and Lars Willnat. 2001. "Dark Questions: Waco, the Media, and Public Opinion." Paper prepared for the annual meeting of the American Political Science Association. San Francisco.

Brody, Richard A. 1984. "International Crises: A Rallying Point for the President." *Public Opinion* 6 (1): 41–43.

———. 1991. *Assessing the President.* Stanford University Press.

Brown, Sherlon P. 1996. "Black Female Adolescents' Career Aspirations and Expectations: Rising to the Challenge of the American Occupational Structure." *Western Journal of Black Studies* 20 (1): 89–95.

Brown, Thad A. 1988. *Migration and Politics: The Impact of Population Mobility on American Voting Behavior.* University of North Carolina Press.

Browning, Rufus, Dale Rogers Marshall, and David H. Tabb. 1984. *Protest Is Not Enough: The Struggle of Blacks and Hispanics for Equality in Urban Politics.* University of California Press.

Burns, Nancy, Kay Lehman Schlozman, and Sidney Verba. 1997. "The Public Consequences of Private Inequality: Family Life and Citizen Participation." *American Political Science Review* 91 (2): 373–89.

Burns, Nancy, and others. 2001. *National Election Studies, 2000: Pre-/Post-Election Study* (dataset). University of Michigan, Center for Political Studies.

Cain, Bruce E., D. Roderick Kiewiet, and Carole J. Uhlaner. 1991. "The Acquisition of Partisanship by Latinos and Asian Americans." *American Journal of Political Science* 35 (2): 390–22.

Caliendo, Stephen M. 2000. *Teachers Matter: The Trouble with Leaving Political Education to the Coaches.* Praeger.

Callaghan, Karen J., and Simo Virtanen. 1993. "Revised Models of the 'Rally Phenomenon': The Case of the Carter Presidency." *Journal of Politics* 55 (3): 756–64.

Campbell, Angus, Gerald Gurin, and Warren E. Miller. 1954. *The Voter Decides.* Evanston, Ill.: Row, Peterson.

Campbell, Angus, and others. 1960. *The American Voter.* John Wiley & Sons.

Campbell, David E. 2002. "Getting Along versus Getting Ahead: Why the Absence of Party Competition Leads to High Voter Turnout." Paper presented at the annual meeting of the Midwest Political Science Association Convention. Chicago.

Campbell, Donald T., and H. Laurence Ross. 1970. "The Connecticut Crackdown on Speeding." In *The Quantitative Analysis of Social Problems*, edited by Edward R. Tufte, 110–25. Addison-Wesley.

Chaffee, Steven H., Scott Ward, and Leonard Tipton. 1970. "Mass Communication and Political Socialization." *Journalism Quarterly* 47 (3): 647–59.

Chalfant, H. Paul, and C. W. Peek. 1983. "Religious Affiliation, Religiosity, and Racial Prejudice: A New Look at Old Relationships." *Review of Religious Research* 25 (2): 155–61.

Citrin, Jack, Beth Reingold, and Donald P. Green. 1990. "American Identity and the Politics of Ethnic Change." *Journal of Politics* 52 (4): 1124–54.

Clarke, James W. 1973. "Family Structure and Political Socialization among Urban Black Children." *American Journal of Political Science* 17 (2): 302–15.

Cohen, Cathy J., and Michael C. Dawson. 1993. "Neighborhood Poverty and African American Politics." *American Political Science Review* 87 (2): 286–302.

Cohen, Steven Martin, and Robert E. Kapsis. 1977. "Religion, Ethnicity, and Party Affiliation in the U.S.: Evidence from Pooled Electoral Surveys, 1968–1972." *Social Forces* 56 (4): 637–53.

Coleman, James S. 1966. *Equality of Educational Opportunity*. Washington: National Assessment Governing Board, Council of Chief State School Officers.

———. 1988. "Social Capital in the Creation of Human Capital." *American Journal of Sociology* 94: S94–S120.

Converse, Philip E. 1964. "The Nature of Belief Systems in Mass Publics." In *Ideology and Discontent*, edited by David Apter, 206–61. Free Press.

Conway, M. Margaret, A. Jay Stevens, and Robert Smith. 1975. "The Relation between Media Use and Children's Civic Awareness." *Journalism Quarterly* 57 (1): 45–54.

Conway, M. Margaret, and others. 1981. "The News Media in Children's Political Socialization." *Public Opinion Quarterly* 45 (2): 164–78.

Corbett, Michael. 1991. *American Public Opinion*. Longman.

Cowan, Gloria, Livier Martinez, and Stephanie Mendiola. 1997. "Predictors of Attitudes toward Illegal Latino Immigrants." *Hispanic Journal of Behavioral Sciences* 19 (4): 403–15.

Damon, William. 2001. "To Not Fade Away: Restoring Civil Identity among the Young." In *Making Good Citizens: Education and Civil Society*, edited by Diane Ravitch and Joseph P. Viteritti, 122–41. Yale University Press.

Dannefer, Dale, and R. K. Schutt. 1982. "Race and Juvenile Justice Processing in Court and Police Agencies." *American Journal of Sociology* 87 (4): 1113–32.

Davis, Nancy J., and Robert V. Robinson. 1996. "Are the Rumors of War Exaggerated? Religious Orthodoxy and Moral Progressivism in America." *American Journal of Sociology* 102 (3): 756–87.

Dawson, Richard E., Kenneth Prewitt, and Karen S. Dawson. 1977. *Political Socialization: An Analytic Study*. Boston: Little Brown.

de la Garza, Rodolfo O., Angelo Falcon, and F. Chris Garcia. 1996. "Will the Real Americans Please Stand Up: Anglo and Mexican-American Support of Core American Political Values." *American Journal of Political Science* 40 (2): 335–51.

Della Fave, L. Richard. 1980. "The Meek Shall Not Inherit the Earth: Self-Evaluation and the Legitimacy of Stratification." *American Sociological Review* 45 (6): 955–71.

———. 1986. "Toward an Explanation of the Legitimation Process." *Social Forces* 65 (2): 476–500.

Delli Carpini, Michael X., and Scott Keeter. 1991. "Stability and Change in the U.S. Public's Knowledge of Politics." *Public Opinion Quarterly* 55 (4): 583–612.

———. 1993. "Measuring Political Knowledge: Putting First Things First." *American Journal of Political Science* 37 (4):1179–1206.

———. 1996. *What Americans Know about Politics and Why It Matters*. Yale University Press.

Dennis, Jack. 1968. "Major Problems of Political Socialization Research." *Midwest Journal of Political Science* 12:1: 85–114.

Denver, David, and Gordon Hands. 1990. "Does Studying Politics Make a Difference? Political Knowledge, Attitudes, and Perceptions of School Students." *British Journal of Political Science* 20 (2): 263–88.

Deufel, Benjamin J. 2002. "The Peter Pan Effect: Why Young People Are Voting Less Today." Paper presented at the annual meeting of the Midwest Political Science Association Convention. Chicago.

Dodoo, F. Nij-Amoo, and Patricia Kasari. 1995. "Race and Female Occupational Location in America." *Journal of Black Studies* 25 (4): 456–75.

Easton, David, and Jack Dennis. 1969. *Children in the Political System*. McGraw-Hill.

Easton, David, and Robert D. Hess. 1962. "The Child's Political World." *Midwest Journal of Political Science* 6 (3): 229–46.

Edwards, George C., III, and Tami Swenson. 1997. "Who Rallies? The Anatomy of a Rally Event." *Journal of Politics* 59 (1): 200–12.

Eisinga, R., A. Felling, and J. Peters. 1990. "Religious Belief, Church Involvement, and Ethnocentrism in the Netherlands." *Journal for the Scientific Study of Religion* 29 (1): 54–75.

Elshtain, Jean Bethke. 2001. "Civil Society, Religion, and the Formation of Citizens." In *Making Good Citizens: Education and Civil Society,* edited by Diane Ravitch and Joseph P. Viteritti, 263–78. Yale University Press.

Evans, Francis B., and James G. Anderson. 1973. "The Psychocultural Origins of Achievement and Achievement Motivation: The Mexican American Family." *Sociology of Education* 46 (4): 396–416.

Fallows, James M. 1996. *Breaking the News: How the Media Undermine American Democracy*. Pantheon Books.

Feagin, Joe R., and C. B. Feagin. 1996. *Racial and Ethnic Relations*. Prentice-Hall.

Fernandez-Kelly, M. Patricia, and Richard Schauffler. 1996. "Divided Fates: Immigrant Children and the New Assimilation." In *The New Second Generation*, edited by Alejandro Portes, 30–53. Russell Sage.

Finifter, Ada. 1974. "The Friendship Group as a Protective Environment for Political Deviants." *American Political Science Review* 68 (3): 607–25.

Finifter, Ada, and Paul Abramson. 1975. "City Size and Feelings of Political Competence." *Public Opinion Quarterly* 39 (2): 189–98.

Finkel, Steven E. 1985. "Reciprocal Effects of Participation and Political Efficacy: A Panel Analysis." *American Journal of Political Science* 29 (4): 891–913.

Fouts, Jeffrey T. 1989. "Coaching Athletics and the Social Studies Classroom." *Social Education* 53 (2): 117–19, 122.

Gamm, Gerald, and Robert D. Putnam. 1999. "The Growth of Voluntary Associations in America, 1840–1940." *Journal of Interdisciplinary History* 29 (2): 511–57.

Garcia, F. Chris. 1973. *The Political Socialization of Chicano Children*. Praeger.

Garcia, John A. 1987. "The Political Integration of Mexican Immigrants: Examining Some Political Orientations." *International Migration Review* 21 (2): 372–87.

Garramone, Gina M., and Charles K. Atkin. 1986. "Mass Communication and Political Socialization: Specifying the Effects." *Public Opinion Quarterly* 50 (1): 76–86.

Gecas, Viktor. 1989. "The Social Psychology of Self-Efficacy." *Annual Review of Sociology* 15: 291–316.

Gerber, Alan S., and Donald P. Green. 2000. "The Effects of Personal Canvassing, Telephone Calls, and Direct Mail on Voter Turnout: A Field Experiment." *American Political Science Review* 94 (3): 653–64.

Gibson, Cynthia, and Peter Levine, eds. 2003. *The Civic Mission of Schools: A Report from the Carnegie Corporation of New York and CIRCLE: The Center for Information and Research on Civic Learning and Engagement*. New York: Carnegie Corporation.

Gilens, Martin. 1995. "Racial Attitudes and Opposition to Welfare." *Journal of Politics* 57 (4): 994–1014.

Gimpel, James G. 1999. *Separate Destinations: Migration, Immigration, and the Politics of Places*. University of Michigan Press.

Gimpel, James G., and James R. Edwards Jr. 1999. *The Congressional Politics of Immigration Reform*. Allyn and Bacon.

Gimpel, James G., Irwin L. Morris, and David A. Armstrong. Forthcoming. "Turnout and the Local Age Distribution: Examining Political Participation across Space and Time." *Political Geography*.

Gimpel, James G., and Lewis S. Ringel. 1995. "Understanding Court Nominee Evaluation and Approval: Mass Opinion in the Bork and Thomas Cases." *Political Behavior* 17 (2): 135–53.

Gimpel, James G., and Jason E. Schuknecht. 2002. "Reconsidering Political Regionalism in the American States." *State Politics and Policy Quarterly* 2 (4): 325–52.

———. 2003. *Patchwork Nation: Sectionalism and Political Change in American Politics.* University of Michigan Press.

Ginsberg, Benjamin. 1993. *Jews and the State: The Fatal Embrace.* University of Chicago Press.

Glaser, James M. 1994. "Back to the Black Belt: Racial Environment and White Racial Attitudes in the South." *Journal of Politics* 56 (1):21–41.

Glenmary Research Center. 2001. *Religious Congregations and Membership in the United States, 2000: An Enumeration by Region, State and County Based on Data Reported for 149 Religious Bodies.* Cincinnati.

Greeley, Andrew M. 1975. "A Model for Ethnic Political Socialization." *American Journal of Political Science* 19 (2): 187–206.

Green, Donald P., and Bradley Palmquist. 1994. "How Stable Is Party Identification?" *Political Behavior* 43 (4): 437–66.

Green, Donald P., Bradley Palmquist, and Eric Schickler. 2002. *Partisan Hearts and Minds: Political Parties and the Social Identities of Voters.* Yale University Press.

Greenberg, Edward S. 1970. "Black Children and the Political System." *Public Opinion Quarterly* 34 (3): 333–45.

Griffin, G. A., and others. 1987. "A Cross-Cultural Investigation of Religious Orientation, Social Norms, and Prejudice." *Journal of the Scientific Study of Religion* 26 (3): 358–65.

Guthrie, Patricia, and Janis Hutchinson. 1995. "The Impact of Perceptions on Interpersonal Interactions in an African American/Asian American Housing Project." *Journal of Black Studies* 25 (3): 377–95.

Hahn, Carole L. 1998. *Becoming Political: Comparative Perspectives on Citizenship Education.* State University of New York Press.

Hansen, Susan B. 1997. "Talking about Politics: Gender and Contextual Effects on Political Proselytizing." *Journal of Politics* 59 (1): 73–103.

Harris, Fredrick C. 1994. "Something Within: Religion as a Mobilizer of African-American Political Activism." *Journal of Politics* 56 (1): 42–68.

Hershey, Marjorie Randon, and David B. Hill. 1975. "Watergate and Preadults' Attitudes toward the President." *American Journal of Political Science* 19 (4): 703–26.

Hess, Robert D., and Judith V. Torney. 1967. *The Development of Political Attitudes in Children.* Chicago: Aldine.

Hill, Kim Quaile, and Jan E. Leighley. 1993. "Party Ideology, Organization, and Competitiveness as Mobilizing Forces in Gubernatorial Elections." *American Journal of Political Science* 37 (4): 1158–78.

Hoge, Dean, Gregory Petrillo, and Ella Smith. 1982. "Transmission of Religious and Social Values from Parents to Teenage Children." *Journal of Marriage and the Family* 44 (4):569–80.

Houghland, James G., and J. A. Christenson. 1983. "Religion and Politics: The Relationship of Religious Participation to Political Efficacy and Involvement." *Sociology and Social Research* 67 (3): 405–20.

Howe, Neil, and William Strauss. 2000. *Millennials Rising: The Next Great Generation.* Vintage Books.

Huckfeldt, Robert. 1986. *Politics in Context.* New York: Agathon.

Huckfeldt, Robert, Paul Johnson, and John Sprague. Forthcoming. "Individuals, Dyads and Networks: Autoregressive Patterns of Political Influence." In *The Social Context of Politics*, edited by Alan Zuckerman. Cambridge University Press.

Huckfeldt, Robert, Eric Plutzer, and John Sprague. 1993. "Alternative Contexts of Political Behavior: Churches, Neighborhoods, and Individuals." *Journal of Politics* 55 (2): 365–81.

Huckfeldt, Robert, and John Sprague. 1990. "Social Order and Political Chaos: The Structural Setting of Political Information." In *Information and Democratic Process,* edited by John A. Ferejohn and James H. Kuklinski, 23–58. University of Illinois Press.

———. 1992. "Political Parties and Electoral Mobilization: Political Structure, Social Structure, and the Party Canvass." *American Political Science Review* 86 (1): 70–86.

———. 1995. *Citizens, Politics, and Social Communication: Information and Influence in an Election Campaign.* Cambridge University Press.

Huckfeldt, Robert, and others. 1995. "Political Environments, Cohesive Social Groups, and the Communication of Public Opinion." *American Journal of Political Science* 39 (4): 1025–54.

Hughes, Michael, and David H. Demo. 1989. "Self-Perceptions of Black Americans: Self-Esteem and Personal Efficacy." *American Journal of Sociology* 95 (1): 132–59.

Hunsberger, Bruce, and L. B. Brown. 1984. "Religious Socialization, Apostasy, and the Impact of Family Background." *Journal for the Scientific Study of Religion* 23 (2): 239–51.

Hunter, James Davison. 1991. *Culture Wars: The Struggle to Define America.* Basic Books.

Hurwitz, Jon, and Mark Peffley. 2001. "Racial Polarization on Criminal Justice Issues: Sources and Political Consequences of Fairness Judgments." Paper presented at the annual meeting of the American Political Science Association. San Francisco.

Hyman, Herbert. 1959. *Political Socialization.* Free Press.

Iyengar, Shanto. 1980. "Subjective Political Efficacy as a Measure of Diffuse Support." *Public Opinion Quarterly* 44 (2): 249–56.

Jackman, Robert W. 1972. "Political Elites, Mass Publics, and Support for Democratic Principles." *Journal of Politics*. 34 (2): 753–73.

Jelen, Ted G. 1992. "Political Christianity: A Contextual Analysis." *American Journal of Political Science* 36 (3): 692–714.

Jencks, Christopher. 1972. *Inequality: A Reassessment of the Effect of Family and Schooling in America.* Basic Books.

Jencks, Christopher, and Susan E. Mayer. 1990. "The Social Consequences of Growing up in a Poor Neighborhood." In *Inner City Poverty in the United States,* edited by L. Lynn Jr. and M. G. H. McGeary. National Academy Press.

Jennings, M. Kent. 1996. "Political Knowledge over Time and across Generations." *Public Opinion Quarterly* 65 (1): 228–52.

Jennings, M. Kent, and Gregory B. Markus. 1984. "Partisan Orientations over the Long Haul: Results from a Three-Wave Political Socialization Panel Study." *American Political Science Review* 78 (4): 1000–08.

Jennings, M. Kent, and Richard G. Niemi. 1968. "The Transmission of Political Values from Parent to Child." *American Political Science Review* 62 (1): 169–84.

———. 1971. "The Division of Political Labor between Mothers and Fathers."*American Political Science Review* 65 (1): 69–82.

———. 1974. *The Political Character of Adolescence: The Influence of Families and Schools.* Princeton University Press.

———. 1981. *Generations and Politics: A Panel Study of Young Adults and Their Parents.* Princeton University Press.

Jennings, M. Kent, Laura Stoker, and Jake Bowers. 1999. "Politics across Generations: Family Transmission Reexamined." Paper presented at the annual meeting of the American Political Science Association. Atlanta.

Jo, Moon H. 1992. "Korean Merchants in the Black Community: Prejudice among the Victims of Prejudice." *Racial and Ethnic Studies* 15 (3): 395–411.

Johnson, Benton. 1966. "Theology and Party Preference among Protestant Clergymen." *American Sociological Review* 31 (1): 200–08.

Johnson, Colleen L. 1977. "Interdependence, Reciprocity, and Indebtedness: An Analysis of Japanese Kinship Relations." *Journal of Marriage and the Family* 39 (2): 351–63.

Johnson, Doyle P. 1977. "Religious Commitment, Social Distance, and Authoritarianism." *Review of Religious Research* 18 (1): 99–113.

Johnson, Martin, W. Phillips Shively, and R. M. Stein. 2002. "Contextual Data and the Study of Elections and Voting Behavior: Connecting Individuals to Environments." *Electoral Studies* 21 (2): 219–33.

Kelley, Jonathan, and Ian McAllister. 1985. "Social Context and Electoral Behavior in Britain." *American Journal of Political Science* 29 (4): 564–87.

Kelly, Rita Mae, and Bernard Ronan. 1987. "Subjective Culture and Patriotism: Gender, Ethnic, and Class Differences among High School Students." *Political Psychology* 8 (4): 525–46.

Kennedy, Randall. 1997. *Race, Crime, and the Law.* Pantheon Books.

Kernell, Samuel. 1986. *Going Public: New Strategies of Presidential Leadership.* Congressional Quarterly Press.

Key, V. O., Jr. 1949. *Southern Politics in State and Nation.* Alfred A. Knopf.

———. 1956. *American State Politics: An Introduction.* Alfred A. Knopf.

Kinder, Donald R., and Lynn M. Sanders. 1996. *Divided by Color: Racial Politics and Democratic Ideals.* University of Chicago Press.

Kinder, Donald R., and David O. Sears. 1981. "Prejudice and Politics: Symbolic Racism versus Racial Threats to the Good Life." *Journal of Personality and Social Psychology* 4 (3): 414–31.

King, Gary. 1996. "Why Context Should Not Count." *Political Geography* 15 (2): 159–64.

Kish, Leslie. 1987. *Statistical Design for Research.* John Wiley & Sons.

Kline, Paul. 1994. *An Easy Guide to Factor Analysis.* Routledge.

Kohlberg, Lawrence. 1958. "The Development of Modes of Moral Thinking and Choice in Years Ten to Sixteen." Ph.D. dissertation. University of Chicago.

———. 1984. *The Psychology of Moral Development: The Nature and Validity of Moral Stages.* Harper & Row.

———. 1987. *Child Psychology and Childhood Education: A Cognitive-Developmental View.* New York: Longman.

Kramer, Judith. 1970. *The American Minority Community.* Crowell.

Kuklinski, James H., Michael D. Cobb, and Martin Gilens. 1997. "Racial Attitudes and the 'New South.'" *Journal of Politics* 59 (2): 329–43.

Kuzma, Lynn M. 2000. "The Polls–Trends: Terrorism in the United States." *Public Opinion Quarterly* 64 (1): 90–105.

Lamare, James. 1982. "The Political Integration of Mexican American Children: A Generational Analysis." *International Migration Review* 16 (1): 169–88.

Langton, Kenneth P. 1969. *Political Socialization.* Oxford University Press.

Langton, Kenneth P., and M. Kent Jennings. 1968. "Political Socialization and the High School Civics Curriculum in the United States." *American Political Science Review* 62 (3): 852–67.

Layman, Geoffrey C. 1997. "Religion and Political Behavior in the United States: The Impact of Beliefs, Affiliations, and Commitment from 1980 to 1994." *Public Opinion Quarterly* 61 (2): 288–316.

———. 2001. *The Great Divide: Religious Cultural Conflict in American Party Politics.* Columbia University Press.

Lee, Valerie E., and Anthony S. Bryk. 1989. "A Multilevel Model of the Social Distribution of High School Achievement." *Sociology of Education* 62 (3): 172–92.

Leege, David C., and Michael R. Welch. 1989. "Religious Roots of Political Orientations: Variations among American Catholic Parishioners." *Journal of Politics* 51 (1): 137–62.

Levey, Geoffrey Brahm. 1996. "The Liberalism of American Jews—Has It Been Explained?" *British Journal of Political Science* 26 (3): 369–401.

Lian, Bradley, and John R. Oneal. 1993. "Presidents, the Use of Military Force, and Public Opinion." *Journal of Conflict Resolution* 37 (2): 277–300.

Lipset, Seymour Martin, and William Schneider. 1983. "The Decline of Confidence in American Institutions." *Political Science Quarterly* 98 (3): 379–402.

Litt, Edgar. 1963. "Civic Education, Community Norms, and Political Indoctrination." *American Sociological Review* 28 (1): 69–75.

Luskin, Robert C. 1990. "Explaining Political Sophistication." *Political Behavior* 12 (3): 331–61.

Lyons, Schley R. 1970. "The Political Socialization of Ghetto Children: Efficacy and Cynicism." *Journal of Politics* 32 (2): 288–304.

Ma, Ying. 1998. "Black Racism." *American Enterprise* 9 (6): 54–56.

MacIntyre, Alasdair. 1995. "Is Patriotism a Virtue?" In *Theorizing Citizenship*, edited by Ronald Beiner, 209–29. State University of New York Press.

MacKuen, Michael, and Courtney Brown. 1987. "Political Context and Attitude Change." *American Political Science Review* 81 (2): 471–90.

MacLeod, Jay. 1995. *Ain't No Makin' It*. Westview Press.

Mann, Sheilah, and John J. Patrick, eds. 2000. *Education for Civic Engagement in Democracy: Service-Learning and Other Promising Practices*. Bloomington, Ind.: ERIC Clearinghouse for Social Studies.

Markus, Gregory B. 1979. "The Political Environment and the Dynamics of Public Attitudes: A Panel Study." *American Journal of Political Science* 23 (2): 338–59.

Maruyama, Geoffrey M. 1998. *Basics of Structural Equation Modeling*. Sage.

McClosky, Herbert, and Dennis Chong. 1985. "Similarities and Differences Between Left-Wing and Right-Wing Radicals." *British Journal of Political Science* 15 (2): 329–63.

McDonald, Michael P., and Samuel L. Popkin. 2001. "The Myth of the Vanishing Voter." *American Political Science Review* 95 (4): 963–73.

McLanahan, Sara S. 1985. "Family Structure and the Intergenerational Transmission of Poverty." *American Journal of Sociology* 90 (4): 873–904.

McLanahan, Sara S., and Larry Bumpass. 1988. "Intergenerational Consequences of Family Disruption." *American Journal of Sociology* 94 (1): 130–52.

McLanahan, Sara S., and G. D. Sandefur. 1994. *Growing Up with a Single Parent*. Harvard University Press.

McVeigh, Rory, and David Sikkink. 2001. "God, Politics, and Protest: Religious Beliefs and the Legitimation of Contentious Tactics." *Social Forces* 79 (4): 1425–58.

Medding, Peter Y. 1977. "Towards a General Theory of Jewish Political Interests and Behaviour." *Jewish Journal of Sociology* 19 (1):115–44.

Miller, Joanne M., and Jon A. Krosnick. 2000. "News Media Impact on the Ingredients of Presidential Evaluations: Politically Knowledgeable Citizens Are Guided by a Trusted Source." *American Journal of Political Science* 44 (2): 301–15.

Miller, Warren E., and J. Merrill Shanks. 1996. *The New American Voter.* Harvard University Press.

Morris, Irwin L. 2002. *Votes, Money, and the Clinton Impeachment.* Westview Press.

Morrison, A., and D. McIntyre. 1971. *Schools and Socialization.* Penguin.

Mueller, John E. 1970. "Presidential Popularity from Truman to Johnson." *American Political Science Review* 64 (1): 18–34.

———. 1973. *War, Presidents, and Public Opinion.* John Wiley & Sons.

Mutz, Diana C. 1998. *Impersonal Influence: How Perceptions of Mass Collectives Affect Political Attitudes.* Cambridge University Press.

———. 2002a. "Cross-Cutting Social Networks: Testing Democratic Theory in Practice." *American Political Science Review* 96 (1): 111–26.

———. 2002b. "The Consequences of Cross-Cutting Networks for Political Participation." *American Journal of Political Science* 46 (4): 838–55.

Mutz, Diana C., and Jeffrey J. Mondak. 1997. "Dimensions of Sociotropic Behavior: Group-Based Judgments of Fairness and Well-Being." *American Journal of Political Science* 41 (1): 284–301.

———. 2001. "Choosing Partners: Co-Workers as Political Discussants." Paper presented at the annual meeting of the Midwest Political Science Association. Chicago.

Nie, Norman, and D. Sunshine Hillygus. 2001. "Education and Democratic Citizenship." In *Making Good Citizens: Education and Civil Society,* edited by Diane Ravitch and Joseph P. Viteritti, 30–57. Yale University Press.

Nie, Norman H., Jane Junn, and Kenneth Stehlik-Barry. 1996. *Education and Democratic Citizenship in America.* University of Chicago Press.

Nie, Norman H., Sidney Verba, and John Petrocik. 1979. *The Changing American Voter.* Harvard University Press.

Niemi, Richard G., and M. Kent Jennings. 1991. "Issues and Inheritance in the Formation of Party Identification." *American Journal of Political Science* 35 (4): 970–88.

Niemi, Richard G., and Jane Junn. 1998. *Civic Education: What Makes Students Learn?* Yale University Press.

Noelle-Neumann, Elisabeth. 1993. *The Spiral of Silence: Our Social Skin.* University of Chicago Press.

Oliver, J. Eric. 1999. "The Effects of Metropolitan Economic Segregation on Local Civic Participation." *American Journal of Political Science* 43 (1): 186–212.

Oyserman, Daphna, and Izumi Sakamoto. 1997. "Being Asian American: Identity, Cultural Contructs, and Stereotype Perception." *Journal of Applied Behavioral Science* 33 (4): 435–53.

Parker, Keith D., Anne B. Onyekwuluje, and Komanduri S. Murty. 1995. "African Americans' Attitudes toward the Local Police: A Multivariate Analysis." *Journal of Black Studies* 25 (5): 396–409.

Parker, Suzanne L. 1995. "Toward an Understanding of 'Rally' Effects: Public Opinion in the Persian Gulf War." *Public Opinion Quarterly* 59 (4): 526–46.

Paskeviciute, Aida, and Christopher Anderson. 2003. "Democracy, Disagreement and the Foundations for Social Capital." Paper presented at the annual meeting of the Midwest Political Science Association, Chicago.

Patterson, Samuel C., and Gregory A. Caldeira. 1983. "Getting Out the Vote: Participation in Gubernatorial Elections." *American Political Science Review* 77 (2): 675–89.

Peek, Charles W., Jon P. Alston, and George D. Lowe. 1978. "Comparative Evaluation of the Local Police." *Public Opinion Quarterly* 42 (3): 370–380.

Peterson, Steve. 1992. "Church Participation and Political Participation: The Spillover Effect." *American Politics Quarterly* 20 (1): 123–39.

Pierce, John C., and Addison Carey Jr. 1971. "Efficacy and Participation: A Study of Black Political Behavior." *Journal of Black Studies* 2 (2): 201–23.

Plutzer, Eric. 2002. "Becoming a Habitual Voter: Inertia, Resources, and Growth in Young Adulthood." *American Political Science Review* 96 (1): 57–74.

Price, Vincent, and John Zaller. 1993. "Who Gets the News? Alternative Measures of News Reception and Their Implications for Research." *Public Opinion Quarterly* 57 (2): 133–64.

Prothro, James W., and Charles M. Grigg. 1960. "Fundamental Principles of Democracy: Bases of Agreement and Disagreement." *Journal of Politics* 22 (2): 276–94.

Putnam, Robert D. 1966. "Political Attitudes and the Local Community." *American Political Science Review* 60 (3): 640–54.

———. 2000. *Bowling Alone: the Collapse and Revival of American Community.* Simon and Schuster.

Quirk, Paul J. 2000. "Scandal Time: The Clinton Impeachment and the Distraction of American Politics." In *The Clinton Scandal and the Future of American Government,* edited by Mark J. Rozell and Clyde Wilcox, 119–42. Georgetown University Press.

Raudenbush, Stephen W., and Anthony S. Bryk. 2002. *Hierarchical Linear Models,* 2d ed. Sage.

Reese, Laura A., and Ronald E. Brown. 1995. "The Effects of Religious Messages on Racial Identity and System Blame among African Americans." *Journal of Politics* 57 (1): 24–43.

Rigby, Ken. 1988a. "Acceptance of Authority, Self, and Others." *Journal of Social Psychology* 126 (4): 493–501.

———. 1988b. "Parental Influence on Attitudes toward Institutional Authority." *Journal of Genetic Psychology* 149 (3): 383–91.

Robinson, Michael J. 1975. "American Political Legitimacy in an Era of Electronic Journalism: Reflections on the Evening News." In *Television as a Social Force: New Approaches to TV Criticism,* edited by D. Cater and R. Adler, 97–139. Praeger.

———. 1976. "Public Affairs Television and the Growth of Political Malaise: The Case of the Selling of the President." *American Political Science Review* 70 (2): 409–32.

Rodgers, Harrell R. 1974. "Toward Explanation of the Political Efficacy and Political Cynicism of Black Adolescents: An Exploratory Study." *American Journal of Political Science* 18 (2): 257–82.

Rodgers, Harrell R., and George Taylor. 1971. "The Policeman as an Agent of Regime Legitimation." *Midwest Journal of Political Science* 15 (2): 72–86.

Rosenstone, Steven P., and John Mark Hansen. 1993. *Mobilization, Participation, and Democracy in America.* Macmillan.

Ross, C. E., J. Mirowsky, and W. C. Cockerham. 1983. "Social Class, Mexican Culture, and Fatalism: Their Effects on Psychological Distress." *American Journal of Community Psychology* 11 (3): 383–99.

Rozell, Mark J., and Clyde Wilcox, eds. 1997. *God at the Grass Roots, 1996: The Christian Right in the American Elections.* Rowman and Littlefield.

———. 2000. *The Clinton Scandal and the Future of American Government.* Georgetown University Press.

Sampson, Robert J., and Dawn J. Bartusch. 1998. "Legal Cynicism and (Subcultural?) Tolerance of Deviance: The Neighborhood Context of Racial Differences." *Law and Society Review* 32 (4): 777–804.

Sampson, Robert J., Stephen W. Raudenbush, and Felton Earls. 1997. "Neighborhoods and Violent Crime: A Multilevel Study of Collective Efficacy." *Science* 277 (4): 918–24.

Sanchez-Jankowski, Martin. 1986. *City Bound: Urban Life and Political Attitudes among Chicano Youth.* University of New Mexico Press.

———. 1992. "Ethnic Identity and Political Consciousness in Different Social Orders." *New Directions for Child Development* 56: 79–94.

Sani, Giacomo. 1976. "Political Traditions as Contextual Variables: Partisanship in Italy." *American Journal of Political Science* 20 (2): 375–405.

Sapiro, Virginia, and Pamela Johnston Conover. 1977. "The Variable Gender Basis of Electoral Politics: Gender and Context in the 1992 U.S. Election." *British Journal of Political Science* 27 (4): 497–523.

Sarat, Austin. 1975. "Reasoning in Politics: The Social, Political, and Psychological Bases of Principled Thought." *American Journal of Political Science* 19 (2): 247–63.

Schattschneider, E. E. 1960. *The Semi-Sovereign People: A Realist's View of Democracy in America.* Holt, Rinehart, and Winston.

Schneider, Barbara, and David Stevenson. 1999. *America's Teenagers: Motivated but Directionless.* Yale University Press.

Schuman, Howard, and Lawrence Bobo. 1988. "Survey-Based Experiments on White Racial Attitudes toward Residential Integration." *American Journal of Sociology* 94 (4): 273–99.

Schuman, Howard, and Amy Corning. 2000. "Collective Knowledge of Public Events: The Soviet Era from the Great Purge to Glasnost." *American Journal of Sociology* 105 (4): 913–56.

Schuman, Howard, Charlotte Steeh, and Lawrence Bobo. 1985. *Racial Attitudes in America: Trends and Interpretations.* Harvard University Press.

Schuman, Howard, and others. 1985. "Effort and Reward: The Assumption That College Grades Are Affected by Quantity of Study." *Social Forces* 63 (4): 945–66.

Schwartz, Audrey James. 1971. "A Comparative Study of Values and Achievement: Mexican-American and Anglo Youth." *Sociology of Education* 44 (4): 438–62.

Searing, Donald, Joel J. Schwartz, and Alden E. Lind. 1973. "The Structuring Principle: Political Socialization and Belief Systems." *American Political Science Review* 67 (2): 415–32.

Searing, Donald, Gerald Wright, and George Rabinowitz. 1976. "The Primacy Principle: Attitude Change and Political Socialization." *British Journal of Political Science* 6 (1): 83–113.

Sears, David O. 1975. "Political Socialization." In *Handbook of Political Science*, vol. 2, edited by Fred I. Greenstein and N.W. Polsby, 93–153. Addison Wesley.

Sears, David O., Jim Sidanius, and Lawrence Bobo, eds. 2000. *Racialized Politics: The Debate about Racism in America.* University of Chicago Press.

Sears, David O., and Nicholas A. Valentino. 1997. "Politics Matters: Political Events as Catalysts for Preadult Socialization." *American Political Science Review* 91 (1): 45–65.

Seeman, Melvin. 1966. "Alienation, Membership, and Political Knowledge: A Comparative Study." *Public Opinion Quarterly* 30 (3): 353–67.

Shapiro, Sheldon. 1976. "Morality in Religious Reformations." *Comparative Studies in Society and History* 18 (4): 438–57.

Shingles, Richard D. 1981. "Black Consciousness and Political Participation: The Missing Link." *American Political Science Review* 75 (1): 76–91.

Skerry, Peter N. 1993. *Mexican Americans: The Ambivalent Minority.* Free Press.

Skocpol, Theda, Marshall Ganz, and Ziad Munson. 2000. "A Nation of Organizers: The Institutional Origins of Civic Voluntarism in the United States." *American Political Science Review* 94 (3): 527–45.

Smidt, Corwin. 1999. "Religion and Civic Engagement: A Comparative Analysis." *Annals of the American Academy of Political and Social Science* 565 (2): 176–92.

Smith, A. Wade. 1981a. "Racial Tolerance as a Function of Group Position." *American Sociological Review* 46 (4): 558–73.

———. 1981b. "Tolerance of School Desegregation, 1954–1977." *Social Forces* 59 (4): 1257–74.

Steeh, Charlotte, and Howard Schuman. 1992. "Young White Adults: Did Racial Attitudes Change in the 1980s?" *American Journal of Sociology* 98 (2): 340–67.

Steenbergen, Marco R., and Bradford S. Jones. 2002. "Modeling Multilevel Data Structures." *American Journal of Political Science* 46 (1): 218–37.

Steinberger, Peter J. 1981. "Social Context and Political Efficacy." *Sociology and Social Research* 65: 129–41.

Stevens, A. Jay. 1975. "The Acquisition of Participatory Norms: The Case of Japanese and Mexican American Children in a Suburban Environment." *Western Political Quarterly* 28 (3): 281–95.

Strate, John M., and others. 1989. "Life Span Civic Development and Voting Participation." *American Political Science Review* 83 (2): 443–64.

Tate, Katherine. 1991. "Black Political Participation in the 1984 and 1988 Presidential Elections." *American Political Science Review* 85 (4): 1159–76.

Taylor, Charles R., Ju Yung Lee, and Barbara B. Stern. 1995. "Portrayals of African, Hispanic and Asian Americans in Magazine Advertising." *American Behavioral Scientist* 38 (4): 608–21.

Torney, Judith V., A. N. Oppenheim, and Russell F. Farnen. 1975. *Civic Education in Ten Countries: An Empirical Study.* John Wiley & Sons.

Torney-Purta, Judith, and others. 2001. *Citizenship and Education in Twenty-Eight Countries: Civic Knowledge and Engagement at Age Fourteen.* International Association for the Evaluation of Educational Achievement, Amsterdam.

Tuch, Steven A., and Ronald Weitzer. 1997. "Trends: Racial Differences in Attitudes toward the Police." *Public Opinion Quarterly* 61 (4): 642–63.

Uhlaner, Carole J., Bruce E. Cain, and D. Roderick Kiewiet. 1989. "Political Participation of Ethnic Minorities in the 1980s." *Political Behavior* 11 (3): 195–227.

Uslaner, Eric M. 2002. *The Moral Foundations of Trust.* Cambridge University Press.

Valentino, Nicholas, and David O. Sears. 1998. "Event-Driven Political Socialization and the Preadult Socialization of Partisanship." *Political Behavior* 20 (3): 127–54.

Verba, Sidney, and others. 1993. "Citizen Activity: Who Participates? What Do They Say?" *American Political Science Review* 87 (3): 303–18.

Wald, Kenneth D., Dennis E. Owen, and Samuel S. Hill Jr. 1990. "Political Cohesion in Churches." *Journal of Politics* 52 (1): 197–215.

Waters, Mary C. 1996. "Ethnic and Racial Identities of Second-Generation Black Immigrants in New York City." In *The New Second Generation,* edited by Alejandro Portes, 171–98. Russell Sage.

Weissberg, Robert. 1972a. "Adolescent Experiences with Political Authorities." *Journal of Politics* 34 (3): 797–824.

———. 1972b. "Adolescents' Perceptions of Political Authorities: Another Look at Political Virtue and Power." *Midwest Journal of Political Science* 16 (1): 147–68.

———. 1975. "Political Efficacy and Political Illusion." *Journal of Politics* 37 (2): 469–87.

Westholm, Anders, Arne Lindquist, and Richard G. Niemi. 1990. "Education and the Making of the Informed Citizen: Political Literacy and the Outside World." In *Political Socialization, Citizen Education, and Democracy*, edited by Orit Ichilov, 430–46. New York: Teacher's College Press.

Wilen, William W., and Jane J. White. 1991. "Interactive Discourse in Social Studies Classrooms." In *Handbook of Research on Social Studies Teaching and Learning*, edited by James P. Shaver, 483–95. Macmillan.

Willis, Paul. 1977. *Learning to Labor: How Working Class Kids Get Working Class Jobs*. Columbia University Press.

Willis-Esqueda, Cynthia. 1997. "European American Students' Perceptions of Crimes Committed by Five Racial Groups." *Journal of Applied Social Psychology* 27 (16): 1406–20.

Wilson, William Julius. 1996. *When Work Disappears: The World of the New Urban Poor*. Alfred A. Knopf.

Wittkopf, Eugene R. 1986. "On the Foreign Policy Beliefs of the American People: A Critique and Some Evidence." *International Studies Quarterly* 30 (4): 425–45.

———. 1987. "Elites and Masses: Another Look at Attitudes toward America's World Role." *International Studies Quarterly* 31 (2): 131–59.

Wuthnow, Robert. 1988. *The Restructuring of American Religion: Society and Faith since World War II*. Princeton University Press.

Yabiku, Scott, William G. Axinn, and Arland Thornton. 1999. "Family Integration and Children's Self-Esteem." *American Sociological Review* 104 (5): 1494–1524.

Zaller, John. 1992. *The Nature and Origins of Mass Opinion*. Cambridge University Press.

Zukin, Cliff. 2000. "Across the Generational Divide: Political Engagement, Civic and Social Attitudes." Paper presented at the annual meeting of the American Association for Public Opinion Research. Portland, Ore.

Further Resources

Abramson, Paul R. 1974. "Generational Change in American Electoral Behavior." *American Political Science Review* 68 (1): 93–105.

———. 1976. "Generational Change and the Decline of Party Identification in America: 1952–1974." *American Political Science Review* 70 (2): 469–78.

———. 1989. "Generations and Political Change in the United States." *Research in Political Sociology* 4: 235–280.

Abramson, Paul R., and Ronald Inglehart. 1987. "Generational Replacement and the Future of Post-Materialist Values." *Journal of Politics* 49 (1): 231–41.

Acock, Alan, Harold D. Clarke, and Marianne C. Stewart. 1985. "A New Model for Old Measures: A Covariance Structure Analysis of Political Efficacy." *Journal of Politics* 47 (4): 1062–84.

Alex-Assensoh, Yvette, and A. B. Assensoh. 2001. "Inner-City Contexts, Church Attendance, and African-American Political Participation." *Journal of Politics* 63 (3): 886–901.

Allen, Jan, Patricia Freeman, and Sandy Osborne. 1989. "Children's Political Knowledge and Attitudes." *Young Children* (January): 57–61.

Alwin, Duane F., and Luther B. Otto. 1977. "High School Context Effects on Aspirations." *Sociology of Education* 50 (1): 259–73.

Anderson, Christopher J., and Aida Paskeviciute. Forthcoming. "Macro-Politics and Micro-Behavior: Mainstream Politics and Political Discussion in Democracies." In *The Social Context of Politics*, edited by Alan Zuckerman. Cambridge University Press.

Apple, Nixon, and D. O'Brien. 1983. "Neighborhood Racial Composition and Residents' Evaluation of Police Performance." *American Sociological Review* 11 (1): 76–84.

Beck, Paul Allen, and M. Kent Jennings. 1975. "Parents as 'Middlepersons' in Political Socialization." *Journal of Politics* 37 (1): 83–107.

Beggs, John J., Wayne J. Villemez, and Ruth Arnold. 1997. "Black Population Concentration and Black-White Inequality: Expanding the Consideration of Place and Space Effects." *Social Forces* 76 (1): 65–91.

Beiner, Ronald, ed. 1995. *Theorizing Citizenship.* State University of New York Press.

Bennett, Stephen E. 1988. "'Know-Nothings' Revisited: The Meaning of Political Ignorance Today." *Social Science Quarterly* 69 (3): 476–90.

———. 1989. "Trends in Americans' Political Information, 1967–1987." *American Politics Quarterly* 17 (3): 422–35.

Bloom, Benjamin S. 1966. "Stability and Change in Human Characteristics: Implications for School Reorganization." *Educational Administration Quarterly* 2 (1): 35–49.

Boocock, Sarane Spence. 1978. "The Social Organization of the Classroom." *Annual Review of Sociology* 4: 1–28.

Brewster, Karin L. 1994. "Race Differences in Sexual Activity among Adolescent Women: The Role of Neighborhood Characteristics." *American Sociological Review* 59 (3): 408–24.

Brint, Steven. 1984. "'New Class' and Cumulative Trend Explanations of the Liberal Political Attitudes of Professionals." *American Journal of Sociology* 90 (1): 30–71.

———. 1985. "The Political Attitudes of Professionals." *Annual Review of Sociology* 11: 389–414.

Brooks-Gunn, Jeanne, and others. 1993. "Do Neighborhoods Influence Child and Adolescent Development?" *American Journal of Sociology* 99 (2): 353–95.

Browning, Sandra, and others. 1994. "Race and Getting Hassled by the Police: A Research Note." *Police Studies* 17 (1): 1–11.

Campbell, Bruce A. 1980. "A Theoretical Approach to Peer Influence in Adolescent Socialization." *American Journal of Political Science* 24 (2): 324–44.

Campbell, Donald T., and Julian C. Stanley. 1963. *Experimental and Quasi-Experimental Designs for Research.* Houghton Mifflin.

Caplow, Theodore, and Howard M. Bahr. 1979. "Half a Century of Change in Adolescent Attitudes: Replication of a Middletown Survey by the Lynds." *Public Opinion Quarterly* 43 (1): 1–17.

Chaffee, Steven H., Xinshu Zhao, and Glenn Leshner. 1994. "Political Knowledge and the Campaign Media of 1992." *Communication Research* 21 (3): 305–24.

Citrin, Jack, and others. 1994. "Is American Nationalism Changing? Implications for Foreign Policy." *International Studies Quarterly* 38 (1): 1–31.

Coleman, James S. 1961. *The Adolescent Society: The Social Life of the Teenager and Its Impact on Education.* Free Press.

Conover, Pamela Johnston, and Virginia Sapiro. 1993. "Gender, Feminist Consciousness and War." *American Journal of Political Science* 37 (4): 1079–99.

Conover, Pamela Johnston, Ivor M. Crewe, and Donald D. Searing. 1991. "The Nature of Citizenship in the United States and Great Britain: Empirical Comments on Theoretical Themes." *Journal of Politics* 53 (4): 800–32.

Converse, Jean M. 1976. "Predicting No Opinion in the Polls." *Public Opinion Quarterly.* 40 (4): 515–30.

Cook, Timothy E. 1985. "The Bear Market in Political Socialization Research and the Costs of Misunderstood Psychological Theories." *American Political Science Review* 79 (4): 1079–93.

Crane, Jonathan. 1991. "The Epidemic Theory of Ghettos and Neighborhood Effects on Dropping Out and Teenage Childbearing." *American Journal of Sociology* 96 (5): 1226–59.

Cummings, Scott, and Thomas Lambert. 1997. "Anti-Hispanic and Anti-Asian Sentiments among African-Americans." *Social Science Quarterly* 78 (2): 338–53.

Dahl, Robert A. 1956. *A Preface to Democratic Theory.* University of Chicago Press.

———. 1961. *Who Governs?* Yale University Press.

Dalton, Russell. 1980. "Reassessing Parental Socialization: Indicator Unreliability versus Generational Transfer." *American Political Science Review* 74 (2): 421–31.

Decker, Scott H. 1981. "Citizen Attitudes toward the Police: A Review of Past Findings and Suggestions for Future Police." *Journal of Police Science and Administration* 9 (1): 80–87.

Dodson, Dan W. 1959. "The Role of the Community in Social Studies." *Journal of Educational Sociology* 33 (1): 85–92.

Dornbusch, Sanford M. 1989. "The Sociology of Adolescence." *Annual Review of Sociology* 15: 233–59.

Easton, David, and Jack Dennis. 1967. "The Child's Acquisition of Regime Norms: Political Efficacy." *American Political Science Review* 61 (1): 25–38.

Ehman, Lee H. 1980. "The American School in the Political Socialization Process." *Review of Educational Research* 50: 99–119.

Exley, Anita R. 1994. "Adolescent Respect for Authority and Attitudes toward the Use of Violence." Ph.D. dissertation, Department of Psychology, University of Toledo (Ohio).

Finifter, Ada. 1970. "Dimensions of Political Alienation." *American Political Science Review* 64: 389–410.

Frank, James, and others. 1996. "Reassessing the Impact of Race on Citizens' Attitudes toward the Police: A Research Note." *Justice Quarterly* 13: 321–34.

Fuchs, Lawrence H. 1956. *The Political Behavior of American Jews.* Free Press.

Furstenberg, Frank F., Jr., and others. 1987. "Race Differences in the Timing of Adolescent Intercourse." *American Sociological Review* 52 (4): 511–18.

Galston, William A. 1988. "Liberal Virtues." *American Political Science Review* 82 (4): 1277–90.

———. 2001. "Political Knowledge, Political Engagement, and Civic Education." *Annual Review of Political Science* 4: 217–34.

Garner, Catherine L., and Stephen W. Raudenbush. 1991. "Neighborhood Effects on Educational Attainment: A Multilevel Analysis." *Sociology of Education* 64 (4): 252–62.

Gerber, Alan S., and Donald P. Green. 1998. "Rational Learning and Partisan Attitudes." *American Journal of Political Science* 42 (3): 794–818.

Gilliam, Franklin D., Jr., and others. 1996. "Crime in Black and White: The Violent, Scary World of Local News." *Harvard International Journal of Press/Politics* 1 (6): 6–23.

Glenn, Charles L., and Ester J. de Jong. 1996. *Educating Immigrant Children: Schools and Language Minorities in Twelve Nations.* New York: Garland Publishing.

Greeley, Andrew M., and Paul B. Sheatsley. 1974. "Attitudes toward Racial Integration." In *Social Problems and Public Policy: Inequality and Justice,* edited by Lee Rainwater, 241–50. Chicago: Aldine.

Greenberg, Anna. 2000. "The Church and the Revitalization of Politics and Community." *Political Science Quarterly* 115 (3): 377–94.

Greenstein, Fred I. 1960. "The Benevolent Leader: Children's Images of Political Authority." *American Political Science Review* 54 (4): 934–43.

———. 1976. "The Benevolent Leader Revisited: Children's Images of Political Leaders in Three Democracies." *American Political Science Review* 69 (4): 1371–98.

Hauser, Robert M. 1974. "Contextual Analysis Revisited." *Sociological Methods and Research* 2 (2): 365–75.

Hawkins, Brett W., Vincent L. Marando, and George A. Taylor. 1971. "Efficacy, Mistrust, and Political Participation: Findings from Additional Data and Indicators." *Journal of Politics* 33 (4): 1130–36.

Herrnstein, Richard J., and Charles Murray. 1994. *The Bell Curve: Intelligence and Class Structure in American Life.* Free Press.

Hinckley, Ronald H. 1988. "Public Attitudes toward Key Foreign Policy Events." *Journal of Conflict Resolution* 32 (2): 295–318.

Hirlinger, Michael W. 1992. "Citizen-Initiated Contacting of Local Government Officials: A Multivariate Explanation." *Journal of Politics* 54 (2): 553–64.

Huckfeldt, Robert, and John Sprague. 1987. "Networks in Context: The Social Flow of Political Information." *American Political Science Review* 81 (4): 1198–1216.

Hurst, Yolander G., and James Frank. 2000. "How Kids View Cops: The Nature of Juvenile Attitudes toward the Police." *Journal of Criminal Justice* 28 (3): 189–202.

Hurst, Yolander G., James Frank, and Sandra Lee Browning. 2000. "The Attitudes of Juveniles toward the Police: A Comparison of Black and White Youth." *Policing: An International Journal of Police Strategies & Management* 23 (1): 37–53.

Iyengar, Shanto. 1987. "Television News and Citizens' Explanations of National Affairs." *American Political Science Review* 81 (3): 815–32.

Jackman, Mary. 1978. "General and Applied Tolerance: Does Education Increase Commitment to Racial Integration?" *American Journal of Political Science* 22 (2): 302–24.

Jackman, Robert W. 1970. "A Note on Intelligence, Social Class, and Political Efficacy in Children." *Journal of Politics* 32 (4): 984–89.

Jennings, M. Kent. 1967. "Pre-Adult Orientations to Multiple Systems of Government." *Midwest Journal of Political Science* 11 (3): 291–317.

Jennings, M. Kent, and Gregory B. Markus. 1977. "The Effect of Military Service on Political Attitudes: A Panel Study." *American Political Science Review* 71 (1): 131–47.

Johnson, Norris. 1973. "Television and Politicization: A Test of Competing Models." *Journalism Quarterly* 51 (3): 447–55.

Kim, Kwang Chung, ed. 1999. *Koreans in the Hood: Conflict with African Americans.* Johns Hopkins University Press.

Kitano, Harry H. L. 1969. *The Japanese Americans.* Prentice-Hall.

Kleck, Gary. 1982. "On the Use of Self-Report Data to Determine the Class Distribution of Criminal and Delinquent Behavior." *American Sociological Review* 47 (3): 427–33.

Kohut, Andrew, and others. 2000. *The Diminishing Divide: Religion's Changing Role in American Politics.* Brookings.

Krassa, Michael. 2000. "Contextual Conditioning of Political Information: Common Themes from Disparate Data." University of Illinois, Department of Political Science, and Merriam Laboratory for Analytic Political Research.

Kwong, Peter. 1996. *The New Chinatown.* New York: Hill and Wang.

Lane, Robert E. 1982. "Government and Self-Esteem." *Political Theory* 10 (1): 5–31.

Langton, Kenneth P. 1967. "Peer Group and School and the Political Socialization Process." *American Political Science Review* 61 (3): 751–58.

Lanoue, David J. 1992. "One That Made a Difference: Cognitive Consistency, Political Knowledge, and the 1980 Presidential Debate." *Public Opinion Quarterly* 56 (2): 168–84.

Lau, Richard R. 1985. "Two Explanations for Negativity Effects in Political Behavior." *American Journal of Political Science* 29 (1): 119–38.

Lau, Richard R., and David P. Redlawsk. 1997. "Voting Correctly." *American Political Science Review* 91 (1): 585–98.

Leiber, Michael J., Mahesh K. Nalla, and Margaret Farnworth. 1998. "Explaining Juveniles' Attitudes toward the Police." *Justice Quarterly* 15 (1): 151–74.

Leshner, Glenn, and Michael L. McKean. 1997. "Using TV News for Political Information During an Off-Year Election: Effects on Political Knowledge and Cynicism." *Journalism and Mass Communication Quarterly* 74 (1): 69–83.

Levin, Martin L. 1961. "Social Climates and Political Socialization." *Public Opinion Quarterly* 25 (4): 596–606.

Lin, Ann Chih. 1998. "The Troubled Success of Crime Policy." In *The Social Divide: Political Parties and the Future of Activist Government*, edited by Margaret Weir, 312–57. Brookings.

Macaluso, Theodore F., and John Wanat. 1979. "Voting Turnout and Religiosity." *Polity* 12 (2): 158–69.

Mackey, James, and Andrew Ahlgren. 1980. "A Pictorial Measure of Adolescent Perceptions of the Police." *Social Education* (March): 224–27, 248.

Madison, James. 1961. "Federalist 57." In *The Federalist Papers,* edited by Clinton Rossiter, 350–56. Penguin Books.

Massey, Douglas S. 1981. "Dimensions of the New Immigration to the United States and the Prospects for Assimilation." *Annual Review of Sociology* 7: 57–85.

Mastrofski, Stephen. 1981. "Surveying Clients to Assess Police Performance." *Evaluation Review* 5: 397–408.

Matsueda, Ross L., and Karen Heimer. 1987. "Race, Family Structure, and Delinquency: A Test of Differential Association and Social Control Theories." *American Sociological Review* 52 (6): 826–40.

Mau, Wei-Cheng. 1995. "Educational Planning and Academic Achievement of Middle School Students: A Racial and Cultural Comparison." *Journal of Counseling and Development* 73 (3): 518–34.

McDill, Edward L., Leo C. Rigsby, and Edmund D. Meyers Jr. 1969. "Educational Climates of High Schools: Their Effects and Sources." *American Journal of Sociology* 74 (3): 567–86.

Merriam, Charles E. 1931. *The Making of Citizens.* University of Chicago Press.

Mondak, Jeffery J. 1995. "Media Exposure and Political Discussion in U.S. Elections." *Journal of Politics* 57 (1): 62–85.

Mueller, John E. 1988. "Trends in Political Tolerance." *Public Opinion Quarterly* 52 (1): 1–25.

Nadeau, Richard, and Richard G. Niemi. 1995. "Educated Guesses: The Process of Answering Factual Knowledge Questions in Surveys." *Public Opinion Quarterly* 59 (3): 323–46.

Nelson, Joel I., and Irving Tallman. 1969. "Local-Cosmopolitan Perceptions of Political Conformity: A Specification of Parental Influence." *American Journal of Sociology* 75 (2): 193–207.

Neuman, W. Russell. 1976. "Patterns of Recall among Television News Viewers." *Public Opinion Quarterly* 40 (1):115–23.

Niemi, Richard G., and Barbara I. Sobieszek. 1977. "Political Socialization." *Annual Review of Sociology* 3: 209–33.

Olzak, Susan. 1989. "Labor Unrest, Immigration, and Ethnic Conflict in Urban America, 1880–1914." *American Journal of Sociology* 94 (4): 1303–33.

———. 1992. *The Dynamics of Ethnic Competition and Conflict.* Stanford University Press.

Owens, Timothy J., Jeylan T. Mortimer, and Michael D. Finch. 1996. "Self-Determination as a Source of Self-Esteem in Adolescence." *Social Forces* 74 (4): 1377–404.

Page, Benjamin, and Robert Y. Shapiro. 1992. *The Rational Public: Fifty Years of Trends in Americans' Policy Preferences.* University of Chicago Press.

Pettey, Gary R. 1988. "The Interaction of the Individual's Social Environment, Attention and Interest, and Public Media Use on Political Knowledge Holding." *Communication Research* 15: 265–81.

Porter, Judith R., and Robert E. Washington. 1979. "Black Identity and Self-Esteem: A Review of Studies of Black Self-Concept, 1968–78." *Annual Review of Sociology* 5: 53–74.

———. 1993. "Minority Identity and Self-Esteem." *Annual Review of Sociology* 19: 139–61.

Powers, Mary G., and J. J. Holmberg. 1982. "Occupational Status Scores: Changes Introduced by the Inclusion of Women." In *Measures of Socioeconomic Status: Current Issues*, edited by Mary Powers, 183–204. Westview Press.

Prewitt, Kenneth, Heinz Eulau, and Betty H. Zisk. 1966. "Political Socialization and Political Roles." *Public Opinion Quarterly* 30 (4): 569–82.

Raudenbush, Stephen W., and Anthony S. Bryk. 1986. "A Hierarchical Model for Studying School Effects." *Sociology of Education* 59 (1): 1–17.

Renshon, Stanley Allen. 1975. "Personality and Family Dynamics in the Political Socialization Process." *American Journal of Political Science* 19 (1): 63–80.

Rigby, Ken. 1982. "A Concise Scale for the Assessment of Attitudes toward Institutional Authority." *Australian Journal of Psychology* 34 (1): 195–204.

———. 1984. "The Attitude of English and Australian College Students towards Institutional Authority." *Journal of Social Psychology* 122 (1): 41–48.

———. 1985. "Are There Behavioral Implications for Attitudes to Authority?" *High School Journal* 68 (4): 365–73.

Rigby, Ken, and E. E. Rump. 1979. "The Generality of Attitudes to Authority." *Human Relations* 32 (3): 469–89.

Roberts, Julian V., and Loretta J. Stalans. 1997. *Public Opinion, Crime, and Criminal Justice.* Westview Press.

Rosenberg, Shawn W. 1985. "Social Psychology and the Study of Political Behavior: The Case of Research on Political Socialization." *Journal of Politics* 47 (2): 715–31.

Sampson, Robert J., and W. Byron Groves. 1989. "Community Structure and Crime: Testing Social-Disorganization Theory." *American Journal of Sociology* 94 (4): 774–802.

Sampson, Robert J., and Stephen W. Raudenbush. 1999. "Systematic Social Observation of Public Places: A New Look at Disorder in Urban Neighborhoods." *American Journal of Sociology* 105 (3): 603–51.

Sanchez-Jankowski, Martin. 1991. *Islands in the Street: Gangs and American Urban Society.* University of California Press.

Scaglion, Richard, and R. Condon. 1980. "Determinants of Attitudes toward City Police." *Criminology* 17 (4): 485–94.

Schooler, Carmi. 1972. "Childhood Family Structure and Adult Characteristics." *Sociometry* 35 (2): 255–69.

Schur, Edwin. 1973. *Radical Non-Interventions: Rethinking the Delinquency Problem.* Prentice-Hall.

Schwartz, Sandra K. 1975. "Preschoolers and Politics." In *New Directions in Political Socialization,* edited by David C. Schwartz and Sandra K. Schwartz, 229–53. Free Press.

Sears, David O., and others. 1978. "Political System Support and Public Response to the Energy Crisis." *American Journal of Political Science* 22 (1): 56–82.

Seltzer, Judith A. 1994. "Consequences of Marital Dissolution for Children." *American Review of Sociology* 20 (2): 235–66.

Shanahan, Suzanne, and Susan Olzak. 1999. "The Effects of Immigrant Diversity and Ethnic Competition on Collective Conflict in Urban America: An Assessment of Two Moments of Mass Migration, 1869–1924 and 1965–1993." *Journal of American Ethnic History* (Spring): 40–64.

Shaw, Greg M., and others. 1998. "Trends: Crime, Police, and Civil Liberties." *Public Opinion Quarterly* 62 (3): 405–26.

Sidanius, Jim, and others. 1997. "The Interface between Ethnic and National Attachment: Ethnic Pluralism or Ethnic Dominance?" *Public Opinion Quarterly* 61 (1): 102–33.

Sidanius, Jim, and others. 1999. "Peering into the Jaws of the Beast: The Integrative Dynamics of Social Identity, Symbolic Racism, and Social Dominance." In *Cultural Divides: Understanding and Overcoming Group Conflict,* edited by Deborah A. Prentice and Dale T. Miller, 80–132. Russell Sage.

Sidelnick, Daniel J. 1987. "Political Attitudes of Secondary School Students: Effects of Grade, Gender, and Ability." *Journal of Social Studies Research* (Winter): 7–14.

———. 1989. "Effects of Ability, Grade, and Gender on Three Measures of Citizenship with High School Students." *Social Studies* (May/June): 92–97.

Sifry, Micah L. 2000. "Finding the Lost Voters." *American Prospect* 11 (6): 23–27.

Silverberg, Susan B., and Laurence Steinberg. 1987. "Adolescent Autonomy, Parent-Adolescent Conflict, and Parental Well-Being." *Journal of Youth and Adolescence* 16 (2): 293–312.

Slaughter-Defoe, Diana T., and Karen Glinert Carlson. 1996. "Young African American and Latino Children in High-Poverty Urban Schools: How They Perceive School Climate." *Journal of Negro Education* 65 (1): 60–70.

Smith, Kathleen Dee. 1995. "Predictors in Late Adolescent College Students' Attitudes towards Police and Their Attitudes towards Parents, Teachers, and Police
as a Function of Self-Esteem." Ph.D. dissertation, Department of Sociology,
Iowa State University, Ames.

Stapinski, Helene. 1999. "Y not Love?" *American Demographics* 21 (2): 62–68.

Stevenson, Zollie, Jr., and Lillian Gonzalez. 1992. "Contemporary Practices in
Multicultural Approaches to Education among the Largest American School
Districts." *Journal of Negro Education* 61 (3): 356–69.

Stewart, Marianne C., and others. 1992. "Arenas and Attitudes: A Note on Political Efficacy in a Federal System." *Journal of Politics* 54 (1): 179–96.

Stoker, Laura, and Jake Bowers. 2002. "Designing Multilevel Studies: Sampling
Voters and Electoral Contexts." *Electoral Studies* 21 (2): 235–67.

Stoker, Laura, and M. Kent Jennings. 1995. "Life-Cycle Transitions and Political
Participation: The Case of Marriage." *American Political Science Review* 89 (2):
421–36.

Suarez-Orozco, Carola, and Marcelo Suarez-Orozco. 1995. *Transformations:
Immigration, Family Life, and Achievement Motivation among Latino Adolescents.*
Stanford University Press.

Suarez-Orozco, Marcelo M. 1989. *Central American Refugees and U.S. High
Schools.* Stanford University Press.

Sullivan, John L., Amy Fried, and Mary G. Dietz. 1992. "Patriotism, Politics and
the Presidential Election of 1988." *American Journal of Political Science* 36 (1):
200–34.

Tedin, Kent. 1980. "Assessing Peer and Parent Influence on Adolescent Political
Attitudes." *American Journal of Political Science* 24 (1): 136–54.

Turner, Julius. 1953. "Primary Elections as the Alternative to Party Competition
in 'Safe' Districts." *Journal of Politics* 15 (1): 197–210.

Tyler, Tom R. 1988. "What Is Procedural Justice? Criteria Used by Citizens to
Assess the Fairness of Legal Procedures." *Law and Society Review* 22 (1): 103–35.

Valentino, Nicholas. 1999. "Crime News and the Priming of Racial Attitudes during Evaluations of the President." *Public Opinion Quarterly* 63 (3): 293–320.

Verba, Sidney, Kay Schlozman, and Henry Brady. 1995. *Voice and Equality: Civic
Voluntarism in American Politics.* Harvard University Press.

Verba, Sidney, and others. 1993. "Race, Ethnicity, and Political Resources: Participation in the United States." *British Journal of Political Science* 23 (3): 453–97.

Waldinger, Roger. 1996. *Still the Promised City?* Harvard University Press.

Warr, Mark. 1995. "Trends: Public Opinion on Crime and Punishment." *Public
Opinion Quarterly* 59 (2): 296–310.

White, Mervin, and B. Menke. 1982. "On Assessing the Mood of the Public
toward the Police: Some Conceptual Issues." *Journal of Criminal Justice* 10 (3):
211–30.

Wilson, Patricia M., and Jeffrey R. Wilson. 1992. "Environmental Influences on Adolescent Education Aspirations." *Youth and Society* 24 (1): 52–71.

Wilson, Robert A. 1971. "Anomie in the Ghetto: A Study of Neighborhood Type, Race, and Anomie." *American Journal of Sociology* 77 (1): 66–88.

Winfree, T., and C. Griffiths. 1977. "Adolescent Attitudes toward the Police: A Survey of High School Students." In *Juvenile Delinquency: Little Brother Grows Up*, edited by Theodore N. Ferdinand, 79–99. Sage.

Wirth, Louis. 1936. "Types of Nationalism." *American Journal of Sociology* 41 (6): 723–37.

World Press Review. 1998a. "Perspectives on 'Fornigate.'" 45 (4): 29–30.

———. 1998b. "Debating Clinton's Legacy." 45 (10): 4.

Yoon, In-Jin. 1995. "Attitudes, Social Distance, and Perceptions of Influence and Discrimination among Minorities." *International Journal of Group Tensions* 25 (1): 35–46.

Young, N. F. 1972. "Changes in Values and Strategies among Chinese in Hawaii." *Sociology and Social Research* 55 (1): 228–41.

Zeigler, Harmon, and Wayne Peak. 1970. "The Political Functions of the Educational System." *Sociology of Education* 43 (2): 115–42.

Zhao, Xinshu, and Steven H. Chaffee. 1995. "Campaign Advertisements versus Television News as Sources of Political Issue Information." *Public Opinion Quarterly* 59 (1): 41–65.

Zill, Nicholas, and John Robinson. 1995. "The Generation X Difference." *American Demographics* 17 (4): 24–33.

Zuckerman, Alan, Laurence Kotler-Berkowitz, and Lucas A. Swaine. 1998. "Anchoring Political Preferences: The Importance of Social and Political Contexts and Networks in Britain." *European Journal of Political Research.* 33 (3): 285–322.

Zuckerman, Alan, Nicholas A. Valentino, and Ezra W. Zuckerman. 1994. "A Structural Theory of Vote Choice: Social and Political Networks and Electoral Flows in Britain." *Journal of Politics* 56 (4): 1008–34.

Index

African American students and populations: economic inequality, 68; family structure, 76–78; gender differences, 87, 88–89; nonparticipation and segregation patterns, 93–94; reaction to researchers, 5; socialization patterns, 38–39, 68–70; and teaching of social studies, 94. *See also* Ethnic and racial identities and communities

The American Voter (Campbell and others), 7

Asian students and populations. *See* Ethnic and racial identities and communities

Attentiveness, political, 187

Authority, attitudes toward: fairness, 145–47, 152, 154–56, 157; government, 162–63. *See also* Law enforcement attitudes

Blair High School, 52, 54

Bobo, Lawrence, 190–91

Brown, Thad, 117

Campbell, Angus, 7

Chauvinism. *See* Nationalism and chauvinism

Churchill High School, 2–3

Citizenship modeling, 201–02

Civic engagement, 6

Clinton impeachment, attitudes toward: and community characteristics, 61–62, 90–91; definition and measurement, 26–28; and efficacy, 200; and ethnicity or race, 82–83, 90–91; and opinions of government, 199; and partisan context, 108–10, 115–18; and political discussion, 199; and religion, 133–35, 140; and school environment, 156–58, 164–66

Community social environment: and classroom, 210–11; and Clinton impeachment attitudes, 61–62; defining characteristics, 44; definition and measurement, 30–32; and diversity attitudes, 58–60, 87–90; importance, 7–8; individual traits vs., 44–46; and law enforcement attitudes, 55–58, 87–90; and media messages, 45; and